G000021288

How to Do Anim

..legally with confidence

Written & Illustrated by
Ben Isacat

First published 2011
This third edition published 2014 by Lulu, Raleigh, NC, USA
© 2014 Lulu. Ben Isacat (aka Roger Panaman). All rights reserved.
ISBN 978-1-291-01592-8

Contents

Chapter 5
The Law & Animal Rights

Chapter 6
Assorted Animal Rights Activists

Chapter 7
Numbers of Animals Raised & Killed

Preface

This book briefs you about doing animal rights as an activity and informs you about animal ethics so that you can defend your actions rationally. This book is for anyone from teen to granny, anarchist to city banker, as well as for experienced rights campaigners wanting to know more about animal rights.

Topics covered in this book include the major problems that humanity is causing animal life, the moral philosophy underlying animal rights, the major methods of campaigning, practical activities for promoting animal rights, how to deal with possible clashes with the police, biographical sketches of animal rights activists from all walks of life, statistics on human usage of animals, and it is rounded off with five extras.

You can work for animal rights high-key or low-key, with like-minded people or by yourself, but above all - do it!

Example of how to cite this book: Ben Isacat (2014). *How to Do Animal Rights*. 3rd edition. Lulu, Raleigh, NC, USA.

Chapter	*Introduction to Doing Animal Rights*
1	*1. The Broad Setting* *2. Mass Extinction* *3. Animal Holocaust*

1. The Broad Setting

Snappy Section Essence
Humanity must expand its circle of moral consideration to include all creatures.

"More than any other time in history, mankind faces a crossroads. One path leads to despair and utter hopelessness. The other, to total extinction. Let us pray we have the wisdom to choose correctly."
Woody Allen (1)

The Big Problem
Humans have been killing animals for millennia and now scientists acknowledge that we are living in a mass extinction of life caused by humanity (2). Added to this is an animal holocaust in which increasing numbers of people endlessly demand animals to eat, wear, kill for sport, experiment on, and more. In almost anyone's definition this is a man-made disaster - a war on animals - undeclared and devastatingly carried. Animals need allies and making active allies for animals is what this online book is about.

Being Active
To be active for animal rights all you need to be is an ordinary person. You do not have to be an 'animal rights terrorist' (see the chapter The Law & Animal Rights, under Terrorism), the stereotype bogeyman of the news media. The media's animal rights archetype is a rare creature because for every bogey animal rights terrorist there is a multitude of concerned people from all walks of life doing their bit for animals. You, too, whether granny, city financier or unemployed anarchist, can make your contribution and be a real ally of animals.

The Best Animal Rights Attitude
As an animal rights activist your attitudes and values will inevitably clash with those of other people. This is where you have to determine what your beliefs are based on. Confused beliefs, inaccurate views and misconceptions fill our minds. The distinguished French writer Francois-Marie Arouet (1694 - 1778),

popularly known as Voltaire, is credited with saying, "If we believe absurdities, we shall commit atrocities." (3) One of the most disturbing visions in the history of human progress is the spectre of the early vivisectors nailing live animals onto dissection boards and cutting them open at leisure to see how they worked...before the era of anaesthetics. The vivisectors conveniently believed that animals do not feel pain even though animals behave as though they do feel pain.

So what is our best attitude for being active for animals? Surely it is always to question what we know, try to understand what we do not know and keep a healthy scepticism about what people tell us. Having the right attitude demands that we constantly question our beliefs, especially when we think we are right, and never be complacent. This is especially important when we consider the moral place of animals.

The Expanding Circle

Expanding the circle is an evocative metaphor that captures the progress of humanity as a moral species. It is a phrase coined by the Irish historian and philosopher William Lecky (1838 - 1903) and means that humanity is enfolding more beings into its moral group as worthy of respect and moral consideration (4). Lecky's reputation gathers dust, yet the moral circle is expanding. Only a few generations ago slaves were excluded from the heart of society and women were devalued chattel. Slavery and woman's repression were once accepted as social norms. Animals are at a much greater disadvantage in the struggle for moral equality because, unlike slaves and women, they are not of our species and cannot fight for their own cause.

Expanding the Circle

The metaphor 'expanding the circle '† captures humanity's progress as a moral species, drawing more beings into humanity's circle of moral concern.

"...the circle expanding includes first a class, then a nation, then a coalition of nations, then all humanity and finally...the animal world."††

The outwardly expanding circle embraced slaves and women. Now it's encompassing animals, too.

†A phrase coined by William Lecky 19th C historian and philosopher.
††History of European Morals. 1:100, 1869.

Ben Isacat 2013

The philosopher Peter Singer puts Lecky's metaphor to use as the title of his book, *The Expanding Circle: ethics and sociobiology.* (5)

The Great Leap

Animals gain when we include them in our moral circle. Looking beyond that, there is another good reason for granting animals rights that is more human-oriented. Humanity is about to make a great leap into the future; blasting off into space, deciphering genomes and implanting synthetic parts in our bodies are some of the signs of this impending leap. These signs signal that we are saying good-bye to our organic roots based on natural selection and are entering a new phase of evolution based on science and technology. We are shaping a transformation of humanity into a powerful super-being that one day (assuming humanity and science survive the next hundred years) will be unrecognisable to the present generation. However, we must not allow our future-being to ravage every creature it meets for its own ends, in the present style of humanity. We must instil in it an enlightened and compassionate morality as a force for good. To this end we must labour to expand our circle of moral consideration to encompass all creatures, whatever and wherever they are in the universe.

2. Mass Extinction

Snappy Section Essence
Humanity is causing a mass extinction of life on Earth, a tragedy for animals, comparable to the mass extinction of the dinosaurs. Few people seem to know or care about it.

"*Homo sapiens* is in the throes of causing a major biological crisis, a mass extinction, the sixth such event, to have occurred in the past half billion years. And we, *Homo sapiens*, may also be among the living dead." Richard Leakey & Roger Lewin (2)

The Sixth Extinction

We are living in a period of mass extinction of life on Earth. This is the greatest extinction since the mass extinction of the dinosaurs 65 million years ago. In the 3.5 billion year evolution of life on our planet there have been five mass extinctions - when close to all species were nearly wiped out. The most massive of these extinctions was the Permian Extinction some 250 million years ago: seventy per cent of land species and ninety per cent of marine species went extinct in less than a million years, close to an instant in Earth's 4.5 billion year evolution.

The common name for the present mass extinction is the Sixth Extinction, popularised in the 1995 book of the same name by Richard Leakey and Roger Lewin. (2) The unique characteristic of the Sixth Extinction is that it is caused by a single species - us: *Homo sapiens*. Scientists calculate that within a hundred years half of Earth's fauna and flora could be treading down the road to extinction. Earth, home to millions of species, may be losing some 30,000 species a year and the rate is increasing as humanity accelerates its devastation of the biosphere. The problem is especially grim for rain forests because they harbour the vast majority of land-living species and humanity is clear-felling forests fast. As the forests shrink away the animals have nowhere to go and die out.

The Mega-Devastators
Humanity has fashioned three mega-devastators that are causing the Sixth Extinction and their combined influence is reaching a climax:

1. Global warming - by releasing carbon dioxide into the atmosphere.
2. Consumption of resources - which includes habitat change/destruction.
3. Human overpopulation - by which every one of us increases the first two devastators

The magnitude of what humanity is doing became apparent in the 1970's. But still the mass extinction crisis is invisible to most people, unaware about it or indifferent. Many scientists are so worried by this lack of concern that in 1992 over 1,500 prominent specialists, among them several Nobel Prize Laureates, endorsed the World Scientists' Warning to Humanity (6) (see Appendix for a copy). But they have made little progress waking people to the looming cataclysm. Likewise, the Doomsday Clock has similarly fallen short. It was originally started in 1947 during the Cold War by a group of scientists concerned about humanity's potential impending self-destruction and is meant to wake us up to fight for our preservation. Currently the minute hand is set at about five minutes to midnight - just a few minutes before annihilation.

Biocide?
Biocide, the massive destruction of life on a worldwide scale, is the ultimate of all human practical and moral violations. Sceptics argue that there is not enough data to support the notion of a Sixth Extinction or that this mass extinction is not of human origin so we need do nothing about it. Other people accept the impending catastrophe and argue that humanity can slow the rate of extinction through proper management of human activity and ecosystems. Still other people maintain that time has expired and there is nothing we can do. But one thing is certain. The disaster of mass extinction is so great do we dare not act? We could not have evolved without animals and

they gave our species food, clothing, shelter and tools. It is payback time. As Woody Allen says at the top of this chapter: "More than any other time in history, mankind faces a crossroads. One path leads to despair and utter hopelessness. The other, to total extinction. Let us pray we have the wisdom to choose correctly."

Homo sapiens is in the throes of causing a major biological crisis, a mass extinction, the sixth such event, to have occured in the past half billion years. And we, Homo sapiens, may also be among the living dead.

R Leakey & R Lewin
The Sixth Extinction

All the wonders of life

Void
Emptiness
Nothingness

Ben Isacat
2013

3. The Animal Holocaust

Snappy Section Essence
Humanity has the attitude and practical capacity to destroy beings on a vast scale. It makes some people stop to consider their role in the Animal Holocaust and even act against it.

"Their suffering is intense, widespread, expanding, systematic and socially sanctioned. And the victims are unable to organize in defence of their own interests." Henry Spira (7)

What is the Animal Holocaust?

Mass extinction is not the only human scourge on animals; animals live in a continuing holocaust. The Animal Holocaust is the mass destruction of animals by humanity and is a direct comparison with Nazi mass murder, particularly of Jews. The animals most often referred to in the Animal Holocaust are domesticated animals that people raise for food. However, more generally, Animal Holocaust victims include any animals and their populations that humans control, systematically abuse, or destroy, such as fur-farmed animals, laboratory animals and free-living wild animals.

The Animal Holocaust resembles the Nazi perpetrated Holocaust in the use of business-like mass slaughter, mediated by transports (trains), factory farms (concentration camps) and slaughterhouses (death camps). Other pertinent comparisons of animals with human Holocaust victims are performing experiments on animal inmates and turning them into commodities, such as fur (skin goods) and fats (soap). Perhaps the most telling comparison is the contempt for the victims' humane treatment and the widespread disregard for their rights. People today generally do not think of animals as beings who are mutilated, tortured or slain; animals are merely 'animals', there for the purpose of satisfying human needs.

The Animal Holocaust is treated in modern books such as Charles Patterson's *Eternal Treblinka* (8). The book's title comes from a quote attributed to author and Holocaust survivor Isaac Beshevis Singer:

"To animals, all people are Nazis. For them it is an eternal Treblinka."

Incredible Killing

No one knows the true figure of how many animals people kill every year, but to get a glimpse see the Chapter 7: Numbers of Animals Raised & Killed. Staggering totals include the two million pigs killed every week in the United States, beaten by the 12 million pigs killed every week in China (9), and the fifty billion chickens killed worldwide every year. (10, 11) Humanity has killed literally trillions of animals since the Second World War and we are killing them at an accelerating rate as our population increases and the mechanisation of the Animal Holocaust gathers pace. The German philosopher Martin Heidegger (1889 - 1976), disgraced for his membership of the Nazi party, is cited in a 1949 lecture of his as saying:

"Agriculture is now a motorized food industry, the same thing in its essence as the production of corpses in the gas chambers and the extermination camps..." (12).

Not Ours

Some animal rights groups juxtapose imagery of the Holocaust and the Animal Holocaust to publicise their campaigns and shock people into admitting the scale and existence of the human abuse of animals. Their message is that animals are not ours to abuse and we must treat them with respect. However, this juxtaposition has angered many people who see it as an inappropriate and corrupting comparison, tasteless and trivialising because of humanity's (assumed unique) moral basis. They say that the Holocaust / Animal Holocaust juxtaposition may gain the cause of animal rights some attention but will lose it support in the long-run. Whether or not you agree, the comparison shows that humanity has the arrogance to destroy beings on a vast scale. It makes some of us stop to consider our role in the slaughter and act against it.

Learn more on the Web

The Sixth Extinction by Niles Eldredge.
www.actionbioscience.org/newfrontiers/eldredge2.html

References

(1) Allen, Woody. *My Speech to the Graduates*. In: Complete Prose. Picador: London. 1997.

(2) Leakey, Richard & Lewin, Roger. *The Sixth Extinction: biodiversity and its survival.* Weidenfield and Nicolson: London. 1996.

(3) Possibly paraphrased from a speech in 1767.

(4) Lecky, William E H. *History of European Morals from Augustus to Charlemagne.* 1869:100–101. Vol 1.

(5) Singer, Peter. *The Expanding Circle: ethics and sociobiology.* Clarendon Press: Oxford. 1981.

(6) *World Scientists' Warning to Humanity.* Union of Concerned Scientists. www.ucsusa.org. (Accessed January 2007.) See Appendix.

(7) Spira, Henry. *Fighting to Win.* In: Peter Singer (editor). In: *Defense of Animals.* Basil Blackwell: New York. 1985:194 - 208.

(8) Patterson, Charles. *Eternal Treblinka: our treatment of animals and the holocaust.* Lantern Books: New York. 2002.

(9) Live Swine Selected Countries Summary. Production (Pig Crop). In: *Livestock and Poultry: World Markets and Trade.* US Department of Agriculture, Foreign Agricultural Service. www.fas.usda.gov. (Accessed February 2008.)

(10) *Livestock and Poultry: World Markets and Trade.* United States Department of Agriculture, Foreign Agricultural Service. www.fas.usda.gov. (Accessed February 2008.)

(11) *The World Egg Industry - a few facts and figures.* International Egg Commission. (Accessed February 2008.)

(12) Lacoue-Labarthe, Philippe. *Heidegger, Art and Politics.* 1990:34. (This quote is sometimes mis-attributed to Heidegger's 1954 essay, The Question Concerning Technology.)

Chapter	*Philosophy: Key Topics*
2	*1. Animal Rights*

Snappy Page Essence

Animal rights are benefits people give to animals to protect them from human use and abuse. Rights can take moral, legal and practical forms.

Animal rights are benefits people give to animals. Benefits include the right of protection from human use and abuse and rights can take moral, legal and practical forms. People who support animal rights believe that animals are not ours to use as we wish, for whatever purpose, be it for food, clothing, experimentation or entertainment. Animal rights supporters also believe that we should consider the best interests of animals regardless of whatever value the animals may have for us.

> "To spread the concept [of animal rights] beyond our species is to jeopardize our dignity as moral beings, who live in judgement of one another and of themselves." Roger Scruton. Animal Rights. City Journal. 2000.

Alternatively:

> "...animal rights must not only be an idea but a social movement for the liberation of the world's most oppressed beings, both in terms of numbers and in the severity of their pain." Steven Best. Essay: Animal Rights and the New Enlightenment.

But what are animal rights specifically, how do animal rights compare with human rights, and are rights a remedy for all moral problems?

Background to Rights

One of the first to distinguish rights was the English philosopher John Lock (1632 - 1704), who thought that people were entitled to the rights of life, liberty and property. People often base their concept of rights on a belief in 'natural' rights that they are given by God or were somehow enjoyed long ago, when people lived in a 'state of nature' before they became civilized. Furthermore, they assume that these rights are universal, that is that they apply to everyone automatically, indisputably and irrevocably. Alternatively, you could claim that human rights are neither natural nor universal. Rights are only what people are willing to confer as they see fit on others, being the granting of particular benefits by people to people.

Modern human rights have four features in that they are:

- **Natural** - rulers do not invent them.
- **Universal** - they apply to everyone.
- **Equal** - they are the same for everyone.
- **Inalienable** - no one can lose them.

Rights are usually contracted between a country's government and its citizens, like the right to vote, the right to fair trial and the right to free speech, and vary from country to country. Many states make utterances about giving their citizens rights but do not fully grant them.

Major Dates for Rights

1776 The *Declaration of Independence* of the United States recognised the right to 'life, liberty and the pursuit of happiness'. This was the world's first major published statement of human rights.

1789 The National Assembly of France approved rights for the common man, including equality before the law, equal opportunity, freedom from arbitrary imprisonment, freedom of speech and religion, security of property, and taxation commensurate with ability to pay.

1948 The United Nations affirmed their *Universal Declaration of Human Rights*, setting out over two dozen rights, including the right of individuals to life, liberty, education, equality in law and freedom of movement, religion, association and information.

Animal Rights

The justification for conferring rights on animals is that animals are in many important ways like humans. Animals are sentient creatures who are subjects of a life: they feel pleasure and pain, experience emotions, remember, anticipate, learn, and what happens to them is important for them, unlike what happens to a rock or a stone. So, if you argue that humans deserve rights, it is rational that animals also deserve rights.

Animal interests, however, are not always the same as human interests. Thus the range of rights that animals need are not always the same as the range of rights that humans need. Animals are not in need of equality before the law, or freedom of speech and religion, or of fair taxation. Nor do animals have an interest in voting or being literate. Hence, it would be meaningless and silly to give animals rights to these affairs. However, this should not prevent people from bestowing relevant and appropriate rights on animals.

Relevant rights for animals can be any benefits appropriate for them that people wish to bestow on them. Relevant rights for animals can include:

- The right to live free in the natural state of the animals' choosing.
- The right to express normal behaviour (eg food searching, grooming, nest building).
- The right to life (ie not be killed for human food or other human use).
- The right to reproduce (ie pass on their genes to the next generation).
- The right to choose their own lifestyle (eg not for people to coerce them into experiments or entertainment).
- The right to live free from human induced harm (eg hunger, thirst, molestation, fear, distress, pain, injury or disease).

If you believe animals have such rights then you would have a doubtful basis for exploiting animals. You would have a moral duty to support those rights and would be morally corrupt if you did not. If animals have these rights, how could you justify, say, eating animals, using them for sport or keeping them in zoos? In practical terms you would have to live your life accordingly, such as become a vegetarian or vegan.

Fundamental Animal Rights Positions
As for the actuality of giving rights to animals there are three fundamental positions: abuse, welfare and liberation.

1. Abuse
Animals have no moral status. We owe nothing to animals except to make use of them as and how we like. This is the position many people held in past centuries and many people still hold today, especially in China and surrounding countries.

2. Welfare
Animals should have welfare. We should treat animals kindly, but humans always come first when there is a conflict of interest, because humans are superior and animals are a resource for humanity. Welfarists acknowledge the need to use animals but try to alleviate 'needless' animal suffering. This is the position most people in the West support today.

3. Liberation

We should liberate animals. This is the avant-garde position: animals deserve moral status similar in some way to human moral status. There are two types of animal liberationist and both want to abolish the use of animals on moral or other grounds. 'New welfarists' regard abolition as a long-term goal and meanwhile try to ease as much animal suffering as possible by introducing practical welfare measures. The 'hard-line abolitionists' believe welfare is a waste of time and pitch straight for abolition of animal use on the grounds that if there is no abuse then there is no need for welfare. Liberationists have a lifestyle quite different to the majority of people, being vegan or vegetarian and reject goods and services based on animals.

Variations on Animal Rights

The concept of animal rights has different levels of definition. So to make any discussion meaningful and avoid talking at cross purposes you need to clarify what people have in mind when they speak about animal rights. For example you can distinguish three basic views: absolute, equal and relative.

1. Relative Animal Rights

We should avoid causing animals 'unnecessary' suffering, but human welfare is more important than animal welfare and we should overrule the interests (rights) of animals if we have good reason to do so. Animal welfarists hold this view.

2. Equal Consideration

We should give equal consideration to the comparable interests of animals and humans. When making a moral decision about the suffering of a dog and a human, neither want pain inflicted on them, so we should give the same weight of consideration to the dog as we would to the human. If we are not prepared to make a human suffer then we should not make a dog suffer. People of a utilitarian philosophy may hold an outlook like this.

3. Absolute Animal Rights

We should always protect the rights of animals, even when doing so is troublesome personally and difficult for society. People should not experiment on dogs to develop a possible life-saving drug even if it might mean delaying the drug's development by some years. This is the view that animal rightists hold.

You need not confine yourself to these three levels when discussing animal rights. Make up nuances as you like, such as broadening animal rights to apparently non-sentient animals, or to the whole of inanimate nature, or by coming up with different definitions of animal rights.

Are Rights a Cure-all?

Rights should be absolute if they are to protect individuals; they cannot be suspended or hacked about to fit in with what someone may happen to want. Yet there seem to be cases for overriding rights during moral dilemmas, such as killing some individuals to save others. This might be when mice are spoiling a harvest and setting off a famine, or when coyotes or foxes are eating the last individuals of an endangered species. How should we react to of conflicts of interest like these? We might respond by temporarily adopting another philosophy, like utilitarianism - that you should act to bring about the greatest good to the greatest number of individuals. Therefore rights may not be a panacea that can cope with all moral conditions all the time; now and then we may have to look outside rights for other solutions to guide us when dealing with moral issues.

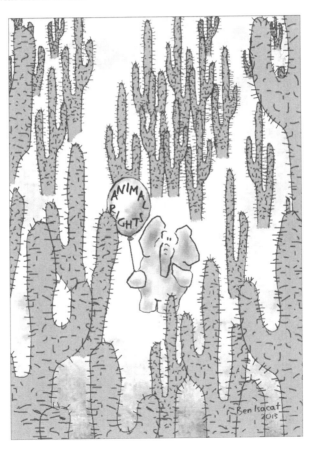

Another problem with rights is that sometimes people say animals have intrinsic value, an importance in themselves irrespective of their value to humans. You might claim that all sentient beings are entitled to rights because they have equal intrinsic value. But does intrinsic value really exist? Intrinsic value may simply be a part of the human value system that values things that have no value or are said to have no value. If you do not believe in intrinsic value then you might have to pursue animal liberation via utilitarianism, not through animal rights. As a utilitarian you could claim that sentient animals have interests and therefore no species (that is humanity) is more important than any other and we should give equal moral consideration to every creature's relevant moral interests.

For & Against: argue your case

Listen to people's arguments for and against animal rights. Break down their arguments into simple statements and add them to these common outlooks to help argue your own case.

1. Drawing the Line

- Claim: If we grant rights to animals then eventually even insects and plants will have rights. That would be ridiculous.
- Claim: Animal rights encompass animals who are sentient (chiefly mammals and birds, but also advanced invertebrates like the octopus, *Octopus vulgaris*). It is Deep ecology that makes the case for giving rights to all of nature.

2. Dependency on Animality

- Claim: Giving rights to animals will severely disrupt society. We would have to undergo enormous changes if we give rights to animals. Every use of animals would have to stop and we would not be able to live normal lives.
- Claim: Most people may want to give absolute animal rights where they can and relative animal rights where they cannot. We must do this with good intention and careful consideration.

3. Moral Sense

- Claim: Animals have no sense of morality. So they do not need moral rights.
- Claim: People should support animal rights because people are moral. Whether or not animals have a sense of morality is not the issue.

4. Comprehension

- Claim: Only creatures who comprehend rights can benefit from them. Only humans understand rights so only humans can have rights.
- Claim: Children and severely mentally impaired people cannot understand rights, yet we do not deny them rights. Therefore we should not hold back from giving rights to animals because they cannot comprehend them.

5. Reciprocation

- Claim: The giving of rights implies reciprocation. You have the right to life so you must respect the right of others to life. But animals cannot reciprocate so they should not have rights.
- Claim: Animal rights are about how humans should treat animals, not about how animals should treat humans. In any case, we respect the rights of our future unborn generations and they cannot reciprocate.

6. Biology vs Rationality

- Claim: Humans kill and eat animals because we evolved to survive by exploiting our environment. It is therefore senseless even to consider giving animals rights and we should continue to exploit them.
- Claim: Unlike other animals, we are not now constrained entirely by biological evolution. We can reflect on how we should act and choose how to behave. Therefore we can behave morally and give animals rights.

7. Food & Territory

- Claim: Animals eat each other and we eat them. We are all part of the food web. So we cannot give animals rights.
- Claim: Animals kill each other because they have to, either for food or to protect their food supplies, or they would die. We can decide not to eat animals. Vegetarians do not die for lack of meat.

8. Mental Capacity

- Claim: People have grater mental capacities than animals and cannot measure up to us. Therefore giving animals rights would demean humanity and we must reject animal rights.
- Claim: We do not use or abuse people who are severely mentally retarded or in a permanent vegetative state. Many animals have mental abilities far better than these people. So we should not withhold rights from animals.

9. Species Differences

- Claim: Animals and humans are obviously different. So we should treat animals differently from us.

- Claim: There is no acceptable difference (whether intelligence, shape, posture or colour) that distinguishes animals from humans on moral grounds. So there is no moral line you can draw that separates animals and humans.

10. Pain & Suffering

- Claim: Animals can experience pain and suffering. But this does not mean we have to give them rights, only that we should not be cruel to them. We can treat animals well and give them adequate legal protection without giving them rights.

- Claim: All children have rights under the United Nations *Convention on the Rights of the Child*, ratified by nearly 200 countries. Mentally handicapped people have rights as people. Now we must broaden our circle of compassion to animals by giving them rights.

11. Sentience

- Claim: Animals are not sentient: they cannot speak, have no thoughts, feelings, desires, emotions or interests. Therefore we should reject animal rights.

- Claim: We should not make our ignorance of animals a basis for insensitivity. But we know that some animals at least have ideas and a measure of speech, and that animals have feelings, like a need to care for their young, remain with their group and feel safe and well. Therefore we should give them rights.

Chapter	*Philosophy: Key Topics*
2	*2. Equal Consideration*

Snappy Page Essence

Equal consideration of moral interests is a moral principle asserting that we should give equal importance to the evaluation of the moral welfare of every individual.

In the context of animal-human relations, equal consideration of interests means giving equal deliberation to the relevant moral welfare of animals as well as humans. Equal consideration of interests is not a new idea, but Peter Singer gave it wide circulation in his 1975 book *Animal Liberation* and defines it thus:

> "Essentially this means that if an animal feels pain, the pain matters as much as it does when a human feels pain - if the pains hurt just as much. How bad pain and suffering are does not depend on the species of being that experiences it." *Singer-Posner Debate*. Slate Magazine. June 2001.

The strong version of equal consideration of interests says that animal and human interests are equally important and when there is moral conflict of interests you must consider animal and human interests equally. Humans should not take precedence over animals automatically and without thought.

Equal Consideration versus Animal Liberation

Many people often use the terms animal rights and animal liberation interchangeably. This might be all right sometimes, but in a strict sense animal liberation is made up of two different approaches to liberating animals: equal consideration of interests and animal rights.

Singer advances animal liberation through equal consideration of interests. Although he often talks about animal rights he does so only as shorthand, what he really means is liberating animals by giving them equal consideration.

The table on the next page points out some of the differences between equal consideration and animal rights.

Comparable Interests

You must apply equal consideration to interests that are comparable (relevant) interests. All animal species and humans share certain major interests in that

Equal Consideration of Interests vs Animal Rights		
	Equal Consideration	**Animal Rights**
Definition	A moral principle stating that you should weigh the comparable moral interests of all creatures who will be affected by your actions.	The bestowal of moral benefits (ie rights) on animals to protect them from human exploitation.
What you should do	You should consider equally the comparable moral interests of all creatures affected by your actions.	You should obey the rights that animals have (eg if animals have a right not to be abused by people then you should not abuse them).
Asserts	Where comparable interests are involved, you can either exploit animals and humans equally or should not exploit either.	You cannot exploit animals. You have a moral duty to support the rights of all animals and would be morally corrupt if you do not.
Criterion of merit	Your action is right if its consequences are good (irrespective of your duty).	Your action is right if your duty is to do it (irrespective of its consequences).
Weaknesses	You must guess which interests are relevant and how to evaluate them.	Not all animals need the same rights (eg monkey vs crab), which makes for lots of different rights to remember.
Can trace roots to	Utilitarianism (see Consequentialism).	Deontology (see this entry).

they need nutrition, freedom of movement and social interaction with peers, for example. However, animals and humans do not share all interests. Animals do not need freedom of speech, voting rights or freedom of religion. These latter interests are not comparable interests so do not consider them. This may seem obvious, but some people like to confuse the issue by trying to compare irrelevant interests ('we should not give rights to pigs because pigs do not need free speech').

Equal Consideration of Moral Interests

"If an animal feels pain, the pain matters as much as when a human feels pain – if the pains hurt just as much. How bad pain and suffering are does not depend on the species that experiences it. When there is moral conflict you must consider animal and human interests equally."

Peter Singer

Some Advantages & Disadvantages

Three advantages of applying the principle of equal consideration when deciding animal-human moral conflicts are:

- Equal consideration counters the view that certain overriding attributes automatically decide in favour of humans, like possessing certain mental abilities, language, high intelligence, or membership of *Homo sapiens.*

- Equal consideration avoids giving moral equality to animals on all issues. You do not have to consider a claim by dogs for equal access to sports or by cats for equal opportunity in arts. Only comparable interests count. So you can limit your consideration to basic claims, such as to life, liberty and procreation.

- Equal consideration avoids giving equal moral status to all creatures. For example, we assume (perhaps wrongly) that insects experience pain in a lesser way than mammals, so that if you cause insects pain you might be harming them less than if you cause chimpanzees pain.

A couple of weaknesses applying equal consideration are:

- Equal consideration does not tell you what interests to consider. Basic interests like staying alive and avoiding pain are obvious, but you have to decide what other interests may be relevant. Children, adults, and mentally retarded adults do not always share the same interests and the difficulty of knowing which interests to consider is compounded when we include animals in our compassion.

- Not everyone might accept that humans and animals have morally equal weight on every comparable interest. Staying alive and avoiding pain would appear to be equally important for animals and humans; however, you might attach more weight to these interests to favour humans. The principle of equal consideration does not tell you how to evaluate relative weights of interests.

Certainly, equal consideration of moral interests is a principle by which we can debate the moral standing of animals, along with equally key concepts, like sentience and speciesism.

Chapter	*Philosophy: Key Topics*
2	*3. Animal Ethics*

Snappy Page Essence
Animal ethics is the systematic study of how we ought to treat animals and therefore is central to animal rights.

"Thinking through, critically and carefully, what most people take for granted is, I believe, the chief task of philosophy, and it is this task that makes philosophy a worthwhile activity." Peter Singer (1)

When you are active in animal rights you should know why you are being active and be able to defend your actions rationally. Simply being emotional about animals is not enough because the opposition may be equally emotional back at you, resulting in a stalemate. However, by stating your case rationally you can convince people of your cause and win converts. This is an important part of doing animal rights. Even the most emotional opponents, if they can be made to see sense, are susceptible to rational arguments. This entry sets out the rational background for animal rights so that you know where you are philosophically and have an idea of where you are going.

Ethics
If you methodically question the meaning and purpose of life you are a philosopher, whether amateur or professional. Ethics is the part of philosophy that asks how people should live their lives and how they should do good and right to each other. Animal ethics is the same but includes animals. Robert Garner in his book *Animal Ethics* says "Animal ethics seeks to examine beliefs that are held about the moral status of non-human animals." (2). You can define animal ethics more broadly, however, by saying that it is about acting for the moral good of animals (including humans) by understanding animal-human moral issues through knowledge and reasoning. Thus animal ethics is a practical pursuit as well as a cognitive study.

Importance of Animal Ethics
Our relationship with animals is based on beliefs we absorb from our upbringing and social customs. We accept these beliefs, often on trust from our elders, without challenging or analysing them. But unexamined beliefs when acted out can do enormous harm (Voltaire pointedly said, "If we believe absurdities we shall commit atrocities.") Everyone has some contact with

animals directly or indirectly, whether farming or shooting animals, eating them, feeding their pets factory farmed animals, going to the zoo, using substances tested on animals or washing with animal-based soap. Yet most people do not realise the suffering and destruction humanity imposes on animals because it goes on largely out of sight and where it peaks above the surface it is tolerated as normal.

Ben Isacat

Here is the point. The harm humans are doing to animals amounts to a holocaust that we must address (see the entry Animal Holocaust). If we are to make civilized progress we must comprehend what we are doing to animals and think about how we should be treating them. All of us must justify and defend our relations with animals in light of animal ethics. An ethical issue is when you think a harm or wrong is happening and something should be done about it. If we harm people then we must justify why we harm them and if we cannot justify our actions then we must not harm them. In the same way, with animal ethics we must critically question our conduct with animals. We must ask what we are doing to animals, why we are doing it, how should we and how can we do better - and take action.

Key Concepts
When thinking about animal ethics these key concepts are helpful to bear in mind.

- **Sentiency**: being able to suffer and feel pleasure.
- **Moral rights**: conferral of protection or privilege.
- **Moral status**: worthy of moral consideration and moral rights.
- **Interests**: a stake in fulfilling a life's natural potential.
- **Intrinsic value**: a value something has independent of its usefulness.
- **Equal consideration of interests**: giving equal weight to everyone's moral interests.
- **Speciesism**: prejudice favouring your own species.
- **Specismo**: an alternative word for speciesism, like machismo or macho. Italian and pronounced speh-chis-mo.

- **Utilitarianism**: theory that states an action is morally right if it benefits with the greatest good the largest number of beings.

Some History

'Animals are made for human use' is the traditional attitude of Western society. This view of human-animal relations has a long tradition extending from at least Old Testament times up to Darwin (1809 - 1882). Aristotle (384 - 322 BC) thought animals exist to provide humans with food and other provisions; Aquinas (1225 - 1274) claimed killing animals is acceptable and we can treat them in any way useful to us; and Descartes (1596 - 1650) asserted that animal are mindless robots that cannot suffer, the corollary being that we can do almost anything to them.

People have always had to emphasise differences between man and beast to maintain and defend their belief in human superiority. Rationally inclined people assert that animals lack reason, intelligence, language and creativity. Spiritually inclined people believe animals are not made in the 'image of God' and, although some of them appreciate and admire animals as God's creatures, many of them are largely unresponsive to animal misfortune and distress. People generally protect some animals, but only if the animals belong to people as property.

Darwin, however, significantly helped begin the demolition of human centredness by convincingly arguing that animals and humans evolved from the same ancestors (although he did not dare publish this overtly). Common evolutionary descent explains why humans share the same appearance as animals, especially with the apes. The notion of a common evolution of humans and primates shocked the Victorian public of Darwin's time but his evolutionary theory in outline is widely accepted today.

Thus an ethical dilemma arose. Animals and humans are similar. Therefore if humans have moral status then animals should have moral status too. For most of the history of Western philosophy just about everyone passed off the moral status of animals as a trivial and insignificant question. However, since the 1970's an energetic debate has been waging about animal moral status, ignited by firebrand philosophers such as Peter Singer (see the chapter Personalities).

The animal moral status debate is founded on basic, common moral principles: it is wrong to cause suffering and it is wrong to discriminate against others by giving greater importance to your own group. Apply these principles consistently, says Singer, and they lead to the logical conclusion that we should morally treat animals like humans, provided the animals have relevant similarities with humans.

Some animal oriented philosophers say the only important morally relevant similarity of animals with humans is that both can feel pain and suffer, that they are sentient. With this in mind the celebrated English philosopher Jeremy Bentham (1748 - 1832) is often quoted:

> "The day may come, when the rest of the animal creation may acquire the rights which never could have been withholden from them but by the hand of tyranny. ...the question is not, Can they reason? not, Can they talk? but, Can they suffer?" (3)

So we must distinguish the relevant similarities of animals and humans (for instance sentiency) and not use inaccurate attributes to justify excluding animals from our moral consideration. Relevant similarities in moral terms boil down to basic requirements, such as the right to reproduce and pass on your genes, the right to liberty and the right not to be forced to suffer for the gain of others (as in experimentation and factory farming).

However, many people today still cannot accept animals on the same moral level as humanity, even while acknowledging the contributions by Darwin. Nevertheless, thanks to Singer and some fellow philosophers, it is said that there is more controversy and discussion about animals in recent years than during the whole of past time.

How to Proceed?

When we make a judgement about the rights or wrongs of a situation our views and actions must be based on knowledge and reason. We must examine our thoughts and feelings carefully. We cannot rely completely on our intuition or feelings because people may be manipulating us for their own purpose without our realising it. We cannot rely on faith, religion, authority, the law, social standards, tradition, fashion, fantasy, immediate impression, emotional illogic, magic and many other reasons that are not necessarily rational.

Reasons for acting ethically can be simple or complex, tempered by intuition or emotion, or whatever. But our reasons for acting ethically must be consistent, comprehensive and based on fact, that is on the truth of the matter as far as we know it. And our reasons for acting ethically must work the 6C Way:

- **Clearly** - can be understood
- **Concisely** - not verbose or diffuse
- **Compatibly** - agreeing with basic sensitivity of what is right and good
- **Consistently** - without contradictions
- **Constructively** - extending our judgement to new or ambiguous areas by building on what we already understand and accept
- **Comprehensively** - not ad hoc but relevant to all kinds of problems

Ethical Theories

Ethical theories help us in two ways: to organise our thoughts when deciding which moral action to take, such as about animal rights, and to understand better other people's moral position. People down the centuries have asked three common moral questions and philosophers have developed three influential theories that attempt a solution. Most ethical positions can be understood in relation to these ethical theories, also called moral systems or moral frameworks.

The three moral questions people ask and the ethical theories philosophers have worked out are:

1. **What outcome should I aim for?**
   Consequentialism (or Consequence Ethics)

2. **What am I required to do?**
   Deontology (or Duty Ethics)

3. **What should I do as a virtuous person?**
   Virtue Ethics (or Virtue Theory)

1. What outcome should I aim for?

Consequentialism says you should act to bring about the best results or consequences. Consequentialism is goal-directed. It asserts that only the good outcome of your goal or action is important, not how you achieve your goal. You need not be dutiful or virtuous - you might even lie, cheat or whatever - so long as the result is morally good.

Say you see a couple of sheep or pigs escape from a slaughterhouse and believe that taking them back to be killed is immoral, so you snatch and hide them and lie that you do not know where they are. Your action focuses on results, the saving of the animals from slaughter. You would believe the outcome is morally more important than stealing and lying.

Consequentialism can also be called by the less cumbersome name of consequence ethics; its traditional name in philosophy is teleology, from the Greek teleos meaning end or purpose.

2. What am I required to do?

Deontology states that you should do whatever is your duty, even if by doing it you harm yourself or others by suffering the consequences. *For King and country, right or wrong,* is a deontology dictum. Deontology counters consequentialism; doing what you consider is your obligation (duty) is more important than the outcome of your action.

As a rancher you might hate shooting predators but accept that you have an obligation to protect your cattle regardless of your action's impact on wildlife. Or you might release laboratory animals waiting to be experimented on because you see your action as your duty to animalkind. (Alternatively you might condemn releasing laboratory animals because you believe your first duty is upholding the law and the standards of society as you see it - moral theories can work both ways!)

You can also call deontology by the more descriptive term of duty ethics.

3. What should I do as a virtuous person?

Virtue ethics claims that making good ethical decisions is based on being a virtuous person and holds that possessing admirable personal qualities - such as compassion, kindness, respect, toleration, honesty and courage - makes you virtuous. Thus, virtue ethics tries to bring in all the qualities of being human to influence your ethical considerations.

Being a virtuous person you might, for instance, approve or reprove individuals or companies and support only those that do not harm animals or nature. Indeed, do these individuals or companies have virtuous qualities themselves? Do they advance or oppose virtue? Are they progressive, admirable and responsible or insensitive, negligent and dishonest?

Virtue ethics, also called virtue theory or value theory, flourished in ancient Greece and Aristotle (BC 384 - 322) is often cited as its main philosophical representative. He argued that a virtue is the mean or middle path between two vices, like courage is midway between, and therefore better than, fearlessness or cowardice. Virtue ethics expired in the fourth century AD when moral theories purporting to be given by God supplanted it. However, the 20th century brought virtue ethics back to life and modernised it. Modern virtue ethics does not emphasise specific moral traits but says you should be virtuous in all aspects of your life and be a good person all the time.

Ethical Theories Compared

The table on the next page contrasts and highlights some of the main features of consequentialism, deontology and virtue ethics. Each theory focuses on a different attitude to morality, reveals a unique insight into moral problems and suggests a different way for resolving moral questions. Consequentialism, deontology and virtue ethics overlap with one another and they each come in several alternative versions (not shown here).

Comparison of Consequence Ethics, Duty Ethics & Virtue Ethics

	Consequence Ethics	Duty Ethics	Virtue Ethics
Asks	How can I make the best outcome or consequence?	What are my duties?	How will my actions support my being a virtuous person?
Morality Is	Doing what may achieve the best results.	Doing my duty.	Doing what a virtuous person would do.
Focuses On	The best outcome I can make.	The duty I am required to do.	What a virtuous person should do.
Main Concern Is	The value of results - not my duty or quality of my character.	Doing my duty - whatever the consequences and whatever my character.	My moral character - not consequences or duty.
Aims to	Produce the most good.	Perform the right duty.	Develop my moral character.
Example	Utilitarianism. Ethical-egoism.	Rights-based ethics. Judaeo-Christianity.	Buddhism. Confucianism. Christian Virtue.

Choosing an Ethical Theory

Which ethical theory (consequentialism, deontology or virtue ethics) should you follow to help you resolve an animal rights issue, or indeed any ethical matter?

The answer may partly depend on your personality. You might be more concerned about the consequences of your action than be oriented to notions of doing your duty, or vice versa. Or you might be more concerned about being virtuous.

Another suggestion commonly put forward for choosing which theory to follow is to use one that feels most natural for your particular set of circumstances. It might be useful to use:

- A **Consequence theory** - for dealing with large numbers.
  You might have to decide to save a majority of some animals at the expense of a minority of other animals - good consequences for some animals, bad consequences for other animals.

- A **Duty theory** - for dealing with conflicting obligations.
  As a livestock farmer you are likely to believe that you have an obligation to send livestock for slaughter to feed people. Thus your primary duty would be to people and a lesser duty would be to animals.

- A **Virtue theory** - for dealing with personal decisions.
  You would apply the range of your mental and emotional faculties to act as a virtuous person would act. So, for example, should you eat animals? You might reckon that as a virtuous person you should be compassionate to all creatures and not cause suffering; therefore you should not eat animals.

There is a third accepted way for choosing which ethical theory to follow. The ethical theories outlined above sometime complement one another. So if two or all three of them support your proposed moral judgement and subsequent action then you can feel more confident of being on the right moral track. People may want to stop whaling because it will upset the ecosystem (consequentialism), or because whaling is illegal (deontology), or because enlightened people do not support whaling (virtue ethics). Thus you would consider each ethical theory in turn to find the best overall solution.

Even if you favour one ethical theory over the others, keep in mind all three theories so that you are better aware of how ethical disagreements can arise, that is when one person advocates one ethical theory that clashes with someone else advocating another ethical theory. A foxhunter or bullfighter might defend their actions as a preservation of tradition; alternatively, you might claim that no one sympathetic to animals would kill foxes or bulls for sport. This can be seen as a case of deontology versus virtue ethics.

Do Philosophical Ideas Work?

Generations of people acquire philosophical ideas and values without realising they are doing so and without knowing where their ideas and values come from. Many of our ideas and values originated from individuals who lived, thought and died before us, examples are John Lock and Karl Marx. Few things in human society are bigger than revolutions and revolutions are made of philosophical ideas. John Locke (1632 - 1704), English physician, public servant and philosopher, significantly helped lay the foundations of liberal society. In his lifetime his ideas about government, tyranny and the rights of man were pivotal in replacing the English monarch in the 'Glorious Revolution' of 1688. Even after his death Locke's ideas played a leading role guiding the American and French revolutions. The other pre-eminent thinker was a German émigré who settled in London and spent much of his time writing there at the British Library. Karl Marx (1818 - 1883) wrote the intellectual foundation of Communism that fuelled the Communist revolutions of Russia and China in the 20th century.

Hundreds of millions of people today still live under the ideas of these two thinkers, ample demonstration of the power and pervasiveness of philosophical ideas. If you are not convinced, where might your ideas of soul and man's place in animal life come from? (Clue: Plato and Darwin.)

References

(1) Singer, Peter. *Applied Ethics.* Oxford University Press: Oxford. 1986:226.
(2) Garner, Robert. *Animal Ethics.* Polity Press. 2005:12.
(3) Bentham, Jeremy. *An Introduction to the Principles of Morals and Legislation.* 1789, chapter xvii.

Further Reading

An excellent, very readable book, that includes animal rights and environmental ethics, is Noel Stewart, *Ethics: an introduction to moral philosophy.* Polity Press. 2009. For more ideas and thoughts, be sure to read the online writings of Peter Singer: www.utilitarian.net/singer

Chapter	*Philosophy: Key Topics*
2	*4. Consequentialism*

Snappy Page Essence

Consequentialism is a theory that evaluates moral actions only by their consequences, and not according to doing your duty or by your being a virtuous person.

What makes your animal rights action good or bad, right or wrong? Consequentialism (or the more descriptive term consequence ethics) is a moral theory stating that the morality of your action depends only on its results or consequences.

Consequentialism is goal-directed because only the outcome or consequence of your action is important, not how you achieve it. You need not be dutiful or virtuous - you might even lie, cheat or whatever - so long as the result of your action is morally good. Consequentialism also goes by the name of teleology, from the Greek teleos meaning end or purpose. You can better understand animal rights and the actions of other people by reflecting on this moral theory.

Say you develop a vaccine that could save the lives of thousands of animals. But as part of the vaccine's development you must test it on tens of laboratory animals and they might die as a result. Consequentialism says it is the end result that is important, in this case you may be saving the lives of many more animals than you might kill, so you might decide it is morally right to go ahead with your tests. Or say a pig escapes from a slaughterhouse. You believe it is immoral to take him back to be killed, so you hide him and lie that you do not know where he is. Your action focuses on its result. Saving the pig from slaughter is morally more important to you than telling lies.

Consequentialism is one of three primary philosophical theories about what constitutes the right action; the other two ethical theories are deontology and virtue ethics. Two varieties of consequentialism are utilitarianism, by which you act to maximise the good for others, and ethical egoism, when you act solely for your own interests.

Consequentialism is a great help to guide how we should act, but like any moral theory it has a number of criticisms, and among them are the following.

Should you base your moral actions on what you vaguely suppose might happen? Given that we have a tendency to make wrong decisions, consequentialism might be especially unreliable when we cannot clearly see what the result of our moral action might be.

Consequentialism sometimes goes against people's sense of justice. Not all ends justify the means, that is the end result of your action, no matter how well-intentioned, may not justify doing a wrong to achieve it. Protecting cattle is worthy, but killing populations of badgers vaguely suspected of infecting cattle with tuberculosis is surely morally wrong (happy farmers but lots of dead badgers). Developing a vaccine to inoculate badgers instead of killing them could be a better outcome.

Consequentialism is concerned only with good results and disregards the motivation for your actions. Yet what you do might still be said to be moral as long as you do it with good intentions, even if your action turns out badly for some reason.

We cannot always judge actions by their results. Some actions seem intrinsically wrong, like killing off innocent people, children or whole populations of animals, even if at times the results seem appropriate.

Even though consequentialism has its weaknesses it is nevertheless a vital mode of thinking when you are involved in practical animal rights. Compare it with the entries in Chapter 2: Deontology and Virtue Ethics.

If we harm people then we must justify why we harm them.
If we cannot justify our actions then we must not harm them.
Similarly, we must question our conduct with animals.
We must ask what humanity is doing to animals,
how should and how can we do right, then act.

Ben Isacat
2015

Chapter	*Philosophy: Key Topics*
2	*5. Deontology*

Snappy Page Essence
Deontology is a theory that evaluates moral actions based only on doing one's duty, not on the consequences of the actions.

Deontology is a theory that evaluates moral actions based only on doing one's duty, not on the consequences of the actions. We are often faced with moral questions concerning animals. Deontology (or the more descriptive term duty ethics) can guide us about what kind of action to take concerning animal rights problems, and with many other moral problems too.

Deontology asserts that the right moral action is founded on an objective duty or obligation. When you do your duty you behave morally; when you fail to do your duty you behave immorally. Deontology asserts that you should do your duty even if you or others suffer as a consequence by your doing it. *'For King and country, right or wrong'*, is a deontology dictum, and you could equally say *'for animal liberation, right or wrong'*.

Two examples of acting deontologically: A rancher might hate shooting predators but accepts that he has an obligation to protect his cattle regardless of his action's impact on wildlife. A researcher might keep an animal in pain because he believes he has a responsibility to find a cure for a disease. Alternatively, however, as your duty to animalkind you might devote yourself to saving wildlife from ranchers or might release laboratory animals used in experiments - moral thinking can work in more than one direction.

The term deontology derives from the Greek *deon*, for that which is necessary or binding, a duty, and *logos*, meaning logic. Deontology is one of three fundamental ethical theories that can guide our thinking about moral questions and how we might resolve them. The other two theories are consequentialism (or more simply consequence ethics) and virtue ethics. Deontology opposes consequentialism by which only the outcome or consequence of your action is important. However, even if your moral action happens to lead to a bad result you will still have acted ethically, according to deontology.

Deontology appeals to an apparently objective source of duty for its authenticity. Deontologists variously believe their duty comes from God, from intuition, from what is 'naturally' right, from the law of their country, from what their society holds as true, from what their leaders say, or from some other apparently 'objective' source.

An ostensible strength of deontology is that it applies equally to everyone. That is, if you have a duty to act in a certain situation then everyone else in the same situation has a duty to act likewise. Some criticisms of deontology are the following.

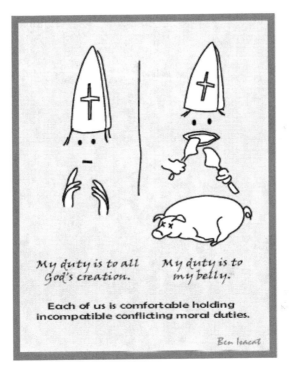

My duty is to all God's creation.

My duty is to my belly.

Each of us is comfortable holding incompatible conflicting moral duties.

Ben Isacat

Where do duties and obligations come from? Duty ethicists say duties are determined objectively and absolutely, not subjectively. However, duties might really be behaviours demonstrated over long periods to give the best results and are now honoured in practice and law. In this case deontology is really a form of Consequentialism, by which moral actions depend only on their consequences.

Emphasise duty and the greatest atrocities are possible, especially in time of war. You might do your duty for animals without regard for any pernicious consequences of your actions. But doing your duty without regard for consequences will at times harm others, perhaps irreparably.

Devotion to duty does not take into account the role of compassion and other emotions. Morality based on rational duty alone, without empathy or pity, could be a moral dead end.

As another criticism of deontology is how can you settle conflict between opposing moral duties? Two common moral duties are to save lives and to tell the truth. You may wish to save a lamb who escaped from a slaughterhouse but cannot lie to the authorities. One course of action is to choose the lesser evil (either save the lamb and lie, or not save the lamb and not lie). But then you will be considering consequences, whereas deontology aspires to be moral guidance resting on duty alone.

Chapter	*Philosophy: Key Topics*
2	*6. Virtue Ethics*

Snappy Page Essence

Virtue ethics is a theory that evaluates moral actions based on what a virtuous person should do, disregarding the consequences of the actions or the duty to carry them out.

Virtue ethics is a theory that evaluates moral actions based on what a virtuous person should do, disregarding the consequences of the actions or the duty to carry them out. Good and right moral acts, according to the moral theory virtue ethics, do not depend on the consequences of your action nor on doing your duty, but instead arise from being a virtuous person. Virtue ethics (also called virtue theory or value theory) prompts the question of how should a moral person act. It replies that a moral act is right if founded on a morally virtuous character and wrong if it stems from a corrupt, depraved or vicious character.

Virtue ethics is an ethical theory about the kind of person you are and as such it differs from the two other basic ethical theories, that of consequentialism (acting for the best outcome) and deontology (doing what duty says you should do). Whereas both these two other theories ask what is the right thing to do, virtue ethics instead brings personality into consideration.

Virtue ethics says you cannot isolate the making of ethical decisions from your personality. Your good actions are the result of good character and possessing admirable personal qualities makes you a virtuous person. Virtue ethics assumes that moral education is important and that childhood is a critical time for developing virtuous character. A person of good character is someone who has good admirable personal qualities, such as empathy, compassion, kindness, loyalty, honesty, prudence, wisdom and courage. Virtue ethics says you should always improve your character to make moral judgements through wisdom and you should always act appropriately morally with the right intention.

A virtuous person is said to hold these moral values:

- Beneficence: doing moral good to others.

- Autonomy: maximising the moral rights of others to make their own decisions.
- Equality: viewing all others as moral equals.
- Finality: taking moral action that overrides the demands of law, religion or social customs.
- Justice: treating all others morally fairly.
- Non-maleficence: causing no harm.
- Respect: consideration for the moral rights of others.
- Tolerance: understanding and accepting the viewpoints of others.
- Universality: basing your moral actions on decisions that hold for everyone, everywhere, for all time.

As a virtue ethicist you might, for instance, approve or reprove individuals or companies. You might only support the ones that do not harm animals and nature. Are these individuals or companies advancing or opposing virtue? Are they progressive, admirable and responsible entities? Or are they insensitive, negligent or dishonest? Do they support virtuous or immoral values? Again, as a virtuous person, you could abstain from eating animals and from wearing fur and could keep a low environmental impact lifestyle.

Virtue ethics flourished in Ancient Greece and Aristotle (BC 384 - 322) is often cited as its main philosophical representative. He said the opposite of a virtue is a vice, and that a virtue lies between two vices, that is between two extremes; courage is better than fearlessness and cowardice. Aristotle argued that a virtue is the mean or middle path between two vices. Virtue ethics expired in the fourth century AD when moral theories purporting to be given by God supplanted it. However, the 20th century brought it back to life and modernised it. Modern virtue ethics does not emphasize specific moral traits but says you should be virtuous in all aspects of your life and be a good person all the time.

An advantage of virtue ethics over consequentialism and deontology is that it brings in all the qualities of being human - like reason, responsibility and emotion - to influence ethical consideration. You can apply virtue ethics in situations where you ask what sort of person you should be.

Some criticisms of virtue ethics are these. What is a good virtue? Some Ancient Greeks said virtues exist in their own right independently of man and are indisputable. Many people today hold that a virtue depends on people's attitudes and since attitudes vary from person to person and from society to society, so virtues must also vary. Thus there is no indisputable list of virtues

and a virtue to one person or culture may be a bane to another. Virtue ethics is therefore relative. It is not a consistent guide on how to act.

Another criticism is that admirable personal qualities or traits do not in themselves tell us how to deal with moral problems. As a virtuous person you would not innately know the right thing to do. You would then have to turn to some other moral theory for guidance, like consequentialism or deontology. Therefore you might claim that virtue ethics is not a basic ethical theory and is redundant.

A final criticism is that even the most virtuous people make wrong moral decisions. So virtue ethics is not infallible.

Chapter 2	*Philosophy: Key Topics*
	7. Comparing Philosophical Ideas

Snappy Page Essence
Know where you stand! See animal rights in perspective. Compare it with animal ethics, animal welfare (and new welfarism), nature conservation…and deep ecology.

How do related animal philosophical outlooks compare with each other? Compare animal rights with fundamentally different approaches: animal ethics, animal welfare (and new welfarism), and nature conservation.

Animal Rights vs Animal Ethics

A primary difference between animal rights and animal ethics is that animal ethics is a theoretical academic pursuit that seeks to understand how humans should relate to animals. It does not advocate any particular ideology or doctrine. It analyses animal rights as one of many viewpoints but does not advocate it. Animal rights, on the other hand, can be studied academically, but it is also a practical doctrine about how we should relate to animals. A musical analogy is appropriate: animal ethics is a bit like exploring musical theory whereas animal rights is like playing a specific musical instrument.

The graphic on the next page explains more by summarising important points for animal rights versus animal ethics.

Ben Isacat

Animal Rights vs Animal Welfare

Animal rights overlaps with animal welfare. But although both outlooks share similarities they have important differences that set them apart and make them conflicting philosophies (see the graphic, below).

Animal rightists often disparage of animal welfare because the two philosophies are worlds apart in important respects. As the radical animal rights academic and activist Stephen Best says:

"Animal 'welfare' laws do little but regulate the details of exploitation." The Epiphanies of Dr Steven Best, Claudette Vaughn. Vegan Voice. 2004. (Accessed online February 2007.)

Animal Rights
They overlap but basically:

1. A practical pursuit applying morality to everyday situations.

2. A doctrine advocating rights for animals.

3. Claims we have a duty to give animals rights which we must respect.

4. Asserts using animals for human gain is morally wrong.

5. Focuses only on rights, a sub-set of animal ethics.

6. Concentrates on sentient animals.

Ben Isacat

Animal Ethics

1. An academic field asking how we should treat animals.

2. Impartial — without any particular moral viewpoint.

3. Attempts to resolve moral animal-human issues with a number of approaches.

4. Explores many ways as to how we should treat animals.

5. Includes animal rights but is broader in scope, eg overlaps with environmental ethics.

6. Considers all animals.

Morality is practical ethics. Ethics is theoretical morality.

An important difference in the practice of animal rights and animal welfare is that one is subjective and the other is objective. We cannot measure animal rights impartially or scientifically. It is a concept and a personal moral choice. It resembles the conviction of the German philosopher Immanuel Kant (1724 - 1804) that we should not harm humans even in the interests of the majority (a deontology philosophy). Animal rights takes Kant's view a step further and applies it to animals. As an ethical concept animal rights is close to duty ethics which Kant advocated.

Animal welfare, on the other hand, has the advantage that we can measure it objectively and manipulate it scientifically. To find which kind of bedding chickens prefer, we can count the number of chickens who seek to live on a straw floor or a wire mesh floor. Then we might provide the chickens with their choice, economic and other constraints permitting the animals' welfare.

In terms of ethics we can see animal welfare as part of consequence ethics (consequentialism) that is conceptually underpinned by utilitarianism.

Animal welfare has a variation called new welfarism, in outlook a cross between animal rights and animal welfare. New welfarism is the view that the best way to prevent animal suffering is to abolish the causes of animal suffering, but that abolition is an ideal long-term goal and meanwhile we must be pragmatic and improve the conditions of animals by advancing their welfare. Thus, for instance, new welfarists want to phase out fur farms and animal experiments but in the short-term they try to improve conditions for the animals in these systems, so they lobby to make cages less constrictive to reduce the numbers of animals used in laboratories.

New welfarism stands somewhere between animal welfare and animal rights. Animal welfarists believe people should use animals but treat them well. Animal rightists say people should not use animals and we must abolish the causes of animal suffering, for if there is no suffering then there is no need for welfare. New welfarists take the view that they support abolishing the causes of suffering but argue pragmatically that it will take a long time to achieve and meanwhile they must do all they can to support the welfare of animals.

A major criticism of new welfarism by animal rightists is that it does not stop the exploitation of animals, even supports it, and therefore is a useless philosophy and the ultimate act of betrayal for animals. New welfarists respond by claiming that new welfarism is more achievable, and therefore of more immediate benefit to exploited animals, than the long-term and perhaps impossible goals of animal rights, such as demanding complete closure of anti-animal industries and changing the entrenched habits of billions of people.

Animal Rights vs Conservation

Animal rights and nature conservation are similar and different. Both became popular with the public in the late 1970's. Both oppose human-centredness (see Anthropocentrism), although not all conservationists do. Both believe that wild animals have intrinsic value (worth or importance independent of human values), though not an attitude shared by all conservationists. And both support conserving the environment, but for different reasons - conservationists for the sake of greater conservation, animal rightists for the animals who live in it. For the differences between these views see the table on the previous page.

Comparison of Animal Rights & Conservation	
Animal Rights	**Conservation**
Focuses on the individual animal as well as on animals in general.	Focuses on levels above the individual (populations, species, ecosystems and the biosphere) except when just a few individuals are the only survivors of their population or species.
Refers usually to sentient animals and not to plants or the physical environment.	Encompasses all creatures (plants etc) and includes the physical part of nature (eg air and water).
Concerned with animals in areas of human activity, such as agriculture, laboratories, fur trade, zoos and circuses.	Not concerned with animals in areas of human activity unless the animals are taken from endangered populations or species.
Tries to minimise suffering of animals, especially when humans cause it.	Conservationists say pain and death are a part of life which individuals must endure and that it is preferable that individuals suffer so long as their population or species survives.

Conclusion

Can you be an exclusive animal rightist, welfarist or conservationist - or for that matter, an exclusive deep ecologist (see next section)? Actually, being exclusively one or another may be the most difficult course. A better approach is to see these philosophies not as necessarily mutually exclusive but as reinforcing one another. We can surely be benignly flexible and adopt the best ideas and activities from each of them depending on the particular circumstances we encounter. Certainly, knowledge about each of them and their antitheses helps us understand the outlook of other people.

Chapter	*Philosophy: Key Topics*
2	*8. Deep Ecology*

Snappy Page Essence

Deep ecology is a philosophical and practical guide that opposes the destruction of nature by materialism and consumerism. It maintains that humanity must change its harmful ways or it will destroy itself and all life. Deep ecology gives us an extra perspective on animal rights.

Deep ecology contrasts with animal rights and helps us see animal rights in perspective. Deep ecology is concerned with fundamental philosophical, practical and personal questions about the ways humans relate to their environment. It relates to animals because of course animals are part of our environment.

Deep ecology opposes the exploitation and destruction of the natural world by materialism and consumerism. It says we should minimise our impact on the world and it appeals for a change in the way we think about the world. Deep ecology predicts that if we do not shift our basic values and customs we will destroy the diversity and beauty of the world's life and its ability to support humanity.

The ideas of deep ecology came about against the background of the nascent Environmentalism of the 1960's. Deep ecology is primarily associated with Norwegian philosopher Arne Naess (1912 - 2009). The 'Deep' in Deep ecology refers to a fundamental or wise questioning of attitudes to nature. Deep ecology questions the root causes of the degeneration of the variety and richness of the world. It calls for a more enlightened approach for humanity to live within the bounds of Nature rather than to depend on technological fixes as remedies for our exploitation / destruction of nature.

Naess coined the term Deep ecology in 1973 in contrast to shallow ecology, a lesser form of environmentalism and typical of societies worldwide today. The nature of shallow ecology has a utilitarian and anthropocentric attitude, based on materialism and consumerism. Shallow ecology focuses on using the world's natural resources for unlimited human growth and comes up with technological solutions to offset environmental problems thus made. For example, shallow ecology promotes recycling of commercial and industrial waste instead of emphasising the prevention of the generation of waste in the first place. Again, shallow ecology supports placing ever increasing demands on the land to produce more food instead of stressing the improvement of human birth control to reduce human numbers.

The Eight Tenets of Deep Ecology

Naess and colleagues proposed eight tenets to form the basis of Deep ecology thought. Their intention was for these points to be agreeable to people from any philosophical, political or religious background. The table below paraphrases the eight tenets and contrasts them with tenets that anyone might make up for shallow ecology.

Some environmental activists, along with some sections of political parties, support the philosophy of Deep ecology and use it as a philosophical basis for change. As a guide for personal growth, Deep ecology invites each individual to intermesh with and identify with all living creatures. But we are not just saving other species and ecosystems; we are really saving ourselves, because nature is a part of us. Deep ecology says that humans are not isolated objects but are part of the whole of Nature.

A criticism of Deep ecology from the animal rights point of view is that it asserts we can use animals to satisfy our basic needs (Tenet 3). 'Deep' (abolitionist) animal rights philosophy forbids the use of animals. We would use up a vast number of animals if all the billions of humans put to use an animal just occasionally.

Can you be an exclusive animal rightist, welfarist, conservationist or deep ecologist? Actually, being exclusively one or the other may be the most difficult course. An alternative approach is not to see these philosophies as mutually exclusive but as reinforcing one another. We can surely be benignly flexible and adopt the best ideas and activities
from each of them depending on the particular circumstances we encounter. Circumstances force us to be pragmatic at times. Certainly, knowledge about each of these outlooks and their antitheses helps us understand the outlook of other people.

The Eight Tenets of Deep Ecology -
paraphrased and contrasted with Shallow Ecology

Deep Ecology	Shallow Ecology
1. All creatures on Earth have intrinsic value.	1. All creatures on Earth have value only for their usefulness to humans.
2. The whole diversity of living beings, simple as well as complex, contributes to life's richness.	2. Complex creatures (ie humans) are more important than simpler ones.
3. Humans should only use other beings to satisfy their basic needs.	3. Humans should use all resources for their material and economic advantage.
4. The health of non-humans depends on decreasing the number of humans.	4. The human population can increase without restraint.
5. Human interference with the world is excessive and worsening.	5. Technological progress will solve all problems.
6. Human policy (economics, technology and ideology) must change radically.	6. Materialism and consumerism should govern human society.
7. Quality of life is more important than standard of living.	7. The standard of living should keep rising.
8. Every human who believes in these points must work for change.	8. Leave environmental problems for the experts to solve.

For & Against: argue your case

Make a note of people's opinions, break them down into simple assertions and add a counter argument to help you defend your corner.

1. Harmony vs Industry

- Claim: Deep ecologists want to stop industrial and technological development in order to embrace a lifestyle that is entirely in harmony with nature. But this would ruin mankind because industrial and technological disintegration would cause great upheaval.

- Claim: We should continue humanity's industrial and technological development but in such a way as radically to take the pressure off biodiversity, particularly by reducing the human birth rate.

2. Anti-human

- Claim: Supporters of Deep ecology say that it is best for nature if humanity disappeared from the face of the Earth. So Deep ecology is anti-human.
- Claim: Deep ecology deplores anti-human statements. Deep ecology affirms that all beings, including humans, have inherent value.

3. Aboriginal Harmony

- Claim: As deep ecologists we should look more to aboriginal people because their values and practices could help us live more wisely.
- Claim: It is a myth that aboriginal people lived in harmony with nature. They exploited their environment to their full advantage. The only thing we can learn from them is also to exploit the environment to our full advantage.

<table>
<tr><td>

Chapter

3

</td></tr>
</table>

Campaigning Methods for Animal Rights

1. Campaigning

Snappy Page Essence
By campaigning you try to change society by persuading and motivating people to act for the better, as you see it. You need to know what you want to achieve, how to do it, a will to act and drive to keep you going.

"Campaigning can be as easy as writing to your local newspaper's letters page, or as elaborate as being at the centre of a busy local group." Animal Aid (1)

Introduction
Campaigning is about changing society for the better by persuading and motivating people to act in some way. Whether you are acting as a group or alone this chapter offers you background and some of the essential techniques for campaigning. Do not think you must campaign by demonstrating at rallies or otherwise by making big noises. You can accomplish a lot effectively in numerous ways from professional or semi-professional work to relatively low-key activities (see Chapter 4 for some examples). The main thing you need for campaigning is a will to act and drive to keep you going. Winston Churchill said 'Persevere to conquer!'

One half of the key to successful campaigning is knowing what you want to achieve. But the other half of the key is knowing how to campaign. Animal rights campaign tactics are no different from their civil rights counterparts in this and past centuries. To make their demands heard activists employed techniques like picketing, lobbying, demonstrating, and today have some novel tools in their arsenal, like email and the Web.

Do not stop at the end of this chapter when finding out how best to campaign for your cause. Let this chapter sharpen your appetite for further inquiry. You can find out a lot more from fellow activists, books and the Web. Seasoned campaigners say there are tried and tested techniques for campaigning based on the experience of many good activists - but they also say there is no infallible guarantee of results! Just get stuck in and good luck.

Your Right to Campaign

In democratic countries we have the right to be involved in decisions that affect society and our lives. Whether you are a student, worker, mother or pensioner we can all campaign to make our voices heard. Each of us has the right to face the powers that be and campaign to bring about changes we think are necessary.

We have the right to influence decision-makers, especially people in powerful positions. We have the right to make them do what we think is best, whether we want change locally or globally, whether our action is high-key or low-key. Much of the change in society comes from a few largely unknown but dedicated people working hard in the background. Working alone or in small groups of committed activists they can stimulate big changes. A few people chucking tea cases into Boston harbour are widely credited for leading the way to the independence of the United States from Britain.

Where to Begin?

Sometimes the most difficult part of taking action is choosing what to champion from the many possible issues. As a starting point, unless something has already fallen into your lap, you can categorise animal rights controversies in a number of ways (which inevitably overlap) and specialise in one that interests you.

- Attire: eg fur, perfume, jewellery, clothing.
- Entertainment: eg circuses, rodeos, zoos, animal baiting.
- Experiment: eg biomedical research, toxicity testing, education.
- Food: eg caged chickens, veal, foie gras, bush meat, vegetarianism.
- Hunting & Sport: eg chasing, trapping, canned hunting, baiting.
- Unintentional: eg motorist kills, habitat destruction, climate change.
- Trade: eg zoos, pets, quack medicine, body parts, trinkets.
- Zoos/Conservation: eg road-side zoos, national zoos, wildlife 'culls'.

Or try picking out a topic from the list (Choosing a Field of Practical Animal Rights Activities) at the end of this section. These are just some fields of interest in animal rights and you can come up with others, among them animal abuse (and its relationship with human abuse), caged hens and open rescue, cruelty-free shopping, and xenotransplantation.

If you are still stumped for an objective to campaign for then contact organisations that take your interest and may want to set up a group in your district.

Keeping Going

Well into your campaigning you could be having fun, but you will also experience workaday frustration when your efforts appear to be falling flat. At times we all get fed up, frustrated and think we are failing. But think again and be heartened for you may simply be going through the normal development of any movement for social change.

Bill Moyer (1933 - 2002) was an American activist for social change during most of 40 years. He outlined several stages that a movement for social change goes through in its development (2). Moyer would say that we in the animal rights movement are at a particular stage in our development. We have successfully passed the initial stages: the animal rights issue is on the social and political agenda and is hotly disputed; citizen groups are growing in number and strength and are educating the public; and some of the public are being alienated by violent activist rebels. However, Moyer would also say that we have not yet won support from the public majority (his stage six) and still have a long way to go before the public will push for change (his stage eight). However, these stages in the development of movements for social change are not clear-cut, as George Lakey, another old-hand American civil rights campaigner reminds us (3). Lakey says that different groups in the same movement for social change may in their development go back and forth a number of times and at different rates.

Knowing the prescriptions that make for successful social change will help us keep going and make us more likely to succeed. Keep Moyer and Lakey in mind and you will despair less in your off moments and when rampaging in frustration.

Ten Essential Campaigning Tips

Here are pointers for success that are common to most campaigns and every campaigner should know from the start.

1. What Is Your Campaign?

What are you ultimately trying to achieve? If you are not completely clear about what you are aiming for you are not likely to achieve it. Your ultimate aim must be clear and precise. A good exercise is to write down your ultimate goal in less than a dozen or so words. You need to record your goal anyway and keep it safe so that over time it does not insidiously change, for it could change into something that seems the same yet in effect is really different. The route to your original goal may not be the same as the route to your changed goal so that you just go round in circles.

2. Break Down Goals Into Manageable Chunks

Break down your ultimate goal into small chunks you know you can attain. For instance, to shut down an animal abusing pet shop or aquarium (ultimate goal), your sub-goals could be: 1. Itemise how the shop may respond to your attack and how you will counter each response. 2. Complete a file of facts that supports your case on the shop. 3. Convince people in the shop's neighbourhood about your cause and document their support. 4. Lobby and win over your local political representative to support your case (see Chapter 3: Lobbying). And so on... Completing each sub-goal will give you a sense of achievement, keep the momentum going, be good for moral, boost your credibility and bring you closer to your ultimate goal.

3. Is It Outrageous?

Outrage is what the news media thrive on and what the public love to read. Issues that may make you fume but for which nothing can be done, or for which everything possible is being done, are not outrages in this sense. An outrage has to be something that nothing or little is being done about yet a great deal can be done about it. Make the focal point of your campaign an outrage and you are more likely to succeed. People who hear about an outraged may turn into fellow campaigners or support you in some other way.

4. Do Sufficient Research

You must convince people generally and policy makers in particular that your campaign issue is important. So get as many relevant and accurate facts that you can about your issue from different perspectives: background, some quantitative figures, the major players, relevant legislation and government policy. Write it in a simple form that people can understand easily. Issues often generate conflict between people because they get their facts wrong or are biased. The more you know, the more expert you will become and people will have more confidence in you. For a regional issue you could get information by carrying out a local survey. For a wider issue a web search might bring up lots of information. Go for reputable, authoritative, primary sources, that is first hand evidence, not what someone says someone else has said.

5. Know Who You Must Influence

Once you know exactly what you are going to campaign on, work out who you need to influence and whose support you need to win. Influencing and winning over 'the public' is too vague. Does your issue involve the people in your locality or region, an institution, a local or national authority, a senator or member of parliament - perhaps a combination? How are you going to reach them? (See Lobbying, Chapter 3.)

6. Your Resources

Do not worry about money - good actions do not necessarily have big budgets, if any budget at all. However, start campaigning with something within your reach. Do members of your group have complementary abilities and experience? Is anyone good at organising events, speaking in public, handling the news media or have expertise in web design? (See Chapter 3: Starting a Group.) If you do not have what you need and cannot get it, think up another campaign.

7. Alternative Viewpoints

No matter how you see your issue, how do the people you must influence see it? Examine the forces, people and organisations at work for and against the change you want to bring about. See things from their points of view. Say you want to save a wood for its animal inhabitants and need to persuade your local authority not to bulldoze it. You might think the wood is important for frogs, owls and weasels, but the local authority see it as a resource for a recreation park and timber. So emphasise the issue in their terms – dog walking and renewable wood felling – and they will be more likely to listen to you.

8. Broaden Your Public

Your campaign is more likely to succeed the greater the number of people who support you. So find a part of your issue that most people can identify with. Say you are campaigning against the building of a new abattoir. Most people tolerate killing animals for food but few willingly endure bad smells. You should therefore concentrate your campaign on the issue of odours rather than on vegetarianism. Better to campaign on five per cent of the problem and get 95 per cent support from the people.

9. Join a Coalition

Individual groups joining together to work toward the same goal make a coalition. By joining a coalition your group may be able to do more than by working alone. You can snap a single stick but you cannot break a bundle of sticks. Look for other groups and ask what they are doing. Introduce your group to them and give them an idea of the benefits your group can offer them.

10. Can't Get No...

You might think that you need hope and passion to change things or that you should have fun and an agreeable time while campaigning. These are important, but what you really need is a measure of satisfaction. Aim for a dose of satisfaction, that is a measure of having achieved something, at least weekly, or daily if possible. You can best get it by setting yourself small goals and achieving them, eg completing a newsletter, bagging a new member, assembling all the bric-a-brac for a fundraising drive. These are solid stepping stones on the way to success that should raise your spirit and keep you going.

Even More Tips

- Selling yourself and your campaign to the news media is a good and free way of telling people you exist and getting their support. The more frequently you appear in the media the more people will know about you and remember your campaign.
- Keep in touch with reality about what you can do. Take off into a world of fantasy and you will be lost.
- Only make accurate claims you can reasonably prove. Be knowledgeable and check your sources. People will then learn they can trust what you say and be more ready to listen to you.
- Do not assume your opponents are depraved. They are likely to be as admirable as you, so respect them. Put yourself in their position and ask what will move them to do what you would have them do.
- Attack obstacles obliquely if you cannot get past them. For instance, if you cannot attack your opponents directly, go for their support.
- The practical campaign is primary. Minimise bureaucracy; don't get stuck in it.
- Build on your reputation and history of successes to take on more or bigger campaigns.

- Bear in mind that you may be mistaken. Someone said, "Don't die for your beliefs - they may be wrong." So keep an open mind and be prepared to alter your campaign course of action if necessary.
- Finally, does your campaign pass the SMART test and have you done a SWOT? See Chapter 3 under Action Planning.

Choosing a Field of Practical Animal Rights Activities
Some Suggestions

General Animal Rights
- Sentience vs non-sentient animals.
- Speciesism vs anthropocentrism.
- Animals as property, legal status as objects.
- Exploitation of animals for food, experimentation, trade.
- Animal rights vs animal welfare vs nature conservation.
- Practical campaigning for animal rights.

Vegetarianism & Veganism
- Why be a vegan or veggie?
- Vegetarian history and demographics.
- Practicalities of organising a veggie/vegan food stall.
- Nutrition and vegan/veggie recipes.
- Health and disease, eg salmonella, bird flu, foot & mouth disease.
- Social impact of the meat industry, eg Third World starvation.

Factory Farming
- The industrial scale of mass slaughter.
- Inhumane housing conditions.
- Gourmet dishes, eg shark fin soup, foie gras, veal.
- Mutilations of farm animals.
- Pollution of the environment.
- Health hazards to humans.
- Deformities induced by confinement or breeding.
- Factory vs traditional vs organic farming.

Animal Experimentation
- Biomedical research & diseases.
- Toxicity testing.

- Animal housing.
- History of animal experimentation.
- Morality & legal history of 'unnecessary' pain.
- National & international animal protection laws.
- Science & ethics.
- The three R's & alternatives to experimentation.

Entertainment

- Kinds of entertainment, eg film industry, rodeos, circuses, bull fighting.
- History & culture of animal entertainment.
- Animals used for entertainment, eg horses, dogs, chicken, wild animals.
- Selective breeding of entertainment animals, eg race horses, greyhounds, beagles, foxhounds, ferrets.
- Fate of retired entertainment animals.

Fur & Skins

- The fur-bearing animals, eg rabbits, racoons, mink, cats.
- Farming fur-bearers.
- Traps & trapping wild fur-bearers.
- Numbers of pelts traded internationally.
- The fashion industry.
- The leather industry: cattle, snakes and crocodiles.
- Fur industry: positive or negative nature conservation?
- Alternative synthetic materials.

Wildlife

- The Sixth Extinction.
- Climate change and animal survival.
- Habitat destruction.
- International trade, eg for body parts, quack medicine, exotic pets.
- Bush meat.
- Hunting wild or canned animals for sport.
- The role of zoos.
- Animal rights vs nature conservation.

Animal Ethics

- Animal moral status.
- The moral community.
- Equal consideration of interests vs intrinsic & instrumental value.
- Consequentialism, deontology and virtue ethics.
- Moral agents & moral patients.
- Moral autonomy & marginal cases.

Pets

- Numbers of animals the pet trade breeds.
- Exotic pets: reptiles, birds, mammals taken from the wild.
- Animals perishing in transit.
- Animals confined in cages & unsuitable quarters.
- Abused, neglected & unwanted pets.
- 'Controlling' pet numbers: neutering & euthanasia.
- Cosmetic surgery or mutation, vanity & tradition.
- Billions of animals killed annually as pet food.

References

(1) *Guide to Campaigning.* July 2007. Animal Aid. (Web site accessed online March 2008.)

(2) Moyer, Bill. *The Practical Strategist: Movement Action Plan* (MAP). Social Movement Empowerment Project, San Francisco. 1990. (Accessed online July 2007.)

(3) Lakey, George. *Strategizing for a Living Revolution.* (Accessed online July 2007.) Also in Solnit, David (ed.) *Globalize Liberation: how to uproot the system and build a better world.* City Lights. 2003.

Chapter	*Campaigning Methods for*
3	*Animal Rights*

2. Civil Disobedience

Snappy Page Essence
Civil disobedience is a form of protest to act on your moral right and correct injustice. The citizen grants the state its authority and the citizen can oppose authority if compelled by conscience.

"So the point isn't to have a victory over somebody else but rather to effect change. And change is a lot more rapid and a lot more enduring if you get the cooperation of what would otherwise be your adversary."
Henry Spira (1)

What Is Civil Disobedience?

Civil disobedience usually entails non-violent actions, such as marches, demonstrations, strikes, sit-ins or occupation of buildings. Civil disobedience is a form of protest. The reason for being a civil resister or dissenter is to act on your moral right and correct an injustice you perceive. You are trying to reverse or stop some process or make an appeal to correct or revoke a law. You are a dissenter every time you deliberately disobey the law or a demand by government, believing that your action is just and the law or government is unfair or harmful.

Henry David Thoreau (1817 - 1862), American philosopher, naturalist and writer, is often cited as articulating the belief that people have a duty not to take part in a perceived injustice and to resist any government or its agent forcing people to participate. Thoreau asserted that it is the citizen who grants the state its authority and the citizen can oppose unjust authority if compelled by conscience.

Dissenters from all kinds of background, including suffragists, feminists, anti-war demonstrators and nuclear bomb protesters, have engaged in civil disobedience. Among the biggest and best known practitioners of civil disobedience are the Indian Mohandas Gandhi (1869 - 1948) and the American Martin Luther King jr (1929 - 1968). Gandhi practised civil disobedience as a weapon in his struggle for independence for India from British rule. King fought peacefully for black-American civil rights. Both men were beaten and jailed - even non-violent acts of civil disobedience risk retaliation and verbal or physical attack by opponents and police - but attracted huge numbers of supporters and co-civil rights rebels.

Gandhi outlined some key rules when carrying out civil disobedience. They convey the flavour of his form of campaigning:

- Tolerate the anger and assaults of your opponents.
- Do not get angry, insult or retaliate against your opponents.
- Submit to arrest.

These are good rules in that they clearly tell you what to do and, all things being equal, do not jeopardise your cause.

Civil Disobedience & Animal Rights
Some animal rights issues attracting civil disobedience actions are:

- Laboratories experimenting on animals: they invite break-ins.
- Factory farms: they attract open and clandestine rescues (see Chapter 4 under Animal Rescuer).
- Fur shops: their locks have been super-glued and windows smashed.
- Fox hunting with hounds: solicit hunt saboteurs to challenge them.

The last of these, campaigning for foxes against fox hunters with hounds, had a successful legal judgement in Britain when the sport was outlawed by Act of Parliament (coming into force in 2003 in Scotland and 2004 in England). This campaigning for foxes had much effort and a long history spanning at least two generations of activists. One kind of campaign took the form of hunt sabotage, a good example of animal rights civil disobedience.

Hunt Sabotage
Hunt sabotage began in 1960's Britain and may have been the first methodical non-violent action to confront organised hunting of animals for sport. The hunt saboteurs (or 'sabs') engaged hunters with hounds (or 'hunts'). The job of the sabs was to make hunting impractical by delaying or confusing the hounds to give the quarry (usually foxes and sometimes deer) a chance to escape. Two sab techniques are blowing hunting horns and covering a quarry's sent with pungent sprays to mislead the hounds.

Sabs were not kindly tolerated by the hunts. Hunts reacted to the sabotage by employing private security firms and their own supporters to take on the sabs, sometimes violently. Police at hunts became a common sight and policing and public order problems emerged. Police sometimes pretended not to notice when hunts attacked sabs, possibly partly because they were unsure of what powers hunts could legally use. The Conservative government, numbering many hunters in their membership, also came down on the sabs by enacting laws specifically obstructing sab action. The sabs replied by disobeying the laws in the field and disputing them the courts. Eventually, a sympathetic (Labour) government pushed through an Act of Parliament banning hunting with dogs. The sabs had pulled through and won (although not alone, as other bodies contributed). Even so, the hunts continue to engage in superficially outwardly legal activities and the hunt sabs continue to engage them.

Arguments For & Against Civil Disobedience

Some people have certain misconceptions and criticisms of civil disobedience. Here are some of the claims and counter claims.

1. Democracy
- Claim: You cannot excuse civil disobedience in a democracy because unjust laws can be changed by democratic procedures.
- Claim: Civil disobedience is a democratic activity. Democratic governments hold power by virtue of the individual citizens who elect them and if change is blocked by a government then dissenters can unblock it with appropriate doses of civil disobedience.

2. Regular Channels
- Claim: Civil disobedience should be the last resort in a democracy. First you must exhaust all existing channels of communication for change.
- Claim: There is a point when appealing through regular channels becomes futile and delays furthering your cause. Besides, regular channels are often part of the problem.

3. Citizenship
- Claim: Being a citizen you enjoy the rights and benefits of your country. Therefore you must in turn obey your country's customs and laws.
- Claim: This is every reason for challenging what you see as unjust, in order to make your country a better place to live.

4. Anarchy
- Claim: Lawlessness and anarchy would reign if everyone were a civil-disobedience activist.
- Claim: If we do not challenge government and its laws we could slip into oppression and despotism.

References
(1) Spira, Henry. The Vegan.com Interview, by Erik Marcus. 1998. (Accessed March 2007.)

Chapter	Campaigning Methods for
3	Animal Rights

3. Direct Action

Snappy Page Essence
Direct action fights for a cause dynamically and directly for immediate change, whereby adversaries must yield significant concessions, and rejects conventional slower methods of social change.

"In moral terms, the granting of rights to animals leads to the conclusion that direct action in their defence is not only permissible but also a moral duty, although whether this justifies some of the more extreme actions involving violence is an open question." Robert Garner (1)

What is Direct Action?
Direct action is activity that fights for a cause dynamically and directly for immediate change. You can view direct action as a strong form of civil disobedience with a capacity for acting illegally. Activists employing direct action aim to create a situation whereby their opponents have to yield significant concessions to the activists' cause. Direct action campaigners often tend to disown the methods of the less dramatic and slower mainstream who advance social change through education and legislative procedures.

Among the issues in addition to animal rights in which direct action is employed are environmental protection, anti-globalisation, nuclear disarmament and asylum-seeker support. People have carried out direct action in labour disputes in Europe and North America since the 19th century and particularly in the 20th century by workers challenging government and big employers for social rights and political power. Strikes, boycotts, picketing, sit-ins, trespass and mass occupation of land or buildings, property damage and sabotage are some of the tools of direct action, with a measure of agitation, sometimes even violence by the more hot headed activists. But employers might also use direct action against activists, such as lockouts and mass dismissal of workers. You might say that governments have also used direct action in the form of mass fines, mass arrest and mass imprisonment.

Examples of Animal Rights Direct Action

Much direct action is perfectly legal. Some of the actions by the more excessive or illegally inclined animal rights activists, however, include:

- Physical assault.
- Posting letter bombs/booby traps.
- Bomb hoaxing.
- Arson of premises (eg at animal breeders, fur shops, laboratories).
- Wrecking equipment (eg at fur farms, laboratories, slaughterhouses, and hunters' traps and shooting platforms).
- Freeing caged or confined animals from properties (eg chickens, minks, rabbits and goats. See Animal Rescuer, Chapter 4).
- Ruining fur apparel.
- Burning or damaging motor vehicles (such as puncturing tyres and paint stripping).
- Breaking or etching windows (eg of pet, fur and butcher shops).
- Painting graffiti or paint bombing (ditto).
- Contaminating commercial products (eg cosmetics, sweets and foodstuff. For more see under Efficacy of Direct Action, below).
- Door lock super-gluing (eg of fur shops and fast food shops).
- Rowdily demonstrating outside animal abusers' homes.
- Reviling people as animal abusers to their neighbours.
- Sending abusive letters and making threatening phone calls.
- Publishing animal abusers' names and addresses on the Web.
- Disrupting phone and email communication of companies.
- Web site hacking.

All these extreme activities can be carried out by just one or two people and most probably are in actuality. Possibly the most serious by far of these actions is arson, which on conviction could land a jail sentence of several years and possibly kill someone trapped in a blazing building.

Some direct actions for animal rights are illegal, but possibly the most successful actions are the legal ones, perhaps because they are sustained over a long period. Good examples are the work of the Sea Shepherd Conservation Society and the Battle of Brightlingsea (as we see below). Another is the assailing of company reputations over the exploitation of animals and nature (more below). One company offensive culminated in the famous case of McDonald's fast food chain with the celebrated McLibel Two (Chapter 6: The McLibel Two). The disruption of animal hunts is also a good example of sustained direct action for animal rights (see Hunt Sabotage, Chapter 3: Civil Disobedience).

Without going into the morality of illegal direct action a criticism can be made about it. Unless an action is methodical and long-term against a particular target, such as with the intention of causing financial ruin and closure of a company, it may be seen by many of the public as wanton vandalism. It is debatable whether such actions have value for animal rights, although they might publicise the cause and stimulate discussion.

Individual vs Mass Direct Action
Sustained direct action needs a certain amount of organisation and long-term effort to be effective. However, you do not need to be a big group or a mass

of citizenry to employ direct action. One activist with a bit of backing can be effective, as demonstrated by Henry Spira (see Chapter 6). Another example is the Rambo affair. The pilot of an airliner at London airport in 2000 would not take off when one of the passengers refused to sit down. The passenger was a member of an activist group protesting the deportation of asylum-seekers from Britain. The pilot only took off when the activist and the object of the action, a deported asylum-seeker, together left the plane (2). The asylum-seeker was Salim Rambo, a 23-year-old political activist from the Democratic Republic of Congo (Zaire), who said he would be killed if he returned to his country of origin. According to later reports, Rambo was granted asylum in Britain.

Sea Shepherd Conservation Society

Sea Shepherd is a seafaring activist organisation based in the United States, operating three ships and a variety of boats. The society's name comes from its first ship, a trawler bought in Britain and renamed the Sea Shepherd. The society engages in direct action to save marine wildlife, especially whales, dolphins, seals and turtles. Its mission is to execute international maritime laws and agreements meant to protect sea species and the marine environment.

A particular aim of Sea Shepherd, the one for which it is best known, is halting illegal whaling. Sea Shepherd's angle is not to protest against whaling as such but to fight illegal whaling operations. Flying a black Jolly Roger Sea Shepherd crews chase and obstruct whalers from illegally harpooning whales, they ram their adversaries' ships on the high seas and sink them in harbour. The organisation's small fleet of ships has battled with whalers from Spain, Iceland, Norway, Japan and other nations. The sea-going activists bring back film of illegal killing of whales to show on television around the world to increase public knowledge of marine issues and the carnage people do on sea animals.

Sea Shepherd rests its legitimacy on its application of the law. Among the international treaties it invokes in the course of its work is the United Nations World Charter for Nature (1982). The Charter mandates individuals to enforce international conservation laws. In particular, under section 21 (c) and (e):

States and, to the extent they are able, other public authorities, international organizations, individuals, groups and corporations shall:
(c) Implement the applicable international legal provisions for the conservation of nature and the protection of the environment.

(e) Safeguard and conserve nature in areas beyond national jurisdiction.

And section 24:

Each person has a duty to act in accordance with the provisions of the present Charter, acting individually, in association with others or through participation in the political process, each person shall strive to ensure that the objectives and requirements of the present Charter are met.

Policing the seas and oceans of the world has its risks. While documenting illegal whaling off Siberia in Soviet territorial waters in 1981 a Sea Shepherd crew was pursued by an aggressive Soviet warship. And in 1994 a Norwegian Navy destroyer lobbed depth charges at another Sea Shepherd boat and rammed it.

Paul Watson, a Canadian and co-founder of Greenpeace, set up Sea Shepherd in 1977. Watson left Greenpeace to be more direct and confrontational in his actions. His radical property-destruction method of ramming and sinking illegal whalers shows that, always taking maximum care, you can sometimes use violent action without endangering human life. Watson is always mindful of the welfare of his and the whaling ships' crews. Sea Shepherd claim they have never caused or taken an injury.

Watson and his colleagues have inflamed their opponents and been incarcerated and sued for crimes on the high seas. But all attempts to lock them up permanently have failed. Sea Shepherd justifies its actions by claiming that it always acts legally within the law. Sea Shepherd says that the ships it sinks are breaking international law by hunting endangered whales and as such are pirates. Sea Shepherd's critics claim the organisation harasses legal harvesting of the sea's resources and call Sea Shepherd crews pirates and eco-terrorists. Indeed, two of Sea Shepherd's ships have been struck off shipping registers, which means they can be boarded and captured as pirates and outlaws.

On the up side, Sea Shepherd has saved the lives of many whales and publicised the plight of whales around the globe. Sea Shepherd says it is the "most aggressive and most successful whale-saving organisation in the world" and in 2000 *Time Magazine* named Watson an Environmental Hero of the 20th Century.

The Battle of Brightlingsea
The Sea Shepard example of direct action was organised and planned, but this example is one of spontaneous action by ordinary residents of a small town, Brightlingsea.

Brightlingsea, on Britain's North Sea coast, is hardly on the map, population less than 50,000. But in the early 1990's the anger of animal rights campaigners was growing at the apathy of politicians to ban live animal export (see the box, below). Campaigners were demonstrating at the points where animals were being exported, such as Coventry airport and seaports at Dover, King's Lynn and Plymouth. Patience was running out. Brightlingsea was one of the exporting sea ports and became a flashpoint.

At Brightlingsea the transport trucks, loaded three tiers high with sheep, had to pass through the town's narrow streets to reach the port. Some local residents turned out spontaneously to stand in front of the trucks to impede them. The confrontation started in January 1995 and no one foresaw that it would develop into a battle lasting nine months. Residents of a town turning out for animals is an almost singular development in animal rights. Among the people were ordinary workers, housewives, school children and grannies, who had never been on a demonstration before.

Protesters and police tried to avoid confrontation with each other but tension was always in the air as the police pushed the convoys forward to the port no matter what the obstruction. One night some protesters managed to drive a 60-seater bus to the gates of the port where they removed the wheels and handcuffed themselves to it.

Some people voiced fears for safety as protesters pressed up against the transports in the narrow Brightlingsea streets. People threw themselves down in front of the trucks and held a sit-down in the road. The police forced back any protesters who tried to get in the way and warned them of arrest. People become casualties in the pushing and were tended by Red Cross medics on hand at the scene. The police arrested many people, even passers-by, and bundled them into vans to the police station at the nearest large town, where activists chanted and waved banners outside the building.

During the Brightlingsea protests activists were carrying out actions at other ports around Britain. Transports were taking calves, destined for the European veal industry, to Coventry Airport and animal rights campaigner Jill Phipps (1964 - 1995) was crushed to death under a transport she tried to hinder (see Chapter 6: Jill Phipps). The next day the Brightlingsea protesters held a candle-light vigil for her.

The final convoy left Brightlingsea towards the end of October. In nine months 250,000 animals were exported through the town and 52 sheep died at the port. The Red Cross treated more than 100 protester casualties. The police

~ Background to Brightlingsea ~

Livestock owners get better payment for stock sold alive. For the animals this means transportation over long distances. The US live animal export market (excluding fish) is worth about $700 million annually. But Australia is the biggest live animal exporter (about A$1.8 billion annually), transporting about 6,000,000 sheep, 850,000 cattle, 100,000 goats per year, mostly for slaughter in other countries. Voyages for Australian livestock take as long as three months at sea in specially adapted freighters. Animals are stacked in tiers, each ship loaded with tens of thousands of animals, to markets in Mexico, the Middle East, south-east Asia and Japan.

Animals going abroad forfeit the protection of the law in their own country and fall subject to the (often unenforced) humane standards of whatever country they are sold to. Animals on route face exposure to weather and climate extremes, often stifle in the heat, cannot lie down or are knocked down and trampled. They suffer thirst and hunger. If they are provided with food or water they cannot always reach them. Conditions and handling can be so poor that many animals die or are seriously injured.

About three million live animals are transported across Europe every year on journeys that can take days. Britain exports over half a million live lambs, sheep and pigs a year. Attempts through the legal system to ban the export of live animals failed after a court ruled that ports cannot refuse to take live animals. In the 1990's seaports and airports in Britain become centres for animal activists fighting on behalf of the exported animals.

made nearly 600 arrests and received a thousand complaints against them. The Brightlingsea protesters did not succeed in stopping a single one of the 150 or so convoys. But the cost of exporting the animals in the face of active protest was too expensive and ceased. The protesters had won. Veal calf exports from Coventry Airport, where Jill Phipps died, also soon closed down when the firm flying out the calves went bankrupt.

Stop Huntingdon Animal Cruelty

SHAC (Stop Huntingdon Animal Cruelty) is an on-going campaign to close down Huntingdon Life Sciences, a company that carries out tests on animals, situated north of London, Britain, with an important branch in New Jersey, USA. Huntingdon is said to be Europe's largest animal testing laboratory and uses cats, dogs and primates, with the majority animals being rodents. Substances like pesticides, drugs and domestic and industrial chemicals are tested on the animals to assess their safety for human use. SHAC was set up in 1999 by seasoned British animal rights activists Greg Avery and Heather James after activists at the Huntingdon laboratory (secretly working for People for the Ethical Treatment of Animals) shot video of animals being abused. SHAC and its activities against Huntingdon have since spread to Europe and the United States.

SHAC says it does not support violence of any kind. However, SHAC's methods are intimidation, harassment and property damage. Targets are Huntingdon itself plus the company's shareholders and business associates, including suppliers, insurers and bankers. SHAC also strikes out at Huntingdon's employees and their families. Thus SHAC targets a wide network of primary targets (Huntingdon), secondary targets (Huntingdon's business associates) and tertiary targets (families and investors). SHAC wants to show all of them that any kind of direct or indirect involvement in animal abuse is a bad investment. (For more about SHAC tactics see Chapter 5: The Law - United States and Britain, under Britain.)

Because of the fear of attack by SHAC supporters, the results so far are that:

- Dozens of companies have stopped trading with Huntingdon.
- Insurers and financial institutions have stopped dealing with Huntingdon (the British government stepped in by ordering the Department of Trade and Industry and the Bank of England to help them).
- Thousands of shareholder have sold their Huntingdon shares.
- The value of Huntingdon's shares collapsed.
- Huntingdon was brought to the edge of bankruptcy.

- The public is divided about the image of Huntingdon as a reputable beleaguered company that should be helped or as a contemptible animal tormentor that should be shut down.

Illegal and violent direct action has had its penalties for SHAC activists, however. Legal actions were brought against SHAC and a small stream of SHAC activists in Britain were jailed. Six SHAC supporters were arrested in the US by the Federal Bureau of Investigation (FBI) and sentenced for up to six years imprisonment for violating Huntingdon's New Jersey facility. Critics of SHAC say it distorts the nature of experiments on animals, excuses and advocates violence and vandalism, uses terror tactics and tries to sway public opinion with hysterical emotional nonsense.

Comparing Direct Actions

The examples of Sea Shepherd, the Battle of Brightlingsea and SHAC demonstrate that effective direct action can be organised (Sea Shepherd and SHAC) or spontaneous (Brightlingsea), with
legal standing (Sea Shepherd), mainly law abiding (Brightlingsea), or pressing against the law (Brightlingsea) and over stepping it (SHAC). And these three examples of direct action share a common motif: potential financial ruin for the targeted companies. Their message for companies may be that companies could face ruin if they annoy enough people who decide to act against them in a concerted fashion. Citizens, not just companies, brandish power.

Direct Action vs Civil Disobedience

Where is the border between direct action and civil disobedience? Civil disobedience tends to be peaceful and within the law, although not inevitably so. Direct action is disposed to be stormy, could be violent, and some activists of a militant mind might decide to cross the line into illegal activity. Some law enforcement agencies, notably the FBI, choose the view that when your direct action includes property damage you become a terrorist. But some direct action proponents argue that violence relates directly to living beings only; property damage is sabotage, not terrorism, because you cannot scare or terrify property.

So the methods of civil disobedience, direct action and terrorism shade into each other. When direct action is peaceful it tends towards civil disobedience, but when it is violent it tends towards terrorism. Critics of direct action, like the FBI, are most vociferous when actions tend towards the terrorism end of the scale. Interestingly, the FBI does not trouble Sea Shepherd, but hounds SHAC. Perhaps this is because the people at Sea Shepherd cleverly harness the law to their cause. SHAC can only fall back on moral justification - and additionally goes against vested American economic interests.

For a discussion and criticism about violence see Chapter 5: Violence or Nonviolence.

Efficacy of Direct Action

Some opponents of direct action claim that it is ineffective or at best just an annoyance, particularly when it is illegal or violent. However, direct action clearly can work and sometimes work well. No business executives worth their salt want their business operations to suffer. Just the idea of being targeted is sufficient for sensible thinking companies to take steps to forestall a direct action attack.

What sort of direct action would send shivers up and down the spine of company executives? Product contamination is a style of attack occasionally used by animal rights activists - but also by the odd individual who is out to make money from blackmail. In one contamination occurrence shopkeepers throughout New South Wales withdrew tens of thousands of Mars and Snickers chocolate bars after an "extortion threat" against the manufacturer suggested that seven bars were deliberately contaminated with a poison (3). There was no mention of whether this was related to animal rights, environmentalism or just to a criminal wanting a ransom. In another contamination event retailers across Britain cleared Savlon skin cream from their shops after animal rights activists claimed to have poisoned the product (4). The Swiss based manufacturer of this product, Novartis, was believed to be a client of the animal testing laboratory Huntingdon Life Sciences.

Contamination perpetrators corrupt a few samples of a retail brand, such as food, drink or lotion, with something harmful like poison or broken glass, then inform the manufacturer or newspapers what they have done. This leaves the manufacturer and the product's retailers with no choice but to withdraw the stock from sale, not knowing the specific batch that was tainted. Some animal activists pick salt as a contaminant as it does the job without making anyone ill. But merely a hoax contamination, given credence by sending actually contaminated samples to the press, is sufficient for a product to be withdrawn.

Ethical Code of Practice

How can companies neutralise a problem like product contamination? The simple fear of being the target of direct action or worse can be enough to make some companies take a more animal-friendly approach to their trading. Companies, by anticipating people's sensitivity and by taking preventative measures to reduce the risk of being struck, may manage to neutralise a problem before it is upon them. Companies could draw up a relevant ethical code of practice, publish it as widely as possible and be seen to live up to it. Four animal-friendly and nature-friendly areas are:

- Animal Ingredients & Testing

A company should state on its product that no animal parts, animal substances or animal derivatives are used in the ingredients and that the product - as a whole and in part – has not been tested on animals.

- Ethical Purchasing

A company should clearly state and demonstrate evidence that they get their supplies from reputable companies, in the sense that their suppliers have a good record for treating animals, nature and their workers well.

- Environmental Policy

A company should state and demonstrate evidence that they do everything possible to avoid and reduce any harm to nature, regarding their development of land and their use of raw materials, their waste generation and waste disposal.

- Ethical Investment

A company should state and demonstrate evidence that their investments are animal friendly and green and that they do not invest in companies with dubious links.

How To Do Animal Rights is not just useful for animal activists - company executives should read and heed it!

References
(1) Garner, Robert. Animals, Politics and Morality. Polity Press. 1993:239.
(2) Guardian, 26 July 2000.
(3) Australian Broadcasting Corporation, 2 July 2005.
(4) Daily Mail, 30 August 2007.

Chapter	*Campaigning Methods for*
3	*Animal Rights*
	4. Action Planning

Snappy Page Essence
An action plan is a simple document that you write as a guide that helps ensure your activities and projects are successful.

What is an Action Plan?

An action plan will help you ensure that your activities will be successful. An action plan guides the day-to-day activities of your project. It is a document that sets out reasons and practical steps to help you achieve your ultimate objective. It helps ensure that things happen when and how you intend them to happen. All action plans are different, varying from one group to another depending on personalities, interests, skills and experience. An action plan relating to a commercial business is often called a business or marketing plan.

You may not want an action plan if you intend just a single quick once-only action. But if you have a long-term project it is useful, even essential, to think ahead about what you intend to do. You need to know matters like:

- What is the actual and specific purpose of your campaign?
- How exactly are you going to accomplish your campaign?
- Who is going to carry out particular responsibilities and for how long?
- What are your opponents' weaknesses and how can you attack them?
- What are your weaknesses and how can you overcome them?
- When and where are actions going to take place?
- What is your timetable for fulfilling actions?
- How will you know that your actions are successful?
- What resources do you have for accomplishing your purpose?
- How can you get more of the resources you lack?

Why an Action Plan?

You could carry all your intentions and actions around in your head, but writing it down concisely on paper helps you think more clearly about them because you must share, explore, clarify and communicate your intentions to colleagues. Through your action plan they will know what to expect and what is expected of them. Writing down your action plan helps keep you on target. With an action plan you are less likely to lose sight of your objective and how you are to reach it. Without a secure record of what you intend to do you might allow your aim to change imperceptibly from one week to the next so that you lose direction, waste your resources and accomplish little of what you set out to do. Should anything go wrong with your campaign you have a concrete document to review and correct so that you can improve your performance. Finally, when concluding your campaign you have an indelible account to look back on to check how well you performed and suggest how you might improve next time.

Who Should Produce the Action Plan?

If you are a one-man-action-group then of course you do everything by yourself. But if you are the organiser or founder of a group then through your action plan you may wish to clarify the basics of your purpose, such as your ultimate objective and method of reaching it. Once you get a team running, everyone should have a chance to assemble and voice their input to your action plan. Usually people can contribute different skills and complementary experiences so that you are more likely to make a better job of the plan. A brainstorming session can elaborate on the plan and establish what is and what is not feasible. One responsible person should write down the action plan so that it is homogeneous and completed.

Before You Begin

Your action plan should not be too long-term because seeing too far into the future is difficult. Depending on what you are doing it could steer a course for the next three, six or twelve months.

So that you do not get bogged down in detail the action plan should be concise, basically a summary, with no excessive or irrelevant detail. If you need to include more information put it in an appendix.

Your action plan should be well thought out and executed but you do not have to spend an overly long time writing it; one or two hours might be enough for a team to contribute their input and for you to make a first draft on paper.

Operations & Administrations

You may find it useful to distinguish two kinds of aims; we might call them operation aims and administration aims. The former relates to your campaign actions and the latter to running your group to make it more effective. They complement and somewhat overlap each other.

Operation aims for example could be:

- Organise a super-massive picket once every two months.
- Decrease the number of customers entering a target shop by fifty per cent for one year.
- Get a news item about our campaign published once a month in the local newspaper.

And administration aims could be:

- Increase the group's membership by twenty per cent this year.
- Raise X amount of money to pay for running costs.
- Establish a second group in a neighbouring town.

You may need to consider your administration aims in order to further your operation aims; however, do not dwell entirely on the former at the expense of the latter or your group may become strong yet ineffective. Again, depending on what you are doing, you could write a separate action plan for your operation aim and your administration aim.

Creating Your Action Plan

Every action plan is different and it is up to you to decide what to include and exclude. But consider the following points for inclusion in your particular plan.

1. Your Objective

Write down your ultimate objective – your final goal. For example, stop people selling fur in your town. Or motivate people to engage in practical animal rights.

2. Your Message

Write down the clear and simple message of your ultimate objective. People forget complicated messages right away, so keep it simple. Remember KISS: Keep It Simple Stupid! For example, 'Animals need their skin as much as you need yours!' Or 'Do more exercise – do animal rights!' Find a positive angle for your message; instead of 'Meat-eating is unhealthy and harmful!' try 'Veganism is healthy and wholesome!'

3. Your Body Targets

Write down the organisations and people you must influence to reach your goal. Deal with the right people the right way; approaching the wrong people is a waste. For example, people of influence could be (re fur shops) shopkeepers and people passing by in the street or they could be (re supplying motivation for animal rights) people sympathetic to animal rights who might be active supporters if given impetus.

4. Your Strategy
Write down how you will achieve your ultimate objective. If your objective is to help stop the fur trade your strategy could be to close down fur-selling shops in your town. Or if your objective is to popularise and get people to do animal rights you could hold an annual animal rights fair in your town.

5. Your Tactics
Write down the steps you must take to reach your ultimate objective. For example, each one of these can be broken down into a number of small steps: use undercover video for exposés, picket each fur seller until they stop selling fur, hold public meetings to publicise and debate animal rights issues.

6. Your Time
Write down realistically how much time you / your group have for your project and when you will do it: For example, six hours per week: about an hour per week for organising plus the rest for picketing.

7. Your Message Distribution
Write down the optimum times when you will give your message to people. For example, hand out your leaflets when most shoppers are about - lunch times – or when you are out demonstrating.

8. Your Management
Write down a list of key tasks (like action-plan planner, leaflet producer, site reconnoitre person, event co-ordinator), who will do them and when tasks will be completed. For example, who will finalise the action plan, monitor its progress and review it in three months time.

9. Your Resources
Write down what resources you need, such as people, space, equipment and funds. For example, half a dozen members for picketing; material for leaflets, banners and placards; storage space; computer and phone.

10. Your Preparedness
Things seldom go perfectly as planned and a good project has a back-up strategy. Imagine and write down a couple of potential disasters and their solutions. For example, if picketing a shop selling furs has no noticeable affect then you might consider driving up the shop's insurance premium so that the

shop cannot pay it and goes out of business. Or, if the police prevent demonstrating at site x then demonstrate at site y or z.

You Should Be Smart

In smart acting business circles they say you should always make sure your goals are SMART: Specific, Measurable, Achievable, Realistic and Time-based. Our goals when doing animal rights should also be smart:

- Specific

Be precise about the ultimate goal you aim to achieve. 'End the fur trade' or 'stop factory farming' is vague. 'Close down this fur shop' or 'stop this restaurant offering foie gras' are precise.

- Measurable

Know when you have reached your goal. To do this your goal has to be something that clearly stops (eg the place you picket closes down or stops selling the stuff) or be something that you can count (eg ten new members recruited).

- Achievable

Your objectives should not be over ambitious but within your reach. Ending factory farming is unattainable for your group; exposing to the press the cruelty of a particular chicken farm could be attainable.

- Realistic

Identify an effective campaign strategy given your group's members, money and other resources. Being realistic makes your campaigning easier to carry out and makes success more likely.

- Time-based

This is the time available to achieve your goal. Is your goal on-going, without a clear end? This is not so good if you want to feel you have achieved a goal and be seen achieving it. You may have to impose a deadline by which time you have accomplished something solid.

So be SMART, or better, BE SMART by adding:

- Believable

You must believe you can achieve your goal - and make others believe it too.

- Ever-flexible

Be willing to modify your actions or goal as necessary.

An example of being smart could be stopping shops in your town selling foie gras (or veal, or frogs' legs, or eggs from caged hens, etc). So what do you do to be smart?

- Be specific

"Our aim is to stop the shops and restaurants in our town selling foie gras." Not "our aim is to stop all shops in the nation selling foie gras" (maybe you have the resources to do that but you might start low down then build on your successes).

- Make things measurable

"We shall count how many places sell foie gras before we begin our campaign, then for comparison count how many places stop selling it." Not "I think some places stopped selling foie gras and some didn't."

- Let it be achievable

"We know we can accomplish our goal because we have the motivation, time and resources we need and can mobilise the manpower." Not "I suppose we can do it so let's have a bash."

- Keep it realistic

"We can do it within our resources because we have queried similar groups elsewhere that have done it." Not "ditto" (as above).

- Set a time scale

"We should be able to accomplish at least half our target within ten months." Not "We shall keep going until we drop or they do."

Follow the above process and you will have more confidence believing in yourself and greater capacity for flexibility to changing circumstances. In practical animal rights you should always BE SMART!

You Should Also SWOT

SWOTing helps you identify your objective and goals and solve problems that may turn up. Strengths, Weaknesses, Opportunities and Threats are factors that affect everyone and every group. Strengths and Weaknesses are elements within your personality or group that you might change whereas Opportunities and Threats are components outside your control. List your Strengths, Weakness, Opportunities and Threats in a few words, such as:

- Strengths

High motivation, persistence, flexible working hours, several potential co-workers to form a group.

- Weaknesses

Only locally mobile, no media contacts, little money, incomplete knowledge of relevant law.

- Opportunities

Several shops selling fur in town, local supermarkets selling eggs from caged chickens, an animal laboratory nearby.

- Threats

The law if we cross the legal line.

Think how you can counter or take advantage of these factors. For instance:

- Strengths

We shall play our strengths and look for opponents with weaknesses we can exploit.

- Weaknesses

We shall decide how we can overcome our weaknesses, perhaps by looking further afield for opportunities. We shall get to know how the news media and the law work. We shall budget and/or seek funding for our campaign.

- Opportunities

We shall look for opportunities that match your strengths and figure out which objectives are the most practicable and achievable to tackle.

- Threats

We shall avoid or neutralise threats. We shall stay within the law or if necessary challenge it by actions that are legally borderline.

Do a SWOT on your opponents from their point of view. Where are they strong and where are they most weak and vulnerable? This may help you attack them.

Make It Happen

Working hard on your action plan will do no good if you do not execute it. When your action plan is complete - do it!

Review

Does your action plan work in practice? From time to time, say after a number of activities or after an appropriate period, dispassionately criticise and analyse it. Get everyone together and ask their opinions about what is going wrong, what is going right and how to do better. Some questions to put are:

- Are we achieving the results we want and if not why not?
- How far have we moved toward our ultimate objective?
- What things can we do better?
- What additional things might we do?
- What lessons can we learn?

Build on experience and rewrite your action plan accordingly.

A Simple Action Plan

To make a start with your action plan write applicable headings like these down the side of a sheet of paper:

- Goal/Target
- Action
- Anticipated Benefits
- Time Scale/Completion Date
- Resources Needed
- Member Responsible for the Activity

You need only a few headings. Other headings according to your needs could be Rational, Expected Outcome, Measure of Performance, Progress Update. Keep your action plan clear and brief. Do not end up with reams of paper!

Chapter	*Campaigning Methods for Animal Rights*
3	*5. Lobbying*

Snappy Page Essence
Lobbying is a democratic process, open to anyone, to communicate to the powerholders to do what you want them to do.

"It is the province of honest men to enlighten the government."
Attributed to Napoleon Bonaparte.

What is Lobbying?

The thrust for changing the human governed world for the better for animals is essentially two-pronged. One prong involves law-making for animals (the other is educating people about animals). In order to make laws you must become a legislator, but we all cannot do this. The next best thing is to influence the legislators and this is what lobbying is about. You go lobbying to persuade the legislators - your political representatives, elected political officials, senators or members of parliament - to do what you want them to do: change or enact laws that benefit animals or otherwise support your cause. The origin of the term lobbying is lost, but it might be connected with cornering and petitioning politicians in the foyers or lobbies of their building. However, lobbying is not confined to political representatives; you can influence local or national institutions, businesses, colleges and any organisation to adopt animal friendly ways for their establishment.

Who Can Lobby?

Lobbying is democratic; it is an important process that gives people a say in political, economic and other polices. Political representatives in democratic countries are elected by the people to serve the people. You are one of the people, so representatives must serve you, especially if you are one of their constituents, by bringing their political standing to bear on your concerns.

The lobbying field is open to anyone or any group. You do not have to be a powerful business corporation that retains professional lobbyists or employs their own specialist staff to lobby for them. Nor do you need any particular experience to go lobbying, just a desire to communicate what you think should be done. No one and no group is too small to make their voice heard. If you do not make yourself heard, the policy makers cannot take into account your opinions and animals will not benefit. By lobbying for animals you change the way society acts by harnessing the power of the law for animals.

What & Who to Lobby

What do you want to lobby for? You may want to:

- Prohibit toxicity testing of substances on animals.
- Change the law to prohibit live exports of animals.
- Ban inhumane jaw traps and snares used by animal trappers.
- Proscribe the production or selling of foie gras, veal and animal body parts.
- Introduce stiffer and more appropriate penalties for animal abusers.
- Change the law about how animals are transported.
- Prohibit the importation and trade of live wild animals or their body parts.
- Propose new laws to regulate breeders of animals.
- Proscribe the mutilation of animals for cosmetic and economic purposes.
- Regulate or make illegal the keeping of wild animals as pets.

You may have to address national political representatives to lobby for such changes as these. But although lobbying is often associated with high-level political representatives, you can just as effectively lobby anyone, such as the figures who have access to the policy makers and legislators. These officials hold a variety of positions from local to national level. Furthermore, you can just as easily lobby institutions and business companies whose activities affect animals more directly or who have the power to help animals. You could persuade your supermarket to change its policy on selling factory farmed produce; lobby your work or school canteen to ban factory farmed food and offer choices for vegetarians; or lobby your college professors to organise courses on animal rights or animal ethics. Representatives of private organisations, unlike our political representatives, are not obliged to assist you but should respond if they want to be seen by the public as honest, caring and open to change.

Start Lobbying

First, ask yourself four questions.

1. Issue: what specific issue shall I campaign about?
For example, livestock transport, entertainment animals, furbearers (for ideas see Chapter 3: Campaigning, under Where to Begin?).

2. Objective: what is my specific campaign objective?
For example, to change a law or to change a procedure, such as governing how animals are kept or used.

3. Authority: which authority shall I lobby?
For example, the Secretary for Agriculture, the Home Secretary, or a company's chief executive officer.

4. Method: what lobbying methods shall I use to persuade the authority?
For example, write letters, arrange private face to face meeting or debates.

Second, find out who your targets are, such as who politically represents you. Good lobbyists do not just know who their representatives are but get to know about them. This way you know you are targeting the right people and can make the best impression on them. For political representatives you should at least know their political party, political status or rank, past and present campaigns, and their involvement with animals.

You can most easily find out who represents you by consulting your library or the Web. Virtually every citizen in the US is represented federally by a member of the House of Representatives and by two members of the Senate. Most US states have this same system of representation. Note that you must lobby federal representatives on federal matters and lobby state representatives on state maters because representatives deal only within their own sphere. Voters in Britain are represented nationally by their Member of Parliament and voters who reside in Scotland or Wales are represented by their member of their particular legislative assembly.

Third, know what your target can do for you. For example your representative in your legislative assembly could:

- Write officially to relevant ministers or other representatives on your behalf.
- Convey your issue at a committee meeting.
- Address the whole political assembly about your campaign.
- Ask a question from the floor on your behalf to elicit information from a minister.
- Propose an early day motion (a petition for representatives to sign) as part of your campaign.
- Set up a committee to study your issue.
- Initiate a parliamentary debate about your cause.
- Introduce a draft law on animals for debate.

- Attempt to alter an existing draft law.
- Propose changes to statutory law.
- Support or impede legislation.
- Attend your public gatherings and make speeches to support your campaign.

How to Lobby

The primary means of lobbying your target is to write, arrange personal meetings, and use the news media.

1. Lobby by Writing

Writing a letter to your representative or other target is possibly the best way to make initial contact and state your case. Paper documents give a target something to study at leisure and refer back to.

- Be concise; one page is probably sufficient. Keep to one subject per letter so as not to cloud the issue.
- Do not make more than two or three points or there will be too much for your representatives to handle.
- Put the main points (the who, why, where or when) in the first paragraph.
- Include supporting information, evidence, photos, but do not overdo it; if you have a lot of data, summarise them on a separate sheet.
- When writing to your representative always include your address and zip/post code so that they can verify that you are one of their constituents, otherwise they may not act for you.
- End by asking politely for a response to your letter.

Make your letter personal. Put one or two specific questions to your target and ask for their opinion; they will take your letter more seriously. If you do not do this, they might simply forward your letter to somebody who seems to them to be a pertinent third party, like a government department that handles such matters that might send you a bland standard reply.

You will have more influence if you get other people to write as well. Your representative might keep count of the letters they receive as a check of public opinion and the more letters they receive on your subject the more influence you will have. If possible try not to send a standard or model letter when writing as part of an organised group. Your representatives will give duplicated letters far less weight and an unfavourable response, even if they get a great many of them on the same topic. If you do use a standard text, get each writer to subtract some remarks from their letter, add singular remarks of their own, and mix it all up to make their letter look personalised.

What about emailing, faxing and phoning? Email is quick and cheap but may not be effective if your target is swamped by them every day. Your particular email may not receive the attention it deserves or might simply get lost in the flood of email. Letter writing is slow and arduous but is likely to get a better response.

A fax is more solid than an email in that it can be held in the hand, put on a desk and filed. But faxes are less legible and less attractive than a well printed letter. Sending a fax can be useful to add further information once your issue is already well known to your target or as a prompt to action, such as to get your target to turn up and vote at an important ballot. Otherwise always send a letter.

Phoning is fast. But you will probably not be able to speak to your representative by phone as they are likely to be out or busy. However, if you are going to phone then jot down and stick to just one or two points that you wish to make. When you get through say you are a constituent and keep your conversation short.

2. Lobby by Personal Meetings
Elected representatives expect to be approached by the public as part of the democratic process, so do not feel inhibited. Go ahead and arrange a meeting with your target to present your case in person. You should certainly meet them if the results of your correspondence are unsatisfactory.

You may visit your representatives alone or, more effectively, as a small group campaigning on your issue. Each member of the group should have a good reason for being at the meeting and with something different to contribute. Decide beforehand who is going to lead the meeting and who is going to say what.

How you come across at the meeting and how you say what you have to say is important. Dress casually or conservatively but dress appropriately. Be rational and objective, not emotional and excitable. Speak clearly and concisely. Know your background facts well and summarise them on a single page to hand to your target. Give duplicate copies to any of their staff. Thank everyone before you depart and leave your target with a good impression of what an animal rights activist is.

Representatives in the US fix a number of public meetings through the year to meet their constituents. At these meetings you should prepare yourself to ask your representative questions in front of a public gathering that may also contain news reporters. Ask your representative to speak about their stand on your issue and make things hot for them if they go against you. Alternatively, your representative might decide to meet you on the side at a private office and a typical meeting could last an hour. You could take the opportunity to hand out leaflets about your campaign to other attendees at the meeting who are not part of your group. Members of Parliament in Britain hold regular sessions in their constituency every few weeks when you can sit with them and speak privately. Check your target's web site for particulars and make an appointment.

3. Lobby via the News Media
Another way of influencing your targets and to strengthen your cause is through the local or national news media. Use the media to:

- Spur lethargic targets to action.
- Make your targets take you even more seriously.
- Pressure your targets into publicly stating their position.
- Give your targets bad publicity if they do bad things.
- Give your targets good publicity if they act well.

Phone or email your newspaper and radio/tv stations and outline what you are doing. News media interest is often short-term, so get your timing right to approach them at the best point in your campaign. Beware that editors simplify issues as black or white, so there is no point going into the minutiae of your case; make your message simple and clear. Use the media to gain widespread public support for your cause, especially if you are not able to achieve your objectives through your target. (Also see Chapter 3: News Media.)

Lobbying Techniques
1.   Learn the House Rules
You must learn the rules of your target organisation (legislative assembly, business company or whatever) to understand their manners and methods to prepare yourself to influence them. If you do not know their rules, ask them.

2.   Set Attainable Goals
Try for goals that are achievable. Stopping egg farming is too sweeping, but phasing out the production and sale of eggs from caged hens is attainable, whether from your supermarket chain or nationally.

3.   Be Flexible & Compromising

Perhaps you cannot make headway or you know your target is not in favour of animal rights, then simply operate under the banner of animal welfare and adjust your goal so that it appears welfare oriented. Politics and influencing people is the art of compromise when you cannot be autocratic.

4.   Pitch the Right Level of Information

Present your target with whatever information is strictly relevant and no more. They will not want to waste time with excessive and non-essential input.

5.   Stick to Facts Not Feelings

You have opinions, but base them on indisputable facts and put them across in reasoned arguments. Know the important arguments for and against your case and be able to refute the latter rationally.

6.   Always Go for Clarity

Do not use abbreviations or unusual, obscure or technical terms that your target may not know. Get your message across simply and quickly, so spell it out fully.

7.   Always Tell Them

Be specific, clear and polite about what action you want your target to take. An action may seem obvious to you but not to them and they will not want to waste their time guessing.

8.   Do Not Rely on Memory

Always make written notes of what is said, the decisions that are made and the names of the people you talk to. Take notes at a meeting even if you are only listening as an observer.

9.   Build Up Your Credibility

You need be an infallible expert but always be open and tell the truth (or at least use your words carefully) to build up your credibility. This is the best way to impress on your target that they can rely on your knowledge.

10. Get the Weight of Authority Behind You

Individuals acting alone can lobby effectively, but you can be more effective if you have authoritative associates to bolster your case. Your target will be more ready and better able to act to influence others if they know your issue has weight behind it.

11. Link to Your Target's Interests

Try to relate your issue to your target's area of personal or professional interests. For instance, you might be lobbying about blood sports and they are keen countryside ramblers or sit on countryside committees. This is where knowing about your target's backgrounds is advantageous.

12. Be Above Party Politics

Eschew party politics when lobbying. Lobby to get the best out of everyone irrespective of their political alliances, affiliations and the party they belong to.

13. Do Not Make Enemies

Your target should listen to you but they do not have to agree with you. Be courteous to them when their views are at odds with your own because you may be able to influence them another time on a different issue. Make enemies of them and you may never be able to enlist their help.

14. Go for the Staff

Always be polite, understanding and patient to your target's personal assistants, secretaries and other office staff. They are your potential allies. They might influence your target for you or reciprocate your kindness by giving you background or other useful information.

15. Analyse Your Progress

Monitor your progress and evaluate your results. You can best do this by setting small practicable goals you must reach on your way to total success. (More in Chapter 3: Action Planning.)

16. Thank People

Thank people who are helpful and if you have the news media involved with your campaign drop them names in praise.

17. Finally...

Keep on going if you do not get the responses you hoped for. Think about reaching the same goal from a different angle. Be persistent and do not give up easily!

Chapter	*Campaigning Methods for*
3	*Animal Rights*

6. Picketing

Snappy Page Essence
Picketing is a legal protest, organised, peaceful and sometimes lively, outside a target's premises to demand change, eg that a business stops selling foie gras. Well organised animals rights picketing can effectively change bad practices.

What is Picketing?
Picketing is a form of demonstration and protest that interest groups employ in a dispute to make their demands accepted by an opposing party. Picketing in animal rights is often about gathering in a small group outside a company's premises to protest the company's actions and demand change. The picketing protesters might harm the company by alerting the company's patrons and the wider public about its misdeeds and persuade as many people they can not to enter the premises. If the company does not handle the situation deftly it risks trade disruption, a tarnished public image and a loss of business standing.

An animal rights activists might picket:

- A retail store - to stop selling fur.
- A fast food restaurant - to stop selling burger meat.
- A restaurant or shop - to stop selling foie gras or veal.
- A supermarket - to stop selling eggs from caged hens.
- A breeding farm for animals - to stop breeding animals for use in experiments.
- A laboratory - to stop doing tests on animals.
- A seaport or airport - to stop importing or exporting live animals.
- The head office of a cargo company - to stop handling animals for trade.

An example of a successful picket by animal rights protesters was the closing down in 2007 of a fur shop (see photo), Schumacher Furs, in Portland, Oregon, a family business since 1895 (1, 2). The owner said he could no longer endure the sidewalk picketing protests of the "terrorists", despite a police presence and an occasional arrest of demonstrators. The owner said the protesters menaced him and his family and he also had bomb threats. His hand written placard on display in the shop window read: "All protesters should be! -beaten -strangled -skinned alive -anally electrocuted". The picketing lasted nearly two years (3).

AR Picketing is Like Industrial Picketing

Picketing is best known in industrial disputes as a recognised form of action. As such it shares many similarities with picketing for animal rights. Picketing workers in industrial disputes stand outside their works forming a 'picket line' at the entrance. They may try to persuade workers who are not taking part in the dispute to stay away and prevent access to the works by replacement workers and their employer's suppliers.

Industrial picketing is legal if carried out according to certain rules, among them are that you must:

- Picket peacefully.
- Not threaten anyone or cause damage.
- Not obstruct people entering or leaving the premises.
- Confine picketing to the employer's workforce.
- Not engage in secondary picketing.

Secondary picketing is when you picket places indirectly connected with your issue. You might picket outside the premises of your employer's suppliers, aiming to persuade the supplier's workers not to deliver goods to your employer. In some countries secondary picketing is illegal.

However, a primary difference between industrial picketing and animal rights picketing is that the former is part of the industrial sector and governed by specific law. Animal rights picketing is a form of public demonstration and handled differently by the authorities.

How to Picket

The first thing to consider when picking is that it takes time, effort and tenacity because it is a long-haul objective (could take months). Therefore you must have high motivation to begin and sufficient impetus to carry you through. So before you decide to go picketing, first try other means of persuading your target to comply with your proposals. Only picket your target when all else has failed to make it move.

Zero in on your target, such as a shop, restaurant or a company head office, once you have decided to stage a picket. Ideally, our target to picket should be within easy reach of your fellow picketers and have many patrons and passers-by you can influence in favour of your proposition. And you must be easily visible to the public for them to see clearly what is going on. The more people you can influence the more quickly your picket may have effect. You must also be able to picket and demonstrate freely in front of your target. Reconsider your use of picketing for an alternative form of action if your target is in some kind of restricted area, like private land with limited rights of access.

How many fellow volunteer picketers do you need to go picketing? You may be able to accomplish everything with just a few supporters, and, in any case, too many picketers may draw unwanted police attention. You may want to keep the number of your picketers to not much more than half a dozen.

What hours will you picket? You cannot picket 24 hours a day. Find out your target's peak activity period and concentrate your picketing during that time.

Try to keep to definite hours and days for picketing so that volunteer picketers know when to appear. Their enthusiasm may be dampened should they turn up and find no one around.

Your picket will be more effective if you:
- Stage frequent picketing sessions.
- Hand out leaflets and brochures to passers-by and display hand-held placards.

- Play a musical instrument (preferably a loud one – get a bagpipe player or drummer) to attract attention.
- Chant short messages to draw attention to yourselves and tell people what you are about.
- Dress up in animal suits and create a fitting tableau for the public to look at.

You will also want to know your legal rights (they differ from one country to another) so that you can stand your ground if challenged with or by the law. You should also ensure that you picket much like your industrial counterparts in that you:

- Comply with any police instructions.
- Act reasonably and politely with passers-by.
- Do not use threatening language and gestures.
- Do not trespass.

Check your national and local laws. How must you adapt to stay legal, eg keep moving, not use a megaphone, not block entrances? Consider:

- Do you need permits?
- Can you picket anywhere? Some places have restrictions or may be private.
- What is the legal maximum number of picketers? Too many may be illegal.
- Where can you position you picket? You must not obstruct certain places, like highways or entrances.
- What constitutes an obstruction? Blocking people from freely going about their business?
- Can you set up a table on site with literature and erect banners?
- What legal influence, strength, authority might the people you are picketing have? Be knowledgeable so that they cannot intimidate you.
- How might your target harass you? Might they hire private security?
- What powers do the police and any private security guards have? Under what circumstances can they tell you to pack up and leave?
- If you are ordered to move on, can you set up at another site close by?

Hitting Back

Bear in mind that companies being picketed can hit back by seeking an injunction from a court of law. An injunction can ban you from picketing in certain areas, limit the number of your picketers and put restrictions on their behaviour (like stopping them shouting abuse). A company might be more likely to win an injunction if picketers are intimidating, violent or in some other way overly anti-social. Animal rights activists set up a picket outside Oxford University's new unfinished multi-million pound animal experiment laboratory. The protesters were seen as noisy and violent by many and in 2004 the University won an injunction against them. The injunction imposed exclusion zones where demonstrating, picketing and loitering were legally banned: from around the building site and from around the property of contractors and the homes of people connected with the work.

Picketing works, as Schumacher Furs found out. Examine the issues thoroughly and chose your target with care.

References

(1) *Local News*. 29 November 2006. www.kgw.com. (Accessed March 2007.)
(2) Former Schumacher Furs building in Portland undergoes extensive. Aaron Spencer, Sept. 2010. *Daily Journal of Commerce*, Portland, Oregon. (Accessed online March 2011.)
(3) Schumacher Furs. www.schumacherfurs.com. (Accessed March 2011.)

Chapter	*Campaigning Methods for Animal Rights*
3	

7. Starting a Group

Snappy Page Essence
You can do many activities alone, but an animal rights group can sometimes be more effective than a soloist, eg members contribute complementary skills and the public may take your campaign more seriously.

Anyone Can Start a Group
Anyone can start being active in animal rights, with friends or alone. You can be successful as a solo animal rights campaigner depending on the nature of your campaign and some examples are *Flyer, Solo Information Centre Worker, Preacher* and *Teacher* in Chapter 4. However, a group can sometimes be more effective than a soloist. A group of people can be an important campaign resource because:

- People may take your campaign more seriously if they see you are backed by a broad membership and consequently may give you more attention.
- Members contribute complementary skills and abilities that a singleton working alone lacks.
- A core of committed campaigners may share your burden and hard work.
- A group is a long-term entity that can outlive the comings and goings of its individual members.
- You might enjoy social company.

Even if you start out alone, acting as a nucleus for kindred spirits to gather round, you may eventually find others to pitch in. Patience and perseverance are assets.

What to Do?
No one and no group can do everything. So chose a section of animal rights that interests you (see Chapter 3: Campaigning, under Where to Begin?) and that you are good at doing, then hack away at it doggedly. An example is example is hair products. Many cosmetic and artists' paint brushes are made from animals, such as shaving brushes from badger hair and paint brushes from sable. Then there are bows of orchestral instruments, like the violin and cello. Most bows are strung with horse hair from China, Mongolia and

Canada. How the hair is obtained is a shady business because most people know nothing about it and the few who know won't tell. Hair is fur, usually of the courser kind, so your specialised niche would be this aspect of the fur trade (great if you are an artist, beautician or musician and wish to influence your colleagues).

Alternatively, your group could work independently by complementing a large animal activist organisation, perhaps under their banner. Just ask them.

Name & Logo

You could give your group a name and design a logo for it as a symbol of your group's individual identity. A well designed logo imparts a sense of common purpose and is good for morale - you can blazen it across your own promotional material, like T-shirts, badges and posters - and if you use letterhead paper it communicates a respectable image on your correspondence - all useful for influencing people.

Finding Members

Look for potential or fellow activists who feel as strongly committed as you and would be keen to play a central role in a campaign. Query friends and acquaintances. Exchange ideas. Arouse their interest; make your enthusiasm infectious. Look everywhere and make allies. Ask potential members for more people you can approach and take the contact details of anyone who really seems interested.

You can pin up notices and hand out leaflets to explain your campaign and why it matters (see Leafleting in Chapter 3). Produce something simple but professional-looking. Put down a campaign title, say what your campaign is about and give your contact address. You may want to hold initial meetings to attract people and acquire members and should put this information about meetings in your notices.

Unless you aim to work clandestinely your group should be loud and visible. People who hear about your campaign may join your group. Get into the public eye often. See News Media and Internet in Chapter 3.

You may find it easier to persuade people to join you if your campaign is achievable and attainable in the near-term. But perhaps your goal is big and long-term? Then split it into segments and concentrate initially on the achievable and the attainable.

A Constitution?

Should your group have a constitution? A constitution is a set of rules that guides the efficient running of a group and settles disputes.

Model Constitution

1. The Group shall be known as ... (hereafter called 'the Group').

2. The purpose of the Group is ... Other activities furthering the purpose of the Group or for the Group's benefit shall be carried out from time to time as its members decide.

3. The area covered by the Group is mainly ... but activities may be undertaken elsewhere as decided by the members.

4. The Group shall cooperate and exchange information with other bodies in similar fields, work in consultation with relevant individuals and organisations, and do such lawful things as are necessary to attain the Group's purpose.

5. Membership of the Group shall be open to everyone engaged in and pledged to the Group's purpose.

6. The Group shall hold regular meetings to discuss all aspects of its work. Meetings shall be fully publicised and all members shall be entitled to attend.

7. Funds shall be raised when necessary for carrying out the purpose of the Group and shall be used as the members decide.

8. There shall be an annual subscription to help pay necessary expenses. The subscription shall be determined at the members' meeting from time to time and at a rate that is considered adequate.

9. When required, officers shall be appointed to conduct the administration of the Group. Officers shall include a Chair, a Secretary, and a Treasurer. They shall be in charge of the day to day running of the Group and shall be answerable to members at the Group's meetings.

10. The Treasurer shall keep the accounts of the Group. Accounts shall be submitted for approval at least once a year at a members' meeting.

11. If the Group shall cease to exist it will be decided by a majority vote at a group meeting. All assets after all bills are paid shall pass to a similar group as the members decide at the meeting.

12. This constitution may be amended only by consent of a majority of the members of the group.

You do not need a constitution if your group consists of just a few close colleagues. Concentrate on your mission, not on your admin. On the other hand, too much rule-making is a mistake that can restrict a group's growth and development. People who are 'rule happy' often err by making too many rules in an attempt to cover all eventualities.

However, if your group is large, internally truculent, or with an already growing jumble of rules to govern its members, then a constitution incorporating the rules in a simple yet formal way may be useful. A constitution may also be necessary to open some banking accounts or for being recognised officially in some capacity.

The previous page points out a simple formal constitution that your group could adopt and modify to suite its purpose.

The Group Committee

If you are going in for a formally and rigorously organised group it should have a number of officers, the members who run the group. These members are called the group's committee. If you wish your group to have a committee then its committee members should keep in touch by meeting every so often. Other interested members should also be able to attend these meetings. Three important posts of the committee are Chair (or Co-ordinator), Secretary and Treasurer.

The Chair is an administrator, responsible for conducting meetings, ensuring they are carried out properly and that order is maintained. Chairing meetings is a skill that improves with practice. The Chair may ultimately be responsible for group decisions and co-ordinates what all the members are doing.

The Secretary is responsible for the efficient day to day running of the group. The Secretary deals with the correspondence and office work, keeps records and minutes of meetings and writes the annual report. The Secretary is the group's executive who carries out the decisions of the group's committee.

The Treasurer is responsible for the group's money and financial transactions. The Treasurer collects subscriptions, pays bills, keeps the accounting books and an eye on expenditure. Accurate financial accounts are essential to any formally organised group; you need to know where the money is coming from and going to and how much you have at any time.

You may want other officers, such as a publicity officer, newsletter editor or liaison officer. But no group need have all these functionaries and one member can combine more than one function. Some responsibilities are best delegated temporarily rather than put an ineffective member permanently in charge of them.

Group Success or Failure

You will not want to set up a group for it to fall to pieces. Therefore paying attention to what can go wrong will pay dividends. Here are some functional tips about organising a group.

1. Mission - Not Admin

Be organised but not to the extent that bureaucracy takes over your group's reason for being. Use the simplest administration to make your group a going concern. Concentrate on the action.

2. 20/80

Any voluntary organisation generally consists of five per cent activists and 95 per cent members; activists do 95 per cent of the work. The familiar '20/80 rule' is more optimistic: 20 per cent of members do 80 per cent of the work. This is human nature and the way with voluntary organisations. So expect to do a lot of the work yourself. Most members may just turn up now and then.

3. Burnout

Beware of your personal drive burning out. No matter how enthusiastic you are now, constant work and stress may exhaust you. Burnout might happen in the far future but watch out for when it comes. Better to work steadily and keep up a good average performance than to explode onto the scene only to extinguish yourself. Should you get burnt out take it easy, thoroughly get over it and then carry on. This applies to anyone getting burn out in your group.

4. Membership Demands

Will you require that prospective members adopt a certain lifestyle before they join your group, that they be vegetarians, vegans or whatever? You might not want to scare them away but let them adapt in their own time. Then you will have more members and they will be more animal-friendly.

5. Assign Tasks

The continuation of any group of activists depends on finding more active members. If you are looking for more members, when new people turn up make them feel wanted and involved. They will be less likely to change their minds about joining you the sooner you give them the opportunity to take part in an activity. So make sure everyone who really wants something to do has something to do.

6.   Contact

You stand to lose contact with your members if you do not see each other reasonably frequently. The longer you delay face to face meetings the greater the likelihood of your membership leaking away. A less forceful alternative to meeting in the flesh is sending out frequent emails, even phoning.

7.   Top Heavy

A big group is not necessarily better than a small one. It is not the vastness of your group that counts but what it accomplishes. If you have many members you could divide them into core activists and a general membership. Communicate with all but work primarily with your 'shock troop' core.

8.   Small Victories

Animal rights opponents often succeed in a conflict because they are well established and therefore can hold-out longer than you simply by carrying on in the same old way. They can ignore you and count on you becoming discouraged and giving up. Therefore you may well need victories from time to time to keep up your member's spirits or they might desert you as a no-hoper and your group will perish. So break down your long-term tasks into small achievable steps you can win. And when you win a small victory let everyone know about it.

9.   Be Dispensable

Efficient managers are dispensable. They can leave their business and relax knowing they will run smoothly in their absence. If you can do this with your group it show how competent you are. So share responsibilities among your group's members. Coach members who are willing and able to take over in your absence. Some members could at least be familiar with the work of the group's officers so that any sudden officer vacancy can be taken over by someone else.

10.   Pleasing Everyone

You cannot please everyone all of the time; if you try you will be seen as a weak leader and your group may fail. Be polite and firm, make the best decisions you can and expect to be wrong sometimes.

11.   Participation

Encourage members to contribute their views and fully take part in the group. Act on their suggestions and let them feel valued members. Otherwise you could lose them to another group.

12. Friction

Fiction within the group may crop up. If you leave friction unresolved it may tear your group open. Recognise you have a problem and discuss it openly in a friendly, non-confrontational way.

13. Positive Criticism

Criticise assertions, arguments or acts but not the individuals behind them. Be on good terms with everyone you disagree with and make sure they know you are not attacking them personally.

14. Diplomacy

If people come to hate you they may turn a blind eye and deaf ear to what you represent and you will make no headway with them. Cultivate good relations within - as well as outside - your group: diplomacy and good humour are always valuable.

15. Fun

No matter the seriousness of your issue, and without being frivolous, take time to have some fun and enjoy your campaigning. Fun reduces stress. With salubrious humour your group will last longer. Socialising can add an extra dimension and enjoyment for many members and make the difference between keeping members and losing them. Social events are better if they depend on members' spontaneous initiative for initiation.

16. Think Ahead

It is vital for the continuity of your group to keep an eye open for potential leaders. Groom them to take over for when the time comes, such as when you step down (no one lasts forever). You should do this even before you think of quitting or at least a few months before you intend to go. All your efforts setting up the group and making it work efficiently will go to waste if the group perishes for want of good leadership when you are gone. You can derive great satisfaction knowing that your work will outlast you.

In summary, make animal rights not admin your target; expect to do most work yourself; watch out for burnout; beware of making membership stipulations; keep members busy; meet every so often; productivity not size matters; motivate troops with achievements on the road to victory; be a dispensable manager; share responsibility with other members; encourage members to participate fully; criticise the act/argument not the person; make decisions without trying to please everyone; recognise internal friction and deal with it; be diplomatic; have fun; and prepare future leaders.

Newsletters

Producing newsletters about your group, what it does and is doing, could be a good idea at some point. A good newsletter evokes a sense of common purpose and is a force for binding together individuals interested in your animal rights issue. A newsletter advertises your group to non-members by telling them what you do and is of value for recruitment. The more well written and produced your newsletter is, the more credible your group will appear to people. Impress them with your conviction, make them laugh at your good humour and subtly redirect their anger about what you are campaigning for.

Give your newsletters to group members. Ask them to distribute copies. Enclose a copy when you correspond with people about your groups business. Stand about town and give them away to passers-by. Leave copies in public places, the town hall and public libraries. Use your newsletter as a calling card.

A simple newsletter need only be one page of news. A bigger newsletter could consist of a larger sheet folded to make four pages. Depending on what you are doing, on your campaigning and on what is happening locally, you could include:

1. Aims and problems.
2. Proposed activities and ideas for future events.
3. Reports of past and continuing activities.
4. Copies of newspaper stories about your group.
5. Pieces about animal-human relations.
6. Letters from members and what individuals are doing.
7. Reviews of your group's financial situation.
8. Dates or social activities for the group.
9. Pinches of light gossip if you want to keep things lively and informal.

- Title

Think of a catchy name for your newsletter's title. Tails Up! is better than The Newsletter of the Grimstown Animal Rights Group. You can always append the longer name as a sub-title in small print below the pithy name to give your readers a better idea of what you are.

- Illustrations

Find a volunteer to illustrate the newsletter and other people to contribute, whether members of your group or not (but sometimes it is simply easier to do everything yourself!).

- Printing

Key everything into a computer and print off from it as many sheets as you need, or print off a single master copy and photocopy it repeatedly.

- Periodicity

How often will your newsletter come out? Four times a year is ample, provided the newsletter is not too difficult to put together and the printing and distribution are easy and cheap. However, twice a year could be sufficient if your newsletter production is long, hard work (but it gets quicker and easier with experience).

- Cost

The cost of the newsletter does not have to come to much with a cheap source of paper and computer print-outs and photocopying. One way of paying for it is to ask members of your group for a small membership subscription, have a whip round, or foot the bill from your own pocket. You might even print prominently on the front page for subscribers.

- Libel

Whatever you write in your newsletter bear in mind that you can be sued for libel. A way around this might be to criticise people's actions rather than make claims about the people themselves. Be circumspect. You can make many points with good humoured jabs and satire.

For related info see Chapter 3: Leafleting.

Fundraising

Much of what your group does may not need funding. Nevertheless, you might require some money to cover your costs. It is up to you to generate funds, so go out and get it.

Do not shy away from asking people for funds or for material you can convert into cash. The fundraiser's first rule is ' if you don't' ask you don't get'. Their second rule is 'ask frequently'. So start asking. With the right frame of mind fundraising can be fun and absorbing - some people do it for a career - and for animal rights fundraising is a virtue. While out and about fundraising, double up by publicising your campaign and bagging new members for your group.

Methods of raising campaigning funds are diverse. Here are perhaps the two most reliable and time honoured ways plus a new one.

- Jumble Sale

Selling jumble may be the number one time-honoured way of raising cash. Book sales are similar and might raise more money with less effort. Make leaflets asking for jumble (or books). Advertise by making four small strip-leaflets, by tearing up an A4 page, and distributing them to the houses in your district. Donors may want to know that their donations will be used to good effect, so tell them you are a voluntary group for animals (they might not agree with the rights bit) and that their jumble is to help animals (which it is!). State your name or the name of your group and the date and time a few days later when you will collect the jumble. You could ask donors to leave the stuff outside so that you need not knock on their door. Hire a stall at a fair or sell your wares at a car boot sale. Adjust your jumble's price to something very reasonable and attractive for people to buy. Your income will depend on the quality and quantity of the jumble and on your expertise selling it.

- Sponsored Event

Carry out an activity, like a cookie-making spin, long-distance walk or bicycle ride, an all-night dance, a marathon run, a litter clean up or something unusual, and get people to pay you for doing it. An excellent system for publicising your event and collecting the money is via an online company, like JustGiving.com, the only catch being that your group must be a registered charity (alternatively you might be able to go through an established registered charity) and have a bank account. JustGiving provide you with your own personalised online fundraising page. Your friends, family, acquaintances and anyone accessing your page from anywhere in the world could sponsor you with a donation of any amount by credit card. JustGiving thank the donor, collect the money and send it to your account for a small cut.

- Sell Merchandise Online

Some online companies, like CafePress.com, provide you with an online 'shop': one or more pages of merchandise that web viewers can look at and buy from. Most wares are clothing, favourite buys are T-shirts and sweat shirts, and there are also coffee mugs and a selection of other things. You characterise your shop with your logo and group details, select the wares to sell, apply graphics and/or a message to them - for instance a T-shirt or mug with your logo and the message *Respect Animals!* across it – and decide on your price tags. When a viewer makes a purchase the company sends them the stuff and forwards you the purchase price minus a per centage. The company handles everything, even returns from unsatisfied customers (should there be any). If your group has its own web site, selling merchandise like this can make it look more interesting and professional. However, you have to sell quite a lot for this way of fundraising to be more than just pocket money.

Chapter	*Campaigning Methods for*
3	*Animal Rights*

8. Leafleting

Snappy Page Essence
Producing and handing out eye-catching, informative flyers you can reach out to
people and tell them what you have to say.

"Publicity, publicity, publicity is the greatest moral factor and force in
our public life." Attributed to Joseph Pulitzer (1847 - 1911).

Why Leafleting?

You might be working in a small group, undercover or alone and may not
want publicity. Alternatively, you may want to reach out to people to influence
them with what you have got to say. A good way to start is by producing good
looking, quick to read and informative leaflets. Leaflets are a kind of open
letter to catch people's eye and be read by anyone. They are an opportunity to
introduce your cause, state your argument and draw attention to your group or
an event you are planning. People can take your leaflets home with them as a
reminder for future action. No doubt many leaflets are quickly discarded but a
single leaflet can be handed around and read my many people.

Design

The design, layout and argument of your leaflet should be interesting,
memorable and persuasive. Well written and attractively designed material
indicate competence. Take a tip from the marketing profession and hit your
audience with 'AIDA' by getting their:

- Attention - to attract their notice.
- Interest - to stimulate their curiosity.
- Desire - to arouse their wish to act.
- Action - to make them do what you want.

Make only one principal message per leaflet, eg wearing fur is cruel or eating
mass factory farmed eggs is a likely health hazard (salmonella). Tell your
readers the what, where, when, why and who of your cause. The more facts
that can be proved the better. Keep what you have to say short and to the
point; the more you write the less your readers will remember and the less

inclined they will be to read it all. Be careful not to libel anyone or they may sue you; for example, call an act cruel, not the people who do it. Tell readers how they can help and remember to add your contact details, whether email, phone or address – easy to forget! Get someone to proofread a mock-up of the final leaflet. Skip this stage and you can expect errors in which case your readers may think you clumsily inefficient and act accordingly.

Make your leaflet uncluttered and look good to the eye. Leaflets are more attractive and easier to read with lots of white (empty) space around text. Break up the text with headings and bullet points. Use colour, graphics or pictures to create interest.

Size of paper? Leaflets should be large enough for your message but small enough for people to handle easily and shove into their pockets. But big leaflets look more important. You can make your leaflet on an ordinary size of paper (such as size A4) that fits a desktop printer or a photocopier. To make a smaller leaflet, fold it in half (size A5) and fold that again for a smaller size if necessary (size A6).

Printing

You do not need a commercial printer. Churn out your leaflets yourself; the learning curve might be steepish but it is quicker and cheaper in the long-term and you have more control over the final result.

Lay out your leaflet on a computer in a normal text editor; you do not need expensive specialist editing software. If you do not have a computer, look for a friend who has, or hire one by the hour at a cafe, or use one free at a public library. The last step is to print off a single copy, you should do this on a good printer, say at a library or at your college or office, then photocopy it as many times as you need.

Distribution

Get rid of your leaflets; no point hoarding them. Stand in the street and hand them out. Spread them on your information table (see Solo Information Worker, Chapter 4). Pass them along at demonstrations and protests. Leave them anywhere they will catch someone's eye, at a cafe or pub. Provided your leaflets do not say inflammatory or rude things, you can ask libraries and other institutions to put them on their notice boards and circulate them to sub-branches. Distribute them to private houses - labour intensive but a way of discussing your issue with householders if they open the door to you and good for drumming up local people for an event.

Pick places relevant to your campaign when distributing your leaflets in the street, such as outside a furrier or a supermarket. Go up to people, make eye contact and with a smile make a brief positive remark such as 'Please read this', or 'Please support our ...', then move on if they do not engage you in conversation. If they ask about what you are doing, reply succinctly in a sentence or two. Prepare some brief answers ahead of time to questions such as, "Who's doing this?" or "What's this all about?" Get into irrelevant and distracting conversation and you will not be able to hand out your leaflets, unless you have bags of time. If people argue, courteously ask them to read the leaflet and contact you later for a discussion. Ensure you have a pen and paper handy to take anyone's contact details if they are interested in joining you.

Posters & Placards

From producing leaflets you can progress to develop your own posters and placards. Posters are like leaflets but much bigger. They are good for promoting an event or strengthening an image, message or slogan: "The greatest threat to people is ignorance - the greatest threat to animals is ignorant people". There are laws about the legality of displaying posters so find out how the law may affect you. Go on to make placards (posters on poles) that you can wave around at demonstrations and rallies; they might find their way in to the press or on to television if the news media are present. Get your message across by other means too, such as printed on T-shirts - see web sites like CafePress.com that provide you with a simple means for doing this.

Chapter	*Campaigning Methods for*
3	*Animal Rights*

9. News Media

Snappy Page Essence
Develop your credibility and reputation with the news media. Write to the editor, write a news release, give interviews, or dress up and do stunts for photo opportunities, but make your story newsworthy: original, with a new twist, or bubbling with human interest.

"Don't hate the media, become the media." Attributed to Jello Biafra, alias Eric Reed Boucher, rock band singer and political activist.

Why the News Media?
Make use of the news media - press, magazines, radio and television - for broadcasting your activities and developing your group's credibility and reputation. Many local newspapers have a free *What's On* section; advertise your meetings and events in it. But you can go a lot further. Newspapers largely depend on the public to supply them with a constant stream of news. Indeed, reporters would be unemployed without a public to give them news. So the media need you as much as you need them and there is no need to be timid when approaching them.

Whether you are a solo campaigner or a group, engaging with the news media can range from writing letters to the editor, providing information, and giving interviews, to dressing up and doing stunts for a photo opportunity. Media publicity reaches a wide audience and can make your campaigning issue a public topic for discussion. The more frequently you figure in the news the more impression you will make with the public. Publicity for your group will raise group member moral ("…we're in the news again - must be getting somewhere!") and could bring in more members.

Make it Newsworthy
Your news story must compete with umpteen other stories to get into the media, so you should make it newsworthy. A newsworthy story tends to be something original or with a new twist, something exciting with a human interest. A newsworthy story concerns people, is happening now or soon, and is controversial or dramatic. The media thrive on disputes and a reporter will contact opposing parties for their opinions. Help the reporter by having to

hand the phone numbers of a few people who oppose you. Give the reporter a few names because not everyone may be available for comment when the reporter calls them.

Media Tips
Here are some tips to help you when reporters come round to interview you about your activities.

- Before the reporter arrives, draw up a checklist of the main points you wish to cover so that you do not leave out anything important.
- Emphasise only one or two main points that you want to get across, they are the purpose of your campaign, and state them clearly to the reporter. Reporters and readers cannot remember more than a couple of arguments, so there is no point spinning off a whole list of them.
- Be clear that your group's name, and if possible some contact address or your web site / blog, are mentioned in the article the reporter will write. This is your payoff for your story.
- Although reporters may seem supportive and interested in your cause, what they are really after is a story. So concentrate on giving them that, your story and not something you might later regret you said (and see the next point).
- Be careful when speaking to reporters because they may report anything you tell them. Nothing is ever 'off the record' (to be withheld from the public) so never say anything you do not want reported. Do not even use this expression (it is a Hollywood contrivance!).
- Always get the reporter's name and thank them by letter or email for their piece when it is published (even if it is awful!). Reporters are only human and being polite will help your media relations.

A Feature Article?
When your campaign really gets going and you have something substantial to report, a newspaper might want to run a feature article, a detailed story, on what you are doing. Be willing to talk about your experiences, to give a human face to the issue, or you could offer a profile of someone who is involved with running your campaign. Photos are important when trying to attract the public's attention. Have some unique, relevant, quality pictures that the newspaper can publish with the story or make an impressive photo opportunity for one of their photographers. This is a 'publicity stunt' that could help your campaign; the newspaper is paying for it so make the best of it.

The Letters Page

A newspaper's Letter to the Editor page is one of the most well-read pages of any newspaper. Write to the page as an individual or on behalf of your group. Make your letter stand out and memorable.

- Be brief and to the point.
- Write in plain English, without exaggeration, jargon or clichés.
- Grab the attention of readers with a good heading (if the newspaper prints headings) and/or with your first sentence.
- Make one or at most two points well; not many points diffusely.

Keep your letter short, about the average length of other letters on the page and no longer than the longest letter. Sign off with your group's name and contact details, either email or web site address, depending on the newspaper's custom, so that readers can contact you.

Check the page for responses from readers to your letter and follow-up with a second letter to the editor in reply to them. Tell members of your group to write their own independent responses to keep the discussion going and spin it out. As a bonus, send a copy of the published letters to newspaper reporters at other newspapers, suggest they write a feature article, and include the latest information about your campaign.

Write letters regularly, get other group members to do so. See Chapter 4: Media Watcher.

News Release

Sending news releases to your national or local news media is one of the main ways of communicating with people broadly. Tell the media something newsworthy about you or your campaign and what you are doing, such as organising a coming event, like a demonstration, picket or other direct action.

Your news release (see the example below) will compete with hundreds of other news releases from other people. So write it in the approved style and in a professional manner for it to stand a chance of being acted on. It may only be scanned briefly for content then chucked out by a harassed member of the newspaper's staff if you do not. There are many books and web articles about the do's and don'ts of news releases but the gist is simple. Most news releases follow this ten step format.

1. Type your news release on your letterhead paper.
2. Type News Release and the date at the top.

3. Then write an attention-grabbing headline in the style of newspapers.
4. The first sentence of your story is the most important, stating what your news release is about.
5. Put the who, where, when and why of your story in the first paragraph.
6. Work a quote into the text; the newspaper may print it and it imparts authority and a personal touch. You can quote yourself or find a celebrity or authoritative figure and ask them for a comment.
7. Throw in some brief evidence to back up your message.
8. Be matter of fact, do not exaggerate or use jargon or clichés.
9. At the bottom put 'For more information' followed by your name and phone number.
10. Fit everything on one side of one page - two sheets might separate and lose each other at the hectic newspaper office. Use regular size type. (An exercise in being concise!)

See below for an example of a news release.

Send your news release a few days before the event and no more than a week. Some newspapers accept news releases by email or fax but many still insist on receiving them by letter only. It is usual to send news release to the News Desk, but check first. Newspaper details are published in various documents, which you can find at main libraries.

Constantly keep close to the phone in the couple of days after they receive your news release. If the newspaper does not phone you during this period then no dice. Try again another time with a different news release.

See below for an example of a news release.

The Radio

Local radio stations are often keen on discussions and phone-ins and want local people to talk about their local issues. Send your local radio stations suitably adapted copies of the news releases you send to newspapers.

If you get on the news you will probably be broadcast live. Actual interviews may only be a few minutes long so stay focused to deliver your two or three key points. But should your interview be recorded, news editors will cut down mercilessly any long message to a few seconds; therefore make sure you deliver a few sound-bites that go straight to the heart of your issue, and be ready to come up with more snappy phrases just in case. Make them simple and memorable so that they stick in people's heads. Humour can sometimes help:

NEWS RELEASE

1 April 2020

Grimstown Citizens Protest For Chickens

Grimstown citizens will gather outside the Town Hall at 12 noon this Saturday 5 April calling for Grimstown supermarkets to stop selling eggs from caged chickens. Members of *Tails Up!* - the Grimstown Animal Rights Group - dressed in chicken suits will stage an 'egg lay-in' confined in mock cages. A petition of over 1,000 signatures of Grimstown shoppers will be handed to the Mayor.

"Eating eggs from battery chickens is morally indefensible," says E.G. Smash, chair of the group. "No one is so poor they cannot afford eggs from free-ranging chickens with access to organic feed and to woodland. Organic eggs are a kinder and healthier option for chickens and people."

Tails Up! is calling on Grimstown supermarkets for an early phase-out of eggs from caged chickens. Members of the public are invited to attend an open air public meeting at Town Hall Square from 12.30 pm, with a speaker from the Chicken Liberation Network.

Global Respect for Farm Animals says there are five billion egg-laying chickens in the top five egg producing countries, the US alone has 280,000,000 egg-laying hens, almost all living in horrifying conditions crammed into tiny bare cages all their lives.

Photo opportunity of protesters with placards and chicken suites: 12 noon at the Town Hall.

For further information:
E.G. Smash, Secretary *Tails Up!*,
Tel 01234 567890

Question: "Do you really think everyone should be a vegetarian?"
Answer (rhyming): "Yes. For man and woman, a veggie diet is healthiest, from the poorest to the wealthiest!"

Radio Tips

Bear these points in mind when speaking on the radio.

1. Speak well but be yourself.
2. Speak slowly, calmly, clearly and let your natural good-natured humour come out.
3. Give short but full answers and make your point as soon as possible.
4. Say if you do not know how to answer a question but then go on to make a related point.
5. Answer a question that seems irrelevant in a word or two then pass on to something else that you want to say.
6. Keep strictly to your reply; do not wander 'off-point'.
7. Stop at once and listen to the interviewer if they interject with a new question.
8. Convince the listeners - get their sympathy; do not try to beat the interviewer should they seem hostile.
9. Remember there is no such thing as 'off the record', even if the interviewer prompts you for such a remark!

Chapter 3	*Campaigning Methods for Animal Rights*

10. Internet

Snappy Page Essence

Communicate to colleagues and win allies all over the globe with the Internet, fast, ceaseless and relatively inexpensive. A number one tool for animal rights activists.

Why the Internet?

The Internet is a communication tool to exchange ideas, inspiration, information, statistics, pictures and drawings, and to find people and organisations. Using the Internet is quick, convenient and relatively cheap. Use it to communicate with your existing and potential supporters to let them know about you, your group and the issues you raise. The Internet has a number of parts and two of the most important are the Web and email.

The Web

The Web is short for World Wide Web (the 'www' that precedes web page addresses), a network of computers around the globe to which anyone can access by connecting to it with a computer. People began using the Web as a popular medium for communication in the mid-1990's. Basically the Web consists of millions of web sites, each of one or more pages where text, graphics and videos are set out for people to view.

Acquiring your own web site may be free, cheap or expensive depending on what you want and how you go about obtaining it. Creating and managing your own web site is not difficult but takes a little time to learn how to handle it. Benefits of your own web site are:

- You can tell your web site viewers what you do and what you think they should do.
- You can send people electronic newsletters in addition to or instead of paper ones sent via the post.
- It is easy to add or delete your web pages and to update, add and delete information to existing pages.
- It will give your group a sense of professionalism and enhance its reputation, especially if your web site is informative and handsome.

Email

Email, short for electronic mail, was invented some years before the Web. You can use email to exchange messages, graphics and video clips within seconds or minutes with any Internet user anywhere in the world who has an email account. Email is so nimble that you will not want to send letters through the post any more and it is often better than using the phone.

When you get a web site you usually also get an email facility that goes with it. You should place your email address on your web site so that people can contact you. However, you do not need a web site to have an email address; web sites and email are separate components of the Internet. To obtain only email you just need to get online using a computer and sign up with a company that provides email, which can be free. You can then send and access from anywhere on any computer that links you to the Internet.

Create Your Own Web Site / Blog

You will need a computer to access the Internet, a computer that you own or can use for a time from a friend, library, your office, an Internet café or some other place. Best to have your own computer because you will be in command of when and how long you stay online. Then you will need two things, first a company that will connect your computer to the Internet, and second a company that will store your web site and send pages to the computers of people who what to look at it. Either company might also provide you with email facilities. Both kinds of company can be found online by searching the Web under 'Internet service provider' and 'web site hosting'. However, the simplest thing is to get a blog as your web site. Blogs are free and easy to use. Just look them up on the Web.

Designing Your Web Site

Making your own blog is easy and instructions come with the blog.

With a regular web site, on the other hand, either you can do it yourself with a bit of flair and resolve, get a friend to do it, or pay someone to design and set it up for you. You will have quicker and more control over your web site by doing it yourself (by cutting out intermediaries). You do not need special software to set out web pages. Instead you can learn to write HTML (short for hyper-text mark-up language), the instructions that professionals type into a computer to lay out Web pages. Special software is only useful if you have hundreds of pages to design. You will still have to lean to use the software, so you may as well learn HTML. Here are some tips for doing it yourself.

- Look around for an easy to read book or two on basic HTML. Big expensive books are unnecessary. You can even find most if not all of what you need free online.
- Read a book about good, simple web page design, or look online for the information, eg how to break up text, which font to use and the application of colour.
- Examine examples online of simple, well designed web sites - and the many web sites with distressingly artless or no design - for inspiration and ideas about what to include and avoid on your web site
- everything simple and you will make progress quickly and your work can look pleasing and professional.
- Once you have typed in your HTML code and completed your page you may want to 'validate' it, ie check that the coding is correct. Download a free HTML Validator from the Web (eg from CoffeeCup.com).

When your web site is more or less complete you will need to upload it to a 'host' (a company that keeps it online 24h a day to show it to people who want to see it). You can upload your web site to your host via their web site or by using your own FTP program (FTP stands for File Transfer Protocol), which you can get free online (eg from CoffeeCup.com).

Capturing Viewers

Now that your blog or web site is online the next step is to get it listed on the Google search engine so that potential Web viewers can discover your site. Google will automatically find your site in due course and list it. You do not have to inform them or any other web search engine. It may take a few weeks but they will find you.

Another method of acquiring viewers is to find relevant web sites (eg connected with animals or nature) and exchange reciprocal links with them. Email a relevant web site. All you have to say is, "Can we exchange reciprocal web links, please? The name of my site is *****, its address is www.*****, and it is about animal rights." It might spur them on if you place a web link to them on your web site before emailing them. Let them know which page it is on.

How many viewers see your web site? Which pages get most viewers? Register with a company offering web counters, software that that computes viewer usage of web sites. An example is StatCounter.com, which is free and excellent. You will be doing well if you get a hundred viewers a day and a thousand plus would be exceptional. Get only half a dozen a day and you may wish to think about how to make more people see your site. And do not be misled by statistics: about 75 per cent of viewers to ordinary web sites (not popular national ones) click off in the first five seconds, having found the site is not what they were looking for. However, a blog / web site is always efficacious for projecting your group and its mission to prospective members, irrespective of how many people land on it.

Discussion Boards

With your web site up and running you could offer viewers a discussion board on it (which are also variously called discussion groups, message boards, forums or newsgroups). There are said to be over 100,000 discussion boards online. (You do not actually have to have a web site to offer people a discussion board. Just go to a specialist discussion board web site and set one up on their site.)

A discussion board is a facility for people to hold discussions online by typing in (or 'posting') and reading messages about topics of interest to them. You can raise questions and answer them with your group members and with anyone viewing your discussion board pages. Contributors can be anonymous if they like and can email each other individually for more confidential discussion.

Discussions are displayed for ease of following in chronological order or are 'threaded', that is questions and answers are displayed in a hierarchical structure along a theme or series of related messages. Discussions are also displayed permanently or archived so that viewers can return to them.

Setting up your discussion group can be free and takes just a few minutes to register with a company online. Select a title and description of what your group discusses. Decide whether the discussion group is open only to your group members or to anyone (you will be able to reach more people if it is open to anyone), and whether you want to 'moderate' it (censor messages before you delete or display them online).

Chapter	*Activities for Animal Rights*
4	*1. Teacher*

Teaching about animal rights is one of the most effective ways of opening minds to the nature of animals and of getting people to question how humans should treat animals. This is especially true when educating children. The field is new and open and you need not be a certified teacher to teach animal rights, although if you choose to teach through an establishment they might require some prerequisite.

Probably the closest thing to teaching animal rights is teaching humane education. Humane educators help their students understand that they have moral choices, that they can act for change, and to explore and develop a respect and compassion for humans, animals and nature. Most humane educators are voluntarily or part-timers. They offer presentations on outreach through their own initiative and/or through non-profit organisations to the wider community and where ever people will listen to them. A few educators teach full-time at schools and teach humane education as an adjunct to their main work.

How to Start
So how do you start teaching animal rights? If you are already a teacher, sound out your school or college about teaching animal rights as a course in addition to your normal duties. Otherwise offer yourself on outreach in the manner of humane educators; explore their web sites and follow up leads they suggest. Also approach animal advocate organisations to offer your services in much the same way as a public speaker (see Chapter 4: Public & School Speaker).

Teaching Animal Rights
As an animal rights teacher you act as facilitator, pointing your students on their way and supplying appropriate material and objective facts. You do not tell them what to think (see Criticism of Animal Rights Teaching, below) but get them to think critically, given their age group, about the issues you raise. You could encourage them to explore animal-human relations, examine the values held by society and held by them personally, question information from all sides in the animal rights debate and argue for and against alternative courses of action.

There are many questions you can set your students, such as:

- What are the harms for animals of humans using them?
- What right do humans have to use animals for human purposes?
- What is speciesism, who benefits from it and is it fair?
- How do we use language to obscure our use of animals?
- What moral arguments challenge the human use of animals?
- What are rights?
- What is natural and should animals have the right to live natural lives?
- Must animals suffer for human advancement and gain?

Test yourself by writing your own one or two page answer for each question!

Should you generalise across animal rights or specialise in a subset of animal rights? Being well-versed in animal rights generally will give you a solid background to build on and from which you can take off in any direction. Being a good all-rounder may be useful especially if you are peripatetic, because each school you visit may want you to adapt your teaching to the specific needs of its students. But on the other hand, you may prefer to teach adults a division of animal rights. For example, animal ethics is relevant to classes that study philosophy or religion; animal experimentation is relevant to classes into biological sciences; and vegetarianism is relevant to classes taking cookery and nutrition, as well to sociology by way of farming and world famine. Demand for your special subject might govern your options.

Criticism of Animal Rights Teaching
Some critics of animal rights say that animal rights activists feed children misinformation and that the children are "propagandized" (1). They claim that animal rights educators are confusing young minds by conflating animal rights with bona fide popular concerns for the environment and healthy eating, such as suggesting that vegetarian children are more considerate and moral for nature than are meat-eating kids. Furthermore, these critics assert that animal rights activists seduce teenagers with popular celebrities who verbalise vacuous emotional appeals for animals. These critics also maintain that animal rights educators are one-sided by not pointing out the usefulness of animals to humanity, as in biomedical research. So, beware. You will inevitably have some critics lambasting you as a slanted animal rights teacher, no matter how even-handed you try to teach!

Teaching Methods
You have several practical teaching methods to choose from, given the age of students and the time allotted for a presentation. Mix your methods if you like; one possibility is presenting a lecture and then a video followed by a debate.

- Lecture

Address your students from the front of the class. This is the usual method for public speakers. It has little scope for input from the audience, although you could leave time for a question and answer session towards the end.

- Debate

Divide the class into two groups. One group argues for a topic, such as the need for fur clothes or animal experiments, and the other group argues against it. Then a vote is taken and discussed by the whole class. Generates ideas and heated involvement.

- Discussion

Get the whole class to discuss a topic. What would they gain by patronising zoos or what problems might they suffer being vegans and how could they overcome the problems? Encourages participation and communication skills.

- Group Work

Divide the class into groups, each group developing and concentrating on its own theme, such as finding out about the international trade in animals or what aquariums do, which it then shares with the rest of the class for contribution. Allows students to participate and helps them think for themselves.

- Questions & Answers

Ask students questions for them to ponder and answer. Encourages a two way student-teacher interaction and you can assess their state of knowledge. Useful at the end of a talk.

- Video

Screen a video and use it in conjunction with some of the methods above. As a window to the outside world a video adds variety to your presentation that maintains the students' interest. Since people are visually oriented, your students may remember a video long after they forget your talk.

- Printed Matter

Supply material that your students can keep and refer to after you leave them. Material may include fact sheets, information booklets and posters. Your students will be able to recall your talk better when referring to them and can pass leaflets and posters to their friends.

Dealing with Disruptive Students

Hopefully it will not always be so, but the subject of animal rights is controversial at present and can generate much emotion between opposing parties. Some older students and adults may have strong views to the point of being openly hostile and disruptive in class. How can you deal with them? Part of your teaching could include how to interact with respect and without hostility when disagreeing with others.

Julie Andrzejewski (2) is one of those rare teachers who have taught animal rights for several years (to students at St Cloud State University, Minnesota). She deals from the outset with potentially disruptive students by giving everyone in class her rules for her course and finds that her code soothes differences of opinion and forestalls hostility. Andrzejewski hands each student a sheet of the rules for referral in case of conflict down the line. A simple rendering of her rules for your students could go like this illustration:

Is there a Code of Conduct for Animal Rights Students

Here is a code of conduct for teachers to keep their students well behaved

You will study ideas that challenge the present human worldview of animals

You may feel these ideas threaten your views and lifestyle

You are not required to agree with these ideas and should decide yourself what to think

To join this course you must accept this code and be positive and respectful

If you are disturbed speak privately with the teacher to explore ways to help you

Now teach with confidence!

Ben Isacat
Human Animal Relations

Material & Training

Various non-profit organisations offer material you may find invaluable. Some non-profits offer teachers free merchandise, including online lessons and activity sheets for teachers to print and copy, plus free videos and DVD's. Of course, not all animal rights videos are suitable for showing to children. Some web sites with useful material for animal rights educators are AnimalAid.org.uk, ShareTheWorld.com and TeachKind.org.

No courses presently exist where you can study animal rights full-time with the intention of teaching it yourself. This situation might change one day as the demand for knowledge about animal rights grows, so keep an eye open. However, a number of law schools in the United States offer the study of animal rights relating to the law (see Animal Lawyer, Chapter 4) and a few universities run short courses for undergraduates on the moral treatment of animals. You may also find some miscellaneous animal rights courses via the Web.

For more about presentations see Chapter 4: Public & School Speaker.

References

(1) Runkle, Deborah & Granger, Ellen. Animal Rights: teaching or deceiving kids. *Science*. 1997. 277:1419. (Accessed August 2007.)
(2) Andrzejewski, Julie. *Teaching Animal Rights at the University: philosophy and practice*. (This paper has at least two different addresses on the web; one is at TeachKind.org. Accessed online 1 July 2007.)

Chapter	***Activities for Animal Rights***
4	*2. Animal Lawyer*

What is an Animal Lawyer?

Animal law is the study and practice of the law relating to animals; as an animal lawyer you apply your country's law to speak for animals and their human associates and allies.

As an animal lawyer you might be contesting animal exploiters, defending animal rights activists and campaigning for the legal status and rights of animals. Specialising in animal law is an unusual but excellent occupation, highly effective for promoting legislative change to advance the rights and welfare of countless animals.

Animal law works at provincial, state, national and international levels and ranges across cases of cruelty, criminal action and negligence, specific contracts and property rights, corporate and criminal matters, and governmental, constitutional and international rulings. The animals who may benefit from the law are as diverse as wild animals, farm animals, pet animals, experimental animals, zoo and captive animals, whether as individuals, populations, species or communities.

Animal law is a growing field as shown by the increase in animal law cases, the enactment of animal welfare legislation, the growth of animal law courses, and the founding of professional associations and student groups for animal law. Animal law has become an independent field of law in the United States, currently taught at dozens of law schools, with animal law clinics, conferences and student organisations. The number of US animal law schools is growing and other countries are following suite.

Animal Legal Standing

Although an ostensible purpose of the law is to protect the vulnerable, this duty is not sufficiently extended to animals. Legal systems throughout the world in reality protect people and their assets. Relatively few laws exist that rigorously define and protect the welfare of animals and there are virtually no laws that have much bearing on protecting animal rights. In fact, laws relating to animals treat animals as property owned by people. In practice this means that animals cannot rectify their grievances and afflictions through the legal system. It would be extraordinary for you as a lawyer to bring a legal action on behalf of animals; you can only represent their human guardians or allies who speak for them, much the same as when adults brings actions to court for children.

Some animal lawyers think animals will attain better protection and appropriate rights without a change in their status as the property of people. Other animal lawyers, however, believe the only way to protect animals from human mistreatment is to abolish the status of animals as property and in a number of court cases have fought for this. These lawyers have appealed to the courts to recognise animals as sentient and to introduce laws accordingly. In 1997 the European Union officially recognised animals as sentient beings and the EU now requires that member states "pay full regard" to animal welfare. Nevertheless, the EU ruling will have to struggle a long way before it translates into practical legal benefits for animals in the face of economic pressures to use animals.

In the United States animal lawyers are doing their bit for animals by collecting signatures to petition congress for an Animal Bill of Rights (1). The Bill would give animals:

- The right to have their interests represented in court and defended by law.
- The right of protection from human exploitation, abuse, cruelty, neglect and 'unnecessary' experiments.
- The right for animals to satisfy their basic physical and psychological needs.
- The right for pets to a wholesome diet and to satisfactory shelter and veterinary care.
- The right for wild animals to a 'natural' habitat sufficient for their ecological needs and to sustain their populations.

Animal Legal Disputes
Protecting animals through litigation in the courts is a route that inevitably leads to statutory reform and in countries like the United States and Britain it has never been easier for animal organisations to mount test cases.

The British Union for the Abolition of Vivisection (BUAV) challenged a decision by the British Government. The Secretary of State had granted planning permission to the University of Cambridge for a new research facility for experimenting on primates. The plaintiff lost but the case may have been a factor that influenced the university to abandon its building project. In another case concerning BUAV vs the British Government and concerning Cambridge University, the court ruled that the Home Secretary had acted unlawfully by licensing invasive brain experiments on marmoset monkeys at the university; the suffering that was caused was not moderate, as the Government claimed, but substantial. The judgement could mean that fewer licenses may be granted to the university's animal experimenters. BUAV based their case on undercover investigation (see Chapter 4: Undercover Investigator) that assembled video and documentary evidence for ten months at the university during 2000/1.

Wild animals also benefit from litigation in the law courts, as demonstrated by the action of Greenpeace in 2005. Greenpeace made use of the European Union's Habitats Directive to challenge the British Government's decision to permit trawling for sea bass within British territorial waters. Greenpeace say the trawling kills over two thousand dolphins annually in the English Channel and that under the European Union directive the British Government is obligated to protect the dolphins.

The majority of animal law cases, however, are smaller and closer to everyday life. A man in Livingston, Montana, was taken to court in 2006 for shooting and beating to death his neighbour's cat. He was charged with cruelty to animals and with firing a gun within the city limits. The judge fined him a small sum of money and sentenced him to a year's jail deferred for a year provided he observed the law for that period. This is a typical example of lenient sentencing in animal cases that animal lawyers want to change so that the punishment fits the crime. Other kinds of everyday animal law are veterinary malpractice: when something goes wrong or someone is negligent; cases when a dog bites back someone who harasses him and is then at risk of being be put down by law; and cases concerning custody of animals in divorce disputes.

Your Work as an Animal Lawyer

In addition to taking on test cases in animal law and fighting local cases in the courts as described above, there are other opportunities for animal lawyers to further the interests of animals and the animal law profession. Animal lawyers:

- Protect the right and civil liberties of people to protest for animals peacefully.

- Prosecute violations of animal-related criminal law and cases of animal cruelty or neglect.
- Provide legal advice about animal law to the public, animal humane societies and other organisations.
- Improve, reform and strengthen animal law legislation.
- Ensure that animal laws are enforced (often they are neglected) and are interpreted as intended (often they are not).
- Educate the public and welfare organisations about animal law.
- Ensure that the public debate about animal rights from a legal point of view is informed and conducted impartially and fairly.
- Take part in consultations and monitor developments in legislative bodies and relevant international institutions.
- Publish scholarly articles in journals of animal law.
- Disseminate information about animal law through professional seminars and popular channels such as radio broadcasts and the Web.
- Plan animal law conferences and workshops and the training of students in animal law.

Taking Up Animal Law

To be an animal lawyer you must first study and train to be a qualified lawyer. You would then specialise in animal law. You should seek up to date information and advice from career counsellors about training in law, and animal law in particular. Also search the Web under 'animal law programs' or 'animal law courses'.

Even if you are not a certified lawyer you might nevertheless counsel on animal law and related procedures provided you do not claim to anyone that you are a lawyer. You might be able to make your way as an independent voluntary 'para-legal', carrying out research, determining facts and providing procedural information for clients. But beware of what the law says you can and cannot do in your state; without a license to practice as a lawyer you may be committing a criminal offence.

Further Information

A number of organisations specialise in animal law. They can best be found on the Web. A few are:

USA
- Animal Legal Defense Fund (they work to develop animal law in law schools.

- International Institute for Animal Law (they encourage legal scholarship and advocacy skills for animals internationally.
- National Centre for Animal Law (situated in Oregon, they train animal law students and are a resource for students, professors, attorneys and anyone in the US.

Britain
- Association of Lawyers for Animal Welfare: they are solicitors, barristers and legal academics who promote animal law, share knowledge and expertise and provide information to animal campaigners and animal welfare organisations.

References
(1)   Animal Legal Defence Fund. www.aldf.org (Accessed May 2008).

Chapter	*Activities for Animal Rights*
4	*3. Undercover Investigator*

Animal abusers are not always willingly open about their treatment of animals. However, as an undercover investigator you can infiltrate their operations and document what they do to bring their activity into the open for public criticism (see Time Magazine article by Kate Pickert in Links, below). Evidence gained from undercover work supplies animal advocate organisations with broadsides they fire at animal abusers. It is on the strength of good documentation that pro-animal campaigns are born and won.

An example of an undercover investigation is the case of the British Union for the Abolition of Vivisection (BUAV), mentioned in Chapter 4: Animal Lawyer. The British Government had granted licences to Cambridge University to experiment on marmoset monkeys and BUAV took the Government to court. BUAV's evidence was based on a ten month undercover investigation of the suffering of the monkeys at the university's animal house. In the ensuing litigation the judge ruled that, considering the monkeys' suffering, the Home Secretary had acted unlawfully in authorising the licences for the university's experiments.

A well-known case of undercover work involved the Institute for Biological Research at Silver Spring, Maryland, in the early 1980's. Alex Pacheco (co-founder of People for the Ethical Treatment of Animals) took a voluntary vacation job at the institute and witnessed abuses on macaque monkeys that violated US animal cruelty laws. He called in the police and the experiments were stopped, resulting in the first impoundment of animals from a US laboratory. The issue went to the US Supreme Court and the news media dubbed it the case of the 'Silver Spring Monkeys'. The laboratory director was the first experimenter in US legal history convicted of animal cruelty and the case contributed to changes in the law for animals. Although Pacheco's role was fortuitous, stumbling upon a corrupt practice rather than undertaking a deliberate pre-planned undercover investigation, the elements are the same: recognising what is going on and acquiring evidence for litigation.

One of the most horrendous exposures by investigators is what is still happening at Chinese fur farms, where foxes, mink, rabbits and other animals are abused and often skinned alive (1). Skinned animals are thrown onto piles, some animals apparently still alive. In this case video documentation was carried out openly with the permission of the fur farmers, but it demonstrates that investigators must observe appalling atrocities and still carry on with their work, outwardly unmoved and apparently willing to go along with whatever they witness.

Ain't animals worth fighting for? Enlist today! ANIMAL RIGHTS

Ups & Downs

Being a spy sounds glamorous; indeed it often is - in fiction novels. The reality is usually just a jot of excitement with long hours of labour. And your jot of excitement comes at a price:

- You will be forced to witness cruelties, unable to do anything about them, and will have to cope emotionally.
- You will work with the people you investigate, but as a secret investigator you are fundamentally alone. You cannot confide in anyone about your undercover work (except perhaps to a 'case officer', see the next point).

- You might do your undercover work through an animal advocacy organisation. If so, you may have a 'case officer' who debriefs you at the end of the day to analyse and collate information and you may have to write reports and make plans for the following day. Even if you are freelancing you will still have to do all this by yourself. Thus you will work evenings in addition to your daytime work.
- You may have to travel anywhere in the country or abroad to carry out your investigations. Not all investigations are around the corner. Therefore you may be away from home for weeks or months and this could disrupt your home and social life.

However, in the long-term you know that what you are doing will help animals and the animal rights cause and that you will not be undercover forever. These thoughts may be your only sustenance. There is, however, a more tangible upside to undercover work: you may be paid twice over! You should be paid by the people you infiltrate (assuming you are infiltrating a company employing you to work for them) and by the animal advocate agency engaging you as an undercover investigator (unless you do it for free).

What It Takes
What are the several qualities and skills you should have as an undercover agent?

- You must be committed and need stamina, determination and persistence to succeed because you must stick with your plan of operation from beginning to end.
- You must be able to pay attention to detail, make your own decisions, and sometimes act fast under pressure to get the evidence.
- You should be informed about animal rights and welfare issues and knowledgeable about relevant animal protection law so that you know what to look for.
- You should be able to keep a secret and not tell strangers, friends or family (except perhaps your partner) that you are an undercover agent. You must be able to live in two worlds. You do not want your cover 'blown'.
- You must be able to work long hours and handle two jobs at once: your day job where the animals are abused and your debriefing at night.
- You must be emotionally stable and able to work with other people. You will see animals suffer yet you will have to masquerade as an unaffected rock, getting along with everyone whatever happens.

- You should be proficient at documenting what you are investigating, whether handling gadgets (see Surveillance Systems, below) or making accurate notes of your observations on paper for people to read.
- You cannot let yourself get paranoid: go about thinking that you are being watched and that you will be found out. If you are the sort who stays cool and rational the tighter the situation gets, then maybe you have the makings of an undercover agent!

Setting-Up as an Undercover Agent

How do you set up as an undercover investigator? There are two ways. Now and then a few organisations advertise employment for undercover agents. One such organisation is People for the Ethical Treatment of Animals; they train you, but you have to have the right background for them.

The other way is to do it yourself. Infiltrate your target in some way. You might get a well-placed job at your target and thus some sort of access to the information you want. Or you might find a sympathetic employee at your target as your inside agent who will act for you (you become their case officer). When you are well placed to get the documentary evidence or once you have it, present yourself to animal advocacy organisations and really sell yourself to them. Build up a reputation as a reliable, willing and able agent and you may get contracts.

Surveillance Systems

Two useful digital surveillance systems are miniature pinhole and button cameras. They are called systems because they are self-contained but are made up of a mixture of different units, basically a camera, a microphone, a recorder, a transmitter and batteries. Wear them secretly on your body, hide them in a bag you carry or conceal them in a room. Properly installed they are difficult for the opposition to find because you can disguise them in various ways and anyway your opponents will not be suspecting you.

- A Pinhole Camera

This is a simple to use camera, smaller than a cigarette packet. You can wear it or plant it where hiding places are limited, like inside a motor vehicle. Or you can carry it in a briefcase or lady's handbag and operate it by remote control when you place the bag unattended at a suitable position. The system offers good picture and sound quality, and records continuously for over six hours onto a gigabyte card the size of a postage stamp. Among the camera's features is a motion sensor that stops the camera recording when there is no action, saving battery power. Just connect the system to a monitor or TV to play back your recordings. The camera will also operate from mains electricity.

- A Button Camera

This camera stays out of sight, literally concealed behind a button. Sew the button onto your jacket and there are different colours and sizes of button for the fussy dresser. Connect the camera to a separate body-worn microphone and battery and to a miniature digital video recorder. Record in colour and store hours of quality audio/video on a minuscule gigabyte card. For playback, plug the card into a monitor or TV. Like the pinhole camera above, this system will also operate from mains electricity. An advantage of this system is that you do not feel you look suspicious by carrying a bag that conceals a camera.

Warning

For every measure there is a counter measure. Might counter surveillance operatives be about? Might they detect your surveillance equipment? A counter surveillance operative sweeping a handheld metal detector over your body will spot any metal you are wearing or concealing in a bag. Furthermore, some camera components emit a weak electronic signal that counter surveillance detectors may pick up. Detectors are small enough to fit into the palm of the hand and anyone can use them without technical knowledge. Just switch on a detector, fiddle a knob or two, and if it blinks it has found a nearby 'bug', a surveillance system. To go undetected you may want to use the latest model surveillance system and test it against existing bug detectors. However, if no one suspects you are carrying surveillance equipment then you may have nothing to worry about - the opposition's defences, if any, will be down!

References

(1) Hsieh-Yi; Yi-Chiao; Yu Fu; Maas B & Rissi, Mark. *Dying for fur: a report on the fur industry in China.* EAST International/Swiss Animal Protection SAP. 2005.

Chapter	*Activities for Animal Rights*
4	*4. Video Activist*

"All that you need to become a true video activist is the necessary equipment, practice to develop your required skills, and, perhaps most importantly, inspiration." Thomas Harding (1)

The miniaturisation and affordability of video technology has brought to the streets and fields the video activist or 'videographer'. Images and sound-bites have the power to seize people's attention and bring home the reality of what is happening around them. Video activists wield the video camera to defend and promote civil rights. You can harness the power of the video camera to bear witness for animal rights. Freelance or work for animal voluntary organisations on their campaigns. Video the odd demonstration or work on a long-term project setting objectives and targeting specific audiences. Set yourself up as a lone video activist or gather a team together. When sufficiently experienced you could train others to be video activists too.

Personal Qualities You Will Need
As a video activist you should or will have to:

- Learn the skills of taking and making a good video. You do not need to be a film producer or photo journalist to be successful.
- Not mind obtruding on people: asking them probing questions and poking your camera into their faces.
- Be confident and courageous when approaching rowdy or aggressive people in hectic situations where you might get hurt physically or when approaching despairing people in desperate conditions where you might get hurt emotionally.
- Feel comfortable ears muffled with headphones, staring through your camera, separate, even alienated, from everyone around you when the action gets hot.
- Be able to stick to your role as video activist should an animal or anyone get beaten or trampled. You will miss getting those video shots if you dilute your task with distractions. You must let others do the aiding work.
- Be willing to cope with tedium and frustration. Your mere presence does not guarantee that interesting incidents will materialise and you will spend

days in the field when nothing of note happens. You have to hang around a lot.

- **What to Video?**

Two basic video activisms for animal rights videographers are recording campaign videos and recording witness videos.

- Campaign videos

You document events and conditions where animals are mistreated, neglected or abused. Your aim is to raise people's awareness, educate and exhort people to act, and persuade people to donate money to fight abuse.

- Witness videos

You record at animal rights demonstrations. Your purpose is to capture evidence of illegal or vicious activity by the opposition or police against activist demonstrators as evidence in court. Taking shots of demonstrations can also be an important part of making a campaign video.

The Campaign Video

You are going to tell a story through video. So where do you find stories? You can easily access some places, like circuses, rodeos and zoos. Factory farms are a bit more difficult and you will have to use your ingenuity to video them, and laboratories and research institutions may be guarded and alert (but see Chapter 4: Undercover Investigator, under the section Surveillance Systems).

Video activists are not in the league of making three-hour documentary films. Depending on your purpose, a five to ten minute video can be long enough, certainly for the Web or to screen at a debate. Your intention is not to bore your viewers but to carry across what you want to say and your video should be just long enough for that. It is said that one picture is worth a thousand words; certainly, one timely five minute video is worth a three hour film. Examples of campaign videos are:

- A Circus Video

Circus Suffering is a video, produced by the Captive Animals Protection Society (CAPS), that juxtaposes circus animals a hundred years ago with circus animals today. The video carries the message that we have advanced tremendously in our understanding of wildlife yet 'wild' circus animals still live in shackles. The video was shot at circuses across Europe, features elephants, baboons, ponies, lions, bears and tigers, and captures, says CAPS, "the confinement, deprivation and violence in these animals' lives." A television presenter narrates the twelve minute video, which also has a five minute Web version.

- A Foie Gras Video

The San Diego City Council was deciding on a proposed law in 2006 to ban the sale of foie gras. The California based Animal Protection and Rescue League presented the Council with a 15 minute video as testimony, made in association with two other animal rights bodies. The Council passed the ban almost unanimously.

- A Rescue Video

Go out on an animal rescue (see the Animal Rescuer, Chapter 4). Video the rescue team posing together and show them setting out and arriving at their destination (you could include a shot of the location on a map). Get wide angle views of the target premises then close ups of team members getting inside. Show the condition of the place and the state the animals are in. Also show the animals post-rescue being cleaned up at your base and recovering with adoption volunteers. To the whole hog and get the full story on an open rescue you may want to video yourselves being arrested and tried, people's reactions, even yourself in prison. Add narration, and music to match.

Camera work will be only one of your talents when making a campaign video. Planning the video is the most important skill and may take up to eighty per cent of video production time and most of your energy. Professional film makers plan their films with storyboards, drawing sequences of pictures that will make up the complete movie. Storyboarding makes a video a lot easier to direct and edit. You could do it that way. Alternatively, you could sit down, close your eyes and concentrate hard on visualising what your video will be about, shot for shot, searching for potential problems and thinking through how you will overcome them. Then, having sorted that out, open your eyes, make a list of the shots and finally go out and shoot them.

The Witness Video

Record events at animal rights demonstrations and in particular catch problems involving the police and opposition against the demonstrators. By videoing at demonstrations:

- You prevent or restrain by your mere presence any over-reactions and excesses by the police acting heavily against demonstrators or being idle when they should be attentive and competent. Police are accountable and do not want to be caught out on video for the world to see.

- You forestall opposition violence when they see they are being videoed. But keep an eye open for anyone wanting to 'taking you out', hopefully a rare and avoidable occurrence!
- You have video footage on offer to lawyers as evidence in litigation disputes to acquit activists and bystanders of spurious or inflated police accusations.
- You are on hand to capture confrontational fracas to distribute to the news media for publicity in favour of animal rights.

If the police think you are taking part in the demonstration, rather than being an uninvolved reporter, they might decide to arrest you on some trumped up charge, such as trespassing on private property or riotous behaviour. To counter this it may be prudent to shoot footage of both sides' altercations so that you can claim to be unbiased. You may also want something that identifies you as an impartial journalist or as a member of some part of the news media. Ideally you would flaunt an official press card. Failing that you could devise a business card ('Joe Snapitall - Freelance Photojournalist - Times Square.'), or have in your pocket a letter from a video company stating you are on assignment for them.

What you do not want to do is inadvertently record illegal activity that could get animal rights people into trouble. This might happen should your footage be shown publicly and wrongly interpreted or the police confiscate your camera and use your footage for their purposes. Do not think that the police will not seize your video camera, even if their taking it is illegal, as they can always make up an excuse afterwards.

While shooting your witness video speak a calm, objective, running commentary into the video camera's microphone. Start with the time, date and place and at appropriate moments re-state the time and position where you are shooting. Note the identity numbers of individual police antagonists, the identities of anyone they arrest, and the name and contact data of witnesses. Follow up possible opportunities for more shots; find out where arrested or injured people were taken and check other video activists working close by to swap footage.

When the fur is really flying at a demonstration it is useful to have one or more helpers. They can assist you by looking out for good potential shots, protect you by watching your rear, and sneak your video footage out of the area if the police intend to grab it. Further, you might be more effective at demonstrations as part of a team of video activists, each member taking their own footage to make a more complete record of what is happening. Some team members could shoot close up, others from a distance, or take footage from opposite sides of an incident.

Interviewing demonstrators can be enjoyable and interesting. Ask open ended questions, like "what did you see?" or "what did you do?" Whenever they stop speaking just prompt them by repeating "then what happened?" Ask again if what they say is not clear; they must speak credibly. Elbow your way into someone else's witness interview; your job is to get evidence, not to be polite. Get phone numbers or addresses from good witnesses, but expect that they may not want to get involved.

Depending on circumstances you may want to shoot openly or from cover. People are sometimes shy, so you could act as though your camera is turned off and carry it inconspicuously while still shooting, or only use its microphone. A shoulder bag is handy for a lot of covert shooting. Cut a hole for the camera lens at one end of the bag and tape the camera in position making sure you can see the camera's viewfinder with the bag open. Cut another hole for your microphone or clip the mic to your clothes.

You may want to buy a pinhole video camera if your heart is set on covert work. These cameras sit on a dime yet zoom, tilt and pan like their bigger relatives. However, while the camera itself is not too expensive, you may have to buy a tiny recorder to store the images the camera takes and that could cost several times the camera's price tag. You will also need to buy other bits like cables, batteries and battery power adapters.

Basic Video Field Kit
Apart from access to a computer and editing software, you do not need much else for making videos than the basic field kit. The basic field kit of the modern video activist consists of:

- Camera: often a camcorder (a camera with a built-in recording device) that plays back footage and sound.
- Batteries: probably come with the camera, but get a long-life battery as a spare.
- Battery charger: probably comes with the camera.
- Headphones: to monitor your sound recording. Buy them as an extra.
- Kit bag: for carrying your kit conveniently and safely. Buy this as an extra, too.

Video cameras are digital and video technology is a growing and fast-changing industry. Some video cameras record for several hours without needing attention, so you can keep recording without constantly downloading footage to a computer or changing batteries. Almost any brand of video camera (or camcorder) will do. But you may like it to have a good range of manual functions so that you can control it by hand depending on what you want it to do - instead of it choosing automatically and overriding you.

You will also want to consider what the video camera will record its images and sound on. A video camera can record on tape (getting out-dated), DVD or hard drive. DVD's are small disks you slot into the camcorder and you can record over them repeatedly. The newer technology is a hard drive built inside the camera (like a computer's hard drive). A hard drive accepts several hours of recording and is easily transferable to your computer via a memory stick or other device.

12 Tips for Making Videos

1. Start your video with an overall shot to show the context of your subject, such as a landmark, a signpost, a building, or something else relevant and unique to that place.
2. Get ten seconds or more of footage on each of the important shots.
3. Perch your video camera on a monopod or tripod to prevent it (and the footage) shaking. If you do not want a pod to impede you at a fast moving demonstration, brace yourself against something, like a lamppost or a helper's shoulder.
4. Pan slowly and steadily from one scene or subject to another. Do not continually move the camera back the way it came. Your viewers will not want to be motion-sick.
5. Monitor what is going on while shooting by keeping both eyes open, one eye looking through the viewfinder and the other eye checking your surroundings.
6. Learn to shoot while walking backwards.
7. Check that you really are recording. You may have been recording when you thought you had stopped, and stopped recording when you thought you had started.
8. Be discrete and unobtrusive. People may feel uncomfortable and object to you shooting. But sometimes it is worth making a nuisance of yourself for a good shot.
9. Your video camera is also a tape recorder. It will record sounds closer to it better than sounds further away. Experiment with an external microphone. You can point it at sound sources and filter out peripheral sounds.
10. While recording, monitor the sound with headphones to make sure it is not a jumble of noise.

11. Buy a cheap video camera if your equipment might get smashed, eg at a violent demo. But buy quality equipment if you intend your video for television or other public viewing.
12. Prepare for Murphy's Law: if anything can go wrong it will go wrong.

Editing

You do not cut celluloid footage into strips anymore. Nowadays you do your video editing entirely on a computer. Nor is there any need for complicated editing software. Basic video-editing programs are installed on most new computers. Even elementary editing programs enable you to add titles, narration, music and special effects to a video. Choose the best footage and put the bits in order to make your video flow the way you want it. Get the editing right and you will have a lot of satisfaction from your completed video. Bear in mind that a witness video may best be left unedited if it is going to be used in court, otherwise it may appear biased and suspect.

Distributing Your Video

You are not a video activist by shutting your video away in the attic. You must show your work to influence people and therefore you must distribute it.

- Show your video online on your web site or blog, or upload it to a web site that displays people's videos, like YouTube or Google Video.
- Describe your video to web site owners and ask them for a link from their web site to the page on your web site where viewers can see it. (Give a reciprocal link to the web site owners who link to your site.)
- Send out details of your video to potential customers, patrons and to anyone who might be interested in it. Briefly describe it (plus ordering information) and include a web address where they can see a preview.
- Present your video at events arranged by animal activist organisations where audiences can view and discuss it.
- After much experience you may find that you are exceptionally good at video activism. Then you may be in the market to sell footage to television. Who knows, you might hit the jackpot by catching a sensational event that television companies fall over themselves to air!

References

(1) Harding, Thomas. *The Video Activist Handbook*. Pluto Press: London. 2001, xvi. 2nd edition.

Further Reading

Gregory, S; Caldwell, G; Avni, R; Harding, T & Gabriel, P. *Video for Change: a guide for advocacy and activism*. Pluto Press: London. 2005.

Chapter	Activities for Animal Rights
4	5. Animal Preacher

"Poll: Do Animals Go To Heaven When They Die?

> Yes.
> Only if they are 'good'.
> I don't believe in Heaven and Hell.
> Karma effects animals as it does humans.
> No.
> Not sure.
> Other.

About our polls: Because AnimalChaplains.com is an interfaith ministry, we do not claim to know the answers to these important religious questions…" (1)

Many attitudes in the West about animals derive from Judaeo-Christian sources and are deeply human centred. Two common fundamental religious beliefs held for centuries are that God made animals for human use and that humans in every way are more important than animals. People manipulate these ideas to justify exploiting animals while denying animals moral and welfare obligations.

How can you transform this view? Perhaps you are gifted for delivering religious teachings or spiritual exhortations? Then no matter what your religion or religious tradition you can speak up and spread respect for God's creation and preach God's word for animal rights. (If you want to teach but not preach, see Teaching, Chapter 4.)

Can Anyone Preach?

Your goal as a preacher is to articulate to people the expression of God as you understand it. You do not need to be ordained as clergy or be a member of a religious group to do this. Anyone can do it anywhere they like on their own initiative. But if you are a member of a religious group and wish to preach within its congregation then the first step is to talk with your minister to explore opportunities. Some religious orders use lay preachers: non-ordained, part-time volunteers. It is said that because lay preachers live among the ordinary people that they are able to relate to the lives of common people and bring a freshness of interpretation to the scriptures that ordained clergy cannot.

Animal Chaplain

Although you may be able to find some clergy who will take general services for animals, they are the rare exceptions among the Clergy. Clergy preachers for animal rights are even more rare (see Andrew Linzey, bellow). Possibly the closest vocation to animal preacher as such is an animal chaplain. Animal chaplains serve animals and the people who are close to their animals. Animal chaplains are unpaid, often have another job to sustain their worldly needs and offer their chaplaincy part-time. Animal chaplains may be affiliated to a religious body and preach in collaboration with ordained clergy; alternatively, they may preach independently of any religious organisation and set up their own ministry. Being an animal chaplain is a fairly new calling and one that has been developing over the last few years.

Among your duties as an animal chaplain you would:

- Conduct religious services in which animals are welcome.
- Perform animal blessings and memorial ceremonies.
- Provide pet-loss consolation and counselling.
- Pray for sick or injured animals.
- Support pet owners during animal surgery or euthanasia.

Animal chaplains also deliver sermons on the relationship between animals and humans and advance spiritual education and guidance about the responsibilities of humans to animals. From here it is a tiny step to preach animal rights and there is no reason why you should not do so as part of your work as an animal chaplain. Broadly, you will be promoting compassion, respect and rights for God's creatures and the sharing of the environment with all creation in peace and harmony.

Qualities You Need for Animal Rights Preaching

- A sense of calling and a will and commitment to preach.
- Be able to articulate your feelings to other people, project your voice with confidence and express yourself well to deliver your sermons effectively.
- Be a spiritual person, without necessarily being religious, with a love for animals.
- If you are religious you should know your religion, especially by studying and interpreting its holy books to apply them when preaching and answering people's questions.

- Develop your faculties as an acute observer of life and discern links between the scriptures and modern everyday living.
- Enjoy serving others, be a good listener, reliable, mature and emotionally stable.
- Be willing to learn the art of preaching. Study the style and delivery of practising preachers and develop your own technique.
- Be willing to spend time publicising your services in your community (people must know you exist).

Animal Preachers Past & Present

Francis of Assisi (1181 – 1226) is one of the best known religious preachers from history. He lived in present day Italy and was first a soldier then a traveller and finally a Catholic friar who started his preaching career without being ordained. Frances was made a saint and as the patron saint of animals he demonstrates the positive side of Christianity to the animal world.

People are quick to depreciate and exterminate some animals without knowing their true nature. This applies to wolves in particular (2, 3). So the fable of Francis and the wolf has special interest. Francis was visiting Gubbio village when the community was terrorised by a wolf consuming their livestock. The people tried to kill the wolf, but he fought back and they were afraid to leave their houses. Francis met the wolf and explained to him that he must not harm the people or their livestock, in which case past errors would be forgiven and the villagers would not try to kill him. To the surprise of the people the wolf agreed and shook hands with Francis as a pledge. From then on the wolf stopped harming the people and their livestock and the villagers fed the wolf in return. We should each draw our own moral from this story, but one moral could be that destructiveness in man and beast can be redeemed by offering animals understanding and respect.

However, you do not need to rely on legend for inspiration to preach about animals. Andrew Linzey (b 1952) is a real-life British Anglican priest, theologian, academic and a champion for animal rights within Christianity. Widely considered an authority on Christianity and animals, Linzey has been preaching and writing about Christianity and animal rights since the 1970's. Linzey says that his vocation is to change Christian attitudes to animals for the better. Linzey says (4):

> "Anglicans, like most Christians, haven't really woken up to the moral issue of our exploitation of animals."

"All the stuff about animals not having language, not having rational souls, not having culture, not being persons - all of these are human constructions."

"In God's eyes, all creatures have value whether we find them cuddly, affectionate, beautiful or otherwise."

Linzey is distinguished for his accomplishments relating to theology and animals. At Oxford University he held the world's first fellowship in Ethics, Theology and Animal Welfare, the first university position to unite ethics, religion and animals. In 2001 the Archbishop of Canterbury presented him with an honorary degree of Doctor of Divinity, the highest distinction he could make to a theologian. The distinction was granted with particular reference to Linzey's work on the rights and welfare of "God's sentient creatures" and is the first time it has been conferred for work embracing Christianity and animals. Linzey says:

"Animals make a special moral claim upon us because, interalia, they are morally innocent, unable to give or withhold their consent, or vocalise their needs, and because they are wholly vulnerable to human exploitation. These considerations make the infliction of suffering upon them not easier - but harder to justify." (5)

Sermons
The sermon is a valuable primary tool. The typical sermon has a clear cohesive union of introduction, body and conclusion. The introduction grabs your listeners' attention, the body of the sermon makes the points you wish to get across to your audience, and the conclusion is a definite and resounding final, like an exhortation. There are different kinds of sermon:

- Topical: follows a subject of current concern via the scriptures.
- Expository: explains passages from the scriptures.
- Biographical: pursues the life and meaning of a personality in the scriptures.
- Evangelistic: spells out how members of the audience can save themselves.

As well as preaching that animals and humans are morally equal and deserving of rights, another major theme is that people should show respect for animals by taking up vegetarianism. Humanity kills billions of food animals annually and therefore meat-eating is at the forefront of animal rights issues and has moral and spiritual significance for animal rights preachers. Some Christian vegetarians cite parts of the Bible as evidence that Jesus was a vegetarian animal activist. They explain that Jesus' act of expelling animal traders from the temple on the eve of a big feast day (6) was to stop a huge slaughter of animals. Furthermore, they claim, that the New Testament only once describes Jesus as eating meat - and then only a small morsel of fish to make a point to his disciples. However, there are endless topics to choose from for sermons.

A good technique is to phrase the titles of sermons as questions so that you can build up your audience's curiosity and bring each sermon to a decisive answer. Titles for sermons could be:

- What do the scriptures say about the moral standing of animals in relation to humans?
- Can we reconcile discrepancies between being God's 'stewards of creation' and setting up factory farms?
- What can we make of God loving all his creatures and of the suffering imposed on animals by humanity?
- Does not God say the strong should protect the weak and therefore should not humanity protect animality?
- Is human dominion over animalkind a trust by God, for which we shall be called to account, and not an exploitative absolute right?
- Eating animals is not associated with a pure state of humanity - Eden was a vegetarian garden - so should we all be vegetarians?
- Do the scriptures illuminate the meaning of equal consideration of God's creatures in a modern world?

Publicising Yourself

You may be able to publicise yourself as an animal rights preacher by way of your house of worship. Another route to publicise your services is through your own web site or blog (see Chapter 3: The Internet). As well as preaching sermons out loud you can write them for display; your web site is an extension of your pulpit so post your sermons there. Hand out your literature in public places and at religious services and meetings. Teach compassion to animals in school classrooms (see Chapter 4: Public & School Speaker).

Training

Some churches offer training and accreditation to lay preachers. The training may take the form of writing essays, meeting in study groups, periodic homework and associated reading for group discussion. Some of training courses may last more than a year and could involve residential weekends. There are no officially approved training courses to qualify candidates as animal chaplains (writing in 2008), although there are a handful of web sites that offer distant learning opportunities, and there are certainly no courses for animal rights preachers. So be an animal rights preacher now - the field is open and may be calling you.

References

(1) www.AnimalChaplains.com. (Accessed October 2007.)

(2) Linnell, John D C, et al. *The fear of wolves: a review of wolf attacks on humans.* NINA Oppdragsmelding, 731. 2002:1 - 65. (Accessed online May 2004.)

(3) McNay, Mark E. *A Case History of wolf-human encounters in Alaska and Canada.* Alaska Department of Fish and Game. Wildlife Technical Bulletin 13. 2002. (Accessed online May 2004.)

(4) Linzey, Andrew. *Christianity and Animals.* Rynn Berry interviews. 1996. www.satyamag.com. (Accessed May 2006.)

(5) Linzey, Andrew. *The Ethical Case Against Fur Farming. A statement by an international group of academics, including ethicists, philosophers and theologians.* (Accessed online May 2006 at Respect for Animals and other web sites.)

(6) Matthew 21:12; Mark 11:15 - 16; Luke 19:45.

Chapter	*Activities for Animal Rights*
4	*6. Animal Rescuer*

Rescues are actions that liberate abused animals. Often the animals are morally or illegally maltreated and their welfare is disregard by the authorities. Frequent target animals for rescues are hens and pigs at factory farms, dogs and rabbits at animal experiment laboratories, fur-bearers at fur farms, and then there are canned hunts, slaughterhouses and any place where people make animals suffer. Rescues can be open or clandestine. Rescues are open when the rescuers maximise publicity for their cause by revealing their identity to the police and public and by challenging the legal consequences of their actions. Rescues are clandestine or closed when the rescuers hide their identity, sometimes by wearing balaclavas, and evade the law.

Aim of Open Rescues
An aim of rescues is to save suffering animals by giving them veterinary aid if sick and either giving them to caring homes or turning them loose to fend for themselves. Another aim, especially of open rescues, is to make as much publicity as possible for the cause of animal rights. Open rescuers contact the news media and police about their rescue and thoroughly explain their reasons for doing it. Moreover, they are prepared to go to court to defend their actions and if necessary go to prison. Open rescuing goes back at least to the 1980's when Australian Patty Mark, in Melbourne, Australia, organised Animal Liberation Victoria to stage open rescues. Open rescues then spread from Australia to Sweden, Germany, the USA and other countries.

Staging an Open Rescue
It is essential that you prepare in advance when going about an open rescue. First of all you need reliable knowledge of your target property and evidence of the illegal abuses perpetrated there. This you could get by wandering about unannounced, which might amount to a mild trespass, or, if security is tight, you could get a job there. Either way you collect sure documentary evidence with video and/or stills photos of the conditions of the animals (see Undercover Investigator and Video Activist, both in Chapter 4). Your evidence must be able to stand up in a court of law.

Duplicate your evidence and take it to the relevant authorities and demand that they prosecute the abusers for breaking the law. All is well and good should the law actually take effective action; in this case you win and can go and find another target. However, it is likely the law will not take action or be sluggishly slow and do nothing effective, in which case you carry out your open rescue. The aim of the rescue is twofold: to publicise the illegal abuse of the animals and publicise the lack of action of the authorities by not prosecuting the perpetrators.

You return to your target property and set free or take with you at least some of the animals when you leave. Then give copies (prepared in advance) of your printed personal details and why you carried out the raid, plus copies of your evidence to the police, news media and your lawyer. Moreover, demand that the authorities now take action to rectify the illegal abuse to the animals. Declare that you accept and welcome the prospect that you may be prosecuted in court (for trespass or burglary) and that you are ready to fight your case and serve time in prison if necessary in defence of the animals. Your legal defence is that the authorities would take no action (or no effective action) and therefore you had no other course but to bring the issue to public attention by steeling the animals for people to see. Squeeze out as much publicity as you can.

Video clips of rescues online. Track them down via a search engine by keying "open rescue" into its search field.

What You Need to Be a Rescuer

For open rescues you should:
- Know how to operate cameras to collect the evidence.
- Understand the animal welfare laws of your state so that you know whether the animal abuse you see is legal or illegal.
- Be able to gather evidence of your target premises before you raid it in a rescue.
- Know how to handle the news media to make the most of the publicity you can generate. (See Chapter 3: News Media.)
- Be able to say goodbye to your family and job in case you spend time in jail.

For closed rescues some of the above also applies but in addition:
- You should also be good at evading the law.

For both open and closed rescues:
- You need a burning desire to act as a rescuer and accept any consequences that befall you.

Some Good & Bad Points

Open rescues have some good arguments in their favour:

- You do not physically harm anyone or destroy property (although some rescuers have taken it on themselves to damage property) and therefore no one can seriously claim that you the rescuers are animal rights 'terrorists' (see Chapter 5 under *Terrorism* and under *Violence or Nonviolence?*).

- When you do not harm anyone or destroy property the news media are likely to focus on the animals, their suffering and the reluctance of the authorities to enforce the law about animal welfare. If you cause harm then you will have thrown away your moral and legal advantage because the news media are likely to focus on that instead of the animals.

- You can get positive reporting for animal rights from the news media because you are open about your identity. Your honesty, candour and non-aggression encourage a sympathetic response to animal liberation from the public. People can see animal lib as a courageous and compassionate aim. Clandestine rescuers, on the other hand, can keep on freeing animals (provided they avoid prison) but tend not to win over the public or make the law on animal welfare more effectively enforced.

Of course there is always a down side to anything:

- Open rescues take up more time, money and effort than closed rescues because open rescuers may have to defend themselves in law courts and possibly go to prison.

- In prison you are not available to go on more rescues - although you could spend time profitably, such as publishing your experiences and why you are an animal rescuer.

- Open rescue is not a method for everyone; you may not want to jeopardize your career by going to prison or want a criminal record.

Rescuing abused animals is certainly worthwhile, especially for the rescued animals. Comparing open and closed rescues, the former may be more effective in that it not only liberates some animals but in the long-run can stimulate better welfare for more animals through making the law act against illegal animal abusers.

However, rescues have their critics. Some people take the view that you have a responsibility to abide by the law and therefore not engage in rescues, open or clandestine, but should pursue your goals by legal and democratic means. Alternatively, other people will see rescues as a moral good that exposes animal abuse and illegal operators. If you have tried every avenue without success then you may have no alternative but to engage in civil disobedience and direct action (see Chapter 3: Civil Disobedience, and Direct Action). The irony is that too often the law-breaking perpetrators of animal abuse get away with their violation while the open rescuers are nicked by the law and end up in jail - a socio-legal hypocrisy.

Chapter	*Activities for Animal Rights*
4	*7. Investigative Reporter*

Investigative reporters (also called investigative journalists) probe questionable activities that are hidden from public view, appear to go against the public interest and which the public do not know much if anything about. As an investigative reporter you do not publicise mere assertions but obtain reasonable evidence of controversial activity and lay it open for public scrutiny and debate. In our case, as an animal rights investigative reporter, you must expose activities that go against the animal good, which in the long-run also often go against the public good.

Your ultimate goal, whatever wrong-doings you decide to pursue, is to change society's attitude to animals for the better. But you do not need to uncover a national or international conspiracy, just begin locally. Then if you want to take it further you can progress on to bigger jobs. Examples where hidden harms against animals may emerge and should be investigated and challenged are:

- Violations of codes of professional conduct, eg at business companies, circuses, rodeos and abattoirs.
- Animal baiting.
- Animal experimentation laboratories.
- Pet theft.
- Wildlife hunting and destruction.
- Animal trade, nationally or international import and export.
- Animal transport, nationally and internationally.
- Factory farming and fur farming.
- Domestic animal abuse in the home.
- Food and clothing labelling.

You may be motivated to take up your investigation for the sake of animals. However, you will be in a much stronger position if you can present the evidence that you propose to get and any conclusions you that might draw in terms of the interests of people, such as people's health and well-being, their economics or sense of morality. Slant your expose this way and more people, whether animal-oriented or not, will respond to your investigative report.

Investigation Ideas

Where do you get ideas for an investigation?

- Monitor industries such as fur fashion, factory farming, pet food production.
- Look for trends like an increase in foie gras, veal or prosecutions for selling meat unsuitable for human consumption.
- Check the news: examine your local or national press to find a new angle on an existing story.
- Browse the Web and your reference library for ideas.
- Ask acquaintances and brain-storm with colleagues.

Also see under the heading 'Define Your Subject' in Chapter 4: Scientific Investigator.

Publication

The results of your investigation must be published if there is to be any kind of public or official reaction to it. So ask yourself these questions about an investigation you have in mind before you start spending a lot of time on the case.

- Would a reputable animal advocate organisation publish your findings as a report for wide circulation (ask some organisations)?
- Could your findings be published locally or nationally in the media (eg is it newsworthy - see Chapter 3: News Media)?
- Might legal action be taken about your findings (get some legal advice)?

Your subject may be worthwhile investigating if the answer to any of these questions is yes. But if the answer to all three questions is negative then think again; look for a different angle to pitch your investigation or cast about for another subject to investigate. Do not just hope or assume that any of these questions might turn out positive. Time spent getting evidence for and against these considerations is time well spent.

Planning

When you pick out a potential investigation get a clear idea of why you propose doing it. Examine it from as many angles as you can to forestall any problems. Ask yourself of your intended investigation:

- What hidden activities might it reveal and are they illegal?
- What moral values might it question?

157

- Who in power might it challenge?
- Can any perpetrator be held accountable legally or morally?
- Has it already been exposed and is nevertheless continuing? (If it is continuing get the facts on why it is.)
- What must you do to get proof of the activity (eg eyewitness statements, documentation, photography, environmental tests)?
- Will you get the evidence openly or by deception? (Deception can be legal - see Legality & Ethics, below.)
- Will there be any legal infringements getting the evidence, such as trespass or theft? (See Legality & Ethics, below.)
- How will the story be delivered to the public (eg to magazines, newspapers or the television, or to an animal rights organisation)?
- Will there be any legal problems like libel if your report is published? (See Legality & Ethics, below.)

And if you go ahead with your investigation do not forget to follow it up after it is complete. Are the abuses still continuing after you have revealed them to the authorities and the public? Keep checking and reinvestigate if necessary.

Is Investigative Reporting for You?
Investigative reporting may be for you if you:

- Get a lot of satisfaction doing your own thing.
- Have an enterprising nature for uncovering shady activity.
- Are single-minded and focused to keep on track.
- Can educate yourself about the field.
- Can identify key points, think critically and ask the right questions.
- Can react quickly in a tricky situation.
- Can turn out your findings in depth for distribution in print or in some other medium, like photography or video.
- Have self-control when dealing with upsetting conditions.
- Have patience and firmness when handling disagreeable people.
- Are prepared for the possibility of occasional physical assault against yourself.
- Are willing to risk entanglement with the law.

Gadgets?
When on an investigation take notes of what you witness (at the time or immediately afterwards) and never rely on memory alone. You may want a sound recorder and a camera, but going overboard with gadgets is pointless; your eyes and ears are your primary tools.

You could operate a pocket sound recorder, perhaps to catch your targets compromising themselves. But a recorder might only add to your workload if you find yourself having to transcribe hours of recordings onto paper.

In some places you may take photos openly. In other situations you may have to be more secretive. A hidden camera could be invaluable for gaining photographic evidence, such as when snooping for unlawful activity, such as at an animal baiting. Hidden cameras are so small that they can mimic buttons on your jacket. They are not overly expensive to buy and you can connect them to a portable device to store the pictures. For more about cameras see Chapter 4: Undercover Investigator, under Surveillance Systems. Also see Chapter 4: Aerial Snooper, as a possible means of capturing some kinds of photographic shot.

Legality & Ethics

During the course of your enquiries you may at times have to conceal your identity to gain the trust of people in order to expose their dubious operations. Even so, good animal rights investigative reporters obey the law (at least most of the time) and act ethically. You have to obtain information legally so that you can use it openly, as in a published report or in a court of law. You take a risk using illegally obtained information openly; you and anyone else involved in obtaining it may find yourselves in a tangle with the law and with a lawsuit on your hands. The main use of illegally obtained information is that it provides knowledge of something that can be investigated further in a legal way. If you must use illegally obtained information in your report, acquire it in such a way that it cannot reveal to the law how you came by it.

Animal rights investigative reporters must also act ethically. A suitable ethical code can be summed up as:

- Be sincere, frank and fair with truthful and honest people.
- Make your investigative report accurate and objective; stick to the facts and never misrepresent the issue in any way.
- Never reveal your confidential sources of information.

Follow these rules to build up your credibility with your animal rights associates and the public.

Chapter	*Activities for Animal Rights*
4	*8. Media Watcher*

Most people bathe daily in the words of the television, radio and print. The news media are powerful shapers and swayers of opinion. They influence both the man in the street and the decision makers of our society. Nevertheless, although the media are influential they are not difficult to influence. Journalists and their bosses, the controllers of media content, are not so remote that we as ordinary members of the public cannot make them hear us. As a media watcher your task is to influence the media to try and make them objective, fair and accurate about animal rights and make them broadcast more animal rights news and stories.

Animals in the News

There is no end of animal-related topics that you can pick up in the media: drug testing, veal farming, live transport, animal adverts, animals in entertainment, animal racing, activists treated as terrorists, nature conservation, and so on. Even when animals are not the actual topic, you can make some point by digging up a new angle, such as connecting a poor diet that is in the news with a contrasting healthy vegan or veggie diet. Of course, no one can scan all the news media every day, even with helpers this would be a daunting task. Therefore you will need to specialise, for instance on what you can find online in your own language or country.

Influencing the Media

Influence the media by searching for animal rights content and getting as many people you can to send their views to the editors about the material you find. Here is how it works.

1. Regularly monitor the latest news.
2. Set up your own web site (see Chapter 3: The Internet).
3. Paraphrase or summarise on your web site relevant animal-related news items you find.
4. Next to each summary place a link going to the original news item and the email address of the editor or journalist responsible for the original item. You might also provide their phone number, postal address or other contact details. (You may want to give details of where an item was broadcast or published if it does not appear online.)

5. Drive viewers to your web site and invite them to give you their email address (ie to join your mailing list).
6. Email everyone on your mailing list about the summaries and include a link with each summary so that your readers can find them on your web site.
7. People receiving your email will be able to read your summaries, follow the links to the original news items and email their views to the editors or journalists.

What Do Editors Think?

What happens to the mail that your readers send to the journalists and editors? Well aimed and relevant mailings can influence the news media because editors take them as a gauge of public opinion. The media want to be popular and rely on feedback from their audiences. Therefore they take emails and letters seriously and may act on them. Furthermore, each mail that someone sends has more weight and worth than might appear. This is because for each email or letter that editors receive they realise there are several people who would like to send mail but did not for one reason or another. Therefore editors take each mail to represent many people with similar views.

What You Need to Be a Media Watcher

- Making your own animal news information web site may especially appeal to you if you have journalistic flair.
- You should be an avid news vulture.
- You must have sufficient time and an abiding perseverance for grabbing most of the relevant news items most of the time and getting them down onto your web site.

What to Look Out For

In addition to the usual animal items, look out for the sort of perspective, standards, stereotypes and language the media use when reporting news with animal content. For example:

- Unbalanced Perspective

Check where stories come from for imbalances. Both sides of an issue should be represented for a story to be broadcast fairly. For instance, suppose a group of activists are accused of terrorism by officialdom without a contrasting statement from a sympathetic animal activist expert. When you find imbalances in perspective ask the media to widen their point of view.

- Double Standards

Are the media measuring one party against one standard while holding up another party to a different standard? Humans alter whole regions to become largely uninhabitable for wildlife and when a few wild animals turn up they are seen as causing a nuisance or as threatening. Subsequently there is an outcry of 'infestation!' Many news media treat humanity's ravaging of Earth as normal but take exception when animals appear to menace human property. Expose the media's double standards.

- Stereotypes

Are the media portraying animals and activists as stereotypes? Wolves, as an example, are not bloodthirsty ravishers of livestock and innocent people. Scientists (1) have shown that the wolf's reputation is a gross exaggeration (elephants kill more people than wolves yet few people decry these giants) and that wolves significantly contribute to a balanced ecosystem (2). Bring the media up to date with education about animals.

- Loaded Language

How do the media describe animals? Do sharks really 'infest' swimming beaches? Are foxes and rats really 'vermin'? Are crocodiles really 'man-eaters'? The most important message in a story relating to animals may be implicit in the choice of words the media use. Ask the media not to apply distorted or indistinct language that fuels biased opinion against animals.

Mailing Manners

What sort of tone is best adopted when writing to the media? Experts on good communication say you should:

- Be upbeat and concise and stick closely to the point.
- Be factual, not rhetorical.
- Make only one or two points at most, preferably in your opening sentence.
- Make a good humoured remark. It is more memorable and conveys a better impact than verbosity.
- Always be pleasant and diplomatic. Be positive and pay complements when you can, but do not over do it or you will sound false.
- Avoid writing angry or insulting mail or you will antagonise people you might have won over.
- Give your full name, address and phone number. Newspaper editorial staff will want to check with you before they print anything you have written for them to publish.

Standard Form Letters?

You may want to provide sample letters on your web site that your viewers can send to the media. However, editors who receive lots of similarly phrased letters may count the lot as one letter. Editors tend to give more weight to mail from individuals rather than mail that is obviously from a mass writing campaign. So you may wish to goad fellow writers to make their mail uniquely different from each other. You could just outline the points they could make, ask them to choose a few of the points in their letter and write in their own words.

Do not underrate your potential to influence the news media. Show them that you are a perceptive and caring citizen and then they cannot dismiss you as a crude, uneducated extremist (even if you are).

References

(1) Linnell, John D C et al. *The fear of wolves: a review of wolf attacks on humans.* NINA Oppdragsmelding, 731. 2002:1 - 65.
(2) Robbins J. *Lessons from the Wolf.* Scientific American. 2004.

Web Link

DawnWatch.com. An excellent animal media watcher online.

Chapter	*Activities for Animal Rights*
4	*9. Street Theatre Actor*

What is Street Theatre?

You can act for animal rights in more ways than one. Street theatre actors take their performance literally onto the streets: to street corners, market places, town squares and busy shopping centres. Serious street theatre performers use their acting skills as a political weapon by circulating current ideas and exploring controversial social themes to influence social reform. Street theatre is an opportunity for you to probe the social, moral and political questions arising from animal rights.

This is what one street theatre group was doing in the streets of Belfast. Linda McKee, reported for the Belfast Telegraph: "In the drama by the Mac Factor street theatre group, the red-coated, whipcracking hunter pursued a fox in an age-old chase that usually ends with the animal torn apart by hounds. But yesterday, the tables were turned as the cornered fox fought back, bringing the hunter to the ground at Cornmarket." (1) Performances were watched by crowds across the city centre and were co-ordinated by the League Against Cruel Sports as part of their campaign to ban fox-hunting in northern Ireland.

Street theatre is a tradition that people watch around the world where audiences are as diverse and different as cosmopolitan London and remote rural India. It reaches even people who have never been to a regular theatre. Street theatre actors perform for anyone passing by with time to stop and watch them, and there is no entrance free. The genre is not 'outdoor theatre', where an indoor performance is entirely transferred with props, lighting and all to an outdoor arena, such as an amphitheatre, set aside for an audience to pay a fee for admission. Nor do merely acrobats, jugglers and fire-eaters dominate a street theatre.

Your Street Theatre

Your audiences are largely composed of passers-by. They have not come prepared to watch a play and are preoccupied with other things, which imposes a limitation on keeping your plays short. Furthermore, as street theatre actors your performing group is peripatetic, so you use minimal costumes and simple portable stage props. At a performance you could start off by singing or playing a loud instrument to attract people. When a sufficient number of onlookers have gathered around, you can begin. In the bustle and hubbub of a busy street you will have to be loud and larger than life and may employ humour, slapstick, song and lively dance to keep the attention of mixed crowds.

To die, to sleep, to end the heart-ache and thousand natural shocks that (animal) flesh is heir to...

Animal Shakespeare Players

"Of course, animals can act agony superbly. But they can't really feel pain, reason or think."

Ben Isacat

Decide to perform independently or in conjunction with the campaigns of other animal rights groups. Either way deliver your message with more certainty by handing out literature about yourselves, your aims and your plays, and at the end of each play by holding a public discussion questioning its purpose (see The 'Y', below). With many street plays under your belt you may be in a good position to organise workshops to teach the art of street performance to other aspiring street theatre actors.

Where to stage your performances? Not just in the streets. Go on tour to schools, factories and civic centres. Book a place at festivals and fairs. Act outside the headquarters of animal abusing companies, supermarkets, animal laboratories and zoos, especially if they constitute the theme of your act. Find out whether you require a licence from your local authority to stage acts and discussions in the street. If you need a licence and do not have one, be prepared to make a bolt for it if a policeman turns up to watch you!

The 'Y'

An example of a street theatre company is the 'Y Touring Theatre Company', which aimed to shake up people's attitudes by creating quality theatre to highlight serious and perplexing contemporary issues. The theatre company was founded in Britain in 1989 as part of the Central Young Man's Christian Association (known as the Y) and has toured throughout Britain and abroad.

One of the Y's interests is ethics in science. To this end the playwright Judith Johnson wrote Every Breath for the Y. The play raises moral, social and scientific questions inherent in using animals in medical research. It poses fundamental questions like whether you are right to put your kin above the lives of animals. The play is intended for students aged 14 plus as part of their science, drama and religious education curricula. The Y have staged the play for thousands of school children nationally and have performed it for audiences at the annual Edinburgh Festival. Interestingly, Every Breath has received funding by a number of organisations and backing from all sides of the animal experimentation debate.

The setting of the play is with a family in danger of breaking up because of the animal experimentation dispute. The four characters in the play are a teenage vegetarian campaigning peacefully to stop a university animal laboratory being built (shades of Cambridge University, see Animal Lawyer, Chapter 4); his older sister, a research student experimenting on rats; their mother, a single mum dedicated to her children; and the mum's boyfriend, an odd job man from a rough background contemplating Buddhism, who brings some light-heart humour to the serious nature of the performance.

One of the principle aims of the Y Touring Theatre Company is to create an impartial arena for learning through debate. So following a performance they encourage the audience to discuss the issues raised by their play. Before performances the company distributes 'preparatory lessons' for teachers and students to ready themselves with background information to take most opportunity of the play and subsequent debate. The premiere of the play at a school in London was followed by a "rowdy and combative discussion", according to a review in a national newspaper (1).

What You Need

The necessary minimum that you need to be a street actor is:

- A burning desire to act and the recognition that you can satisfy it in the street.
- The skill of projecting your body movements and voice so that scores of people standing around you can comprehend what you are trying to convey. In short, you must be able to act with many distractions in a noisy crowd.
- Dedication and sufficient time, not just for acting but to devote to the planning, organising and rehearsing that go into each performance.
- Your audience will definitely walk away if they get bored or are busy. So you do not want to be over-sensitive to people's coming and going and when playing to a diminishing crowd.

Although onlookers do not pay an entrance fee some of them might throw you a few coins; so financial remuneration is nil or minor and you will have to support yourself some other way. But you never know if an impresario is in the crowd and about to discover you. Add to that the satisfaction of combining show biz with animal rights.

References
(1) Linda McKee, The campaigners who turned a fox hunt protest into performance art. *Belfast Telegraph*, 17 February 2007.
(2) *Guardian*. 14 March 2006.

Web Link
National Association of Street Artists (www.nasauk.org). Artists and companies creating street and outdoor arts work.

Chapter	*Activities for Animal Rights*
4	*10. Blogger*

Blogging in a Nutshell

A blog consists of one or more pages you develop on the Web. On your blog you can display items like stories, news, announcements, revelations, illustrations and video clips about what interests you. Readers of your blog may leave comments and discussions on it about its contents. Blogs are easy to set up, are often free or inexpensive, and have the potential to be read by numerous people around the world.

Anyone, from juvenile jailbird to elder politician, can start one or more blogs. A single blog is sometimes the work of a group of people. The aim of many bloggers is to influence their readers by informing and motivating them. You can find millions of blogs online of all genres and tastes and the informal generic term for blogs on the Web is the 'blogosphere'.

Blogs originally began as online personal diaries in the late 1990's and have evolved as valued contributions to society (authoritarian regimes often try to restrict blogs and penalize bloggers). Some blogs are obviously blogs but some resemble traditional web sites. An advantage of publishing a blog is that you build it using simple-to-understand software without needing to learn the workings behind it. Creating a traditional web site you must know HTML (hyper-text mark-up language), the coding used to layout web pages.

Is Blogging for You?

Do you enjoy reading, writing, creating designs and surfing the Web? Do you enjoy exploring and examining issues, staying abreast of news and ideas, promoting and defending your views and corresponding with people? You can do all these with a blog.

As a blogger for animal rights you promote a subject related to animals. You might know nothing about your subject now but in time could become an acknowledged specialist in it. Appropriate subjects are diverse and could be almost anything, from selling animal-rights-related commercial products to preaching animal-rights-related religion.

There are many books and online tutorials about blogging, but to make a good job of it you will need to draw on your resources from within:

- Time and energy on top of your daily schedule
- Motivation and self-discipline to revise your blog regularly
- Ability to write clearly about your subject
- A capacity to attract new readers and keep them coming back for more
- Of course you need a computer and some associated knowledge.

Which Subject to Blog?

Blogging is a medium to long-term project in which you should keep the content of your blog fresh by updating it reasonably frequently with relevant and interesting material. Therefore, choose a subject that you are hot-blooded about and can pursue until the end of time. As mentioned above, you can do anything from selling goods to evangelizing. A quick round up of some animal rights areas:

- Art (eg animal rights photography, paintings, posters, images of all sorts)
- Commodities (eg selling products like non-leather shoes or animal rights books)
- Conservation & Zoos (eg about extinctions, wildlife management, wildlife 'culls')
- Entertainment (eg animal baiting, circuses, rodeos, zoos)
- Experimentation (eg advocating animal-free biomedical, toxicity and military research)
- Factory Farming (eg about confined animals, disease, environmental contamination, economics)
- Food (eg veal, foie gras, bush meat, vegetarianism, veganism, school meals)
- Fundraising (eg sponsoring people's activities for animals)
- Fur (eg about the national or international trade, cat and dog fur trade)
- Garb (eg relating to fur, feather, leather, perfume, ornaments)
- History (eg of any topics on this list)
- Hunting & Sport (eg about shooting, coursing, trapping, baiting, racing)
- Law (eg the law relating to animal rights/welfare, animal abuse court cases)
- News and Current Affairs (eg digging up news stories about animal rights)
- Personalities (eg about animal rights workers, teachers, philosophers)
- Philosophy (eg of animal rights or more broadly of animal ethics)
- Politics (eg what politicians are doing/saying about animal rights)
- Teaching (eg teaching children about animal rights

- Trafficking (eg for zoos, pets, body parts, quack medicine, trinkets)
- Undercover Investigations (eg clandestine work uncovering illegal doings)
- Unintentional (eg motorist kills, habitat destruction, climate change)

Cannot find a subject? How about writing a blog about animal rights blogs? Do not just write a list of blogs. Find the best and worst blogs. Compare them. Comment about their aims and, as you see it, their effectiveness. Generalise or specialise, for instance concentrate on veggie blogs, animal experiment blogs, or fur blogs.

A blog can be static, with no input from its readers, or it can be 'interactive' in that readers leave comments on it or send you email. With an interactive blog you will need to be receptive and respond to your commentators. Therefore, chose a subject that you are prepared to debate with your readers.

Get to know the blogosphere. You can find out a lot by reading blogs related to your subject - assuming there are related blogs (you might be pioneering a new field). Use search engines and specialist blog indexing sites (like Technorati.com) to find blogs that interest you.

Blog Service Providers

Choose a blog service provider (or 'platform' in blog jargon), a company that supplies the necessary resources for people to start blogging. There are many competing providers, with seemingly similar facilities and levels of service. Some providers are free, others charge a fee, and some are a bit of both, charging for extras. Examples of blog service providers are blogger.com, wordpress (.com & .org), moveabletype.com and typepad.com.

A key feature of blog service providers is provision of pre-designed blog pages, called templates, ready for you to input your text and graphics. You can modify templates with themes, variations of features like colours and fonts. A drawback of free blog service providers is fewer template options; another snag is that you have somewhat less control of your blog overall.

If you are going to be a serious blogger you will want a professional look and may have to use a fee-charging blog service provider. Even so, you might first try the free providers to get to know your way around and what is on offer. Otherwise, you could go straight for more advance services and pay a fee. You can change your blog service provider anytime, but it may be a bit of a nuisance to change once your blog is established.

Setting Up Your Blog

Setting up your blog takes just a few minutes and is straightforward:

- Choose a bog service provider
- Open an account by following their online instructions
- Select your blog's Web address (or 'URL')*
- Choose a title for your blog (it appears at the top of your blog pages and could be the same as your Web address)
- Choose a blog template
- Modify the template's themes
- Fill in your personal profile
- Start writing your posts (entries)

Follow instructions for adding and placing images
Sit back and admire your blog. Keep modifying its design until you are satisfied. Try a different blog service provider if all else fails.

---

* Spend time in advance thinking up a suitable Web address (best addresses use words closely related to your blog's subject). Also, consider that a free blog service provider is likely to combine their company name with your Web address, making it look like part of their Web address. If you want a unique, professional looking address you may have to pay for it.

Design Inspiration

How to come up with a good design for your blog? Find inspiration from the work of other bloggers (and elsewhere). Let them spark your imagination. Build on other people's work by adapting suitable ideas to your needs. Improve on them and make them uniquely your own. Always try to go one better and give sources of inspiration credit where appropriate.

Writing Your Blog

In the influence stakes, your blog is not about you or even animals. It is about your readers. You are trying to influence as many people as possible. Readers scan your posts and will leave your blog if it seems boring or irrelevant. So help them by making your pages interesting and easy to scan.

- Write in plain English (can be understood at the first reading).
- Compose crisp informative titles for posts.
- Break up text into small chunks.
- Think up informative headings and subheadings.
- Keep lines of text shorter than 15 words at most.

171

- Highlight particularly important text
- Display attractive, relevant images
- Employ bullets
- Use lots of white space

Create your own images or search stock photo sites on the Web where you can pick up quality photos and illustrations for a small fee (examples are dreamstime.com, istockphoto.com, fotolia.co.uk, alamy.com). A few web sites offer free photos but of lesser quality or relevance.

Paying for Your Blog
Should you choose to spend some money on your blog then placing ads on it can help pay its way. Adverts can be quite unobtrusive, for instance with Google's AdSense. These adverts appear as text or small static banners. You earn a cent or two every time a reader clicks on one and the money adds up over a year. To some extent you can choose the type of advert that appears on your blog, but some adverts could be inappropriate, such as for leather items or sausages.

Measuring Your Success
How well is your blog reaching out to people and what influence is it having on them? Analytics is a term for software that collects data about your blog's readers. By analysing the data you can make conclusions about the efficacy of your blogging. Among the statistics analytics can tell you are:

- How many and which pages people view
- How visitors found your blog
- Which keywords visitors typed into search engines to find your blog
- How many readers return another day to your blog
- Where visitors come from
- The length of time people spend on your blog

Some of the many analytic web sites are free and some offer more services for a payment. Check statcounter.com (excellent layout), blogpatrol.com (specialises in blogs) or Google Analytics to get the hang of them.

The Law
Copyright offers a measure of legal protection to a work's creator should they wish to engage in litigation if their work is misappropriated. In many countries, like the US and Britain, you automatically possess the copyright of

original work you create (such as an essay or an image) and do not have to do anything to claim copyright.

Often you do not need written permission from a copyright owner when you publish just a small part of their work (like one or two sentences). But for anything substantial it is good practice to obtain written permission, cite its source and provide a link to it. 'Fair use' is a term that covers quoting something more substantial than a couple of sentences. However, what exactly constitutes fair use is a grey, debatable area. People defamed on blogs have prosecuted bloggers through the law courts. So be sensibly and act with tact.

Bloggers' Code of Conduct

There are various codes for bloggers, intended to elevate blogging. Here are a few rules of conduct that convey the flavour:

- Be open about who and what you are
- Be truthful and accurate about what you write
- Provide original material (not rehash)
- Do not plagiarise material
- Cite and give credit to copyright and fair use material
- Respect all your readers and critics
- Promptly reply to reader's comments
- Do not publish email sent to you privately

Examples of Animal Related Blogs

- Animal and Wildlife News: animalblog.co.uk
- Animal Rights Collective: animalrightscollective.wordpress.com
- All Dog Boots: blog.alldogboots.com
- The Animal Rights Blog: animalrights.typepad.com
- Animal Rights Blog: animalrightsblog.org
- Animal Ethics: animalethics.blogspot.com
- House Rabbit Society Blog: rabbit.org/blog/index.php
- Dog News: newsdog.co.uk

Glossary of Blog Terms Used in This Section

Analytics - software that gathers information about the readers of your blog. Analytics give you data about how well your blog is reaching out to people.

Blog - a journal or diary on the Web.

Blogger - someone who keeps a blog or more generally reads and contributes to other people's blogs.

Blogosphere - all the blogs on the Web.

Blog Service Providers - business companies that enable you to publish your blog on the Web. In blogging slang, they and/or their software used to create blogs are called 'platforms'.

Comments - a place on a blog where readers can leave comment about the blog's posts.

Content - what you put on your blog, eg text, graphics, adverts.

HTML - Hypertext Mark-up Language. The coding used to layout the text and graphics on blogs and websites.

Link - a graphic or bit of text that you click on that takes you from a paragraph, page or blog to another one.

Platforms - see Blog Service Providers.

Post - an entry, such as a message or article, on a blog.

Templates - a selection of predesigned pages, offered by blog service providers, that you can choose for your blog to enhance its appearance and usability. Much quicker than designing your own pages from scratch.

Theme - a template may have different themes so that you can change elements, such as font, font colour, background colour.

URL - Uniform Resource Locator. An address on the Web of a web site, blog or page, eg ww.animalethics.org.uk/blogging.html.

Chapter	*Activities for Animal Rights*
4	*11. Philosopher*

Why Philosophy?

Some people shout emotional inanities to bully you to agree with them. More refined people apply smart arguments to make you agree with them. But philosophers do it by critically reasoning for and against the arguments; a more effective strategy.

> "Thus, if we are to grant them an inferior moral status or, indeed, no moral status whatsoever, a justification is required and such a justification must spell out why it is that we are entitled to treat them differently from ourselves and what it is that their moral status entitles us to do to them." Robert Garner (1)

The first Western philosophers lived around 2,500 years ago in south-east Europe in Ancient Greece and surroundings. They were among the first important thinkers of Western society. Unlike other people they did not think dogmatically but reasoned rationally and methodically. Significantly, they expected listeners to disagree with what they said and make opposing assertions to support reasonable counter arguments. This was a tremendous event in the evolution of thought. Until then people explained the world in terms of the supernatural, blind faith or authority, building ideas on emotional illogic, immediate impression, mistaken belief, fantasy and much other irrationality.

Philosophers in ancient times lived and worked among ordinary people. But by the 19th century they had confined themselves within universities and limited their questions to elucidate narrow and obscure matters. However, philosophy has undergone a rebirth since the 1970's as new ideas and directions for exploration broadened its scope. Nowadays a new philosophical avenue is practical ethics, by which people from all walks of life try to resolve everyday moral issues that affect them (see Applying Philosophy, below).

You do not, therefore, have to be a university professor to philosophise; thinking fundamental and deep thoughts is open to everyone. You just need to ask questions rationally and methodically about the nature of life, its ostensible meaning and purpose and come up with rational answers. Philosophising could be for you if you are interested in seeking answers to ultimate questions and enjoy rigorously marshalling arguments for and against ideas and issues.

Landmarks in Animal Philosophy

Many key philosophers of past centuries have damned their moral status by being largely negative about animals. For example:

- Aristotle (384 - 322 BC) said that the most important faculty is the power of reasoning, only humans can reason, therefore they are the most important beings. He concluded that we can use animals without the consideration we would give to people.

- Descartes (1596 - 1650) thought that animals cannot feel pain, even though they act as though they do. He concluded that animals are automata, mere machines.

- Kant (1724 - 1804) believed that animals are not conscious and may therefore be used as a means to an end, as a way of getting something you want.

These and other philosophers spelt tragedy for myriad animals by doing nothing that challenged the deeply rooted assumption held by people, that the claims of humans always have priority over the needs of animals.

Animals do not have it easy even in our own times, as one practising physiologist makes clear, believing that:

> "In contrast to ourselves, animal behaviour is mechanical, driven by the dictates of nature and immune to the processes of reflective cognition that we take for granted. It is a black, silent existence that is not conscious of its own processes or, at the very most, a dark murky experience that does not compare with our own." (2)

However, the 18th century might have witnessed the beginning of rescue for animals. In an often quoted phrase Jeremy Bentham (1748 - 1832) wrote:

> "The question is not can they reason? Nor, can they talk? But can they suffer?" (3)

Bentham thought that animals can feel pain and that the essential attribute qualifying an animal to moral consideration is the capacity for suffering and no other reference is necessary, not the power of reasoning, nor consciousness nor cognition. Then, in the 20th century, Peter Singer (b 1946) opened the floodgates of moral concern for animals by writing his book *Animal Liberation* (1975). Translated into over 17 languages the book started a chain reaction of thought and publications, still expanding, about animals and why they matter morally. Indeed, Singer is widely credited with founding modern practical ethics.

Philosophy & the Real World
Does philosophy influence our material everyday world? Yes it does. The human-world is constantly shaped and re-shaped by philosophical ideas. Ethical reasoning permeates and influences our everyday world. For more see Do Philosophical Ideas Work? in Chapter 2: Animal Ethics.

Applying Philosophy
Areas of practical ethics are diverse and could include almost any area of human activity in which moral dilemmas rear up. Some areas of practical ethics are:

- Environmental ethics: how should humanity relate to and deal with nature?
- Medical ethics: how should we deal with sick people?
- Feminism: how we should behave towards women?
- Education ethics: how and to whom should education be taught?
- Legal ethics: how should lawyers deal with each other and their clients?
- Corporate responsibility: how should businesses engage with individuals and society?
- Internet ethics: how should people use the internet responsibly?

Where does animal rights fit in to all this? Animal rights is a part of the practical field of animal ethics. Animal ethics examines beliefs that are held about the moral status of animals. But animal ethics does not presume that any particular point of view is good and right; it accommodates a number of approaches for trying to resolve animal-human moral issues. Animal rights, on the other hand, is a doctrine about how humans should treat animals and states that animals should have rights, somewhat like but not exactly the same as humans rights. Animal rights concentrates on sentient animals and its basic doctrine is that using animals for human gain is morally wrong and should stop. More in Comparing Animal Philosophies, Chapter 2.

Philosophical Exercises
An essential objective in philosophy is to be able to evaluate ideas and construct reasoned arguments by yourself. So toward this end this is what you can do. Read as much about philosophy, ethics and animal rights as you can.

Clarify the arguments and counter-arguments the writers present. Select and explain which are the more convincing arguments and try to come up with new arguments of your own.

Try the following exercise:

1. Write down your ideas about animal rights or some aspect of the subject.
2. Compare and contrast your ideas with the various points and arguments that one or more philosophers have written on the subject.
3. Think up objections to what these philosophers say and find out objections that other writers have put forward.
4. Rewrite step one in light of steps two and three
5. Get people to criticise what you have written in step four and engage them in friendly critical discussion about what they say.
6. Rewrite step one again.
7. Compare what you first wrote in step one with your final draft and in a few sentences write down what you have leaned.

You may be wondering why you have to write down everything. Expressing your ideas on paper is better than only thinking about them. Writing forces you to think deeper about your subject, enables you to progress without wastefully going over the same ground, and is a basis for circulating your ideas to other people, such as when writing an article or a book.

When philosophising check the assumptions you make and ask yourself if they are valid. Abandon anything that does not stand up to your critical examination. Come up with new ideas as necessary. Keep doing this over the years. Never stop thinking rationally and critically. Do not be afraid to put forward radical ideas. This may be difficult at first but like any accomplishment the more you do it the easier it gets. Be able to accept and learn from criticism and remember that good philosophers attack arguments, not their proponents.

Take Animal Philosophy to the People

As an animal rights philosopher you should communicate your ideas to the public and to anyone who will listen to you. For giving talks see Public & School Speaker, Chapter 4. Also lend your pen to write animal philosophy articles for magazines.

You will need to write at least one book on your philosophical animal rights subject to gain recognition as an animal philosopher. Come up with an original thesis to argue about. Your thesis could be your own original inspiration or your development of someone else's idea in an original way. Write the book as a straightforward philosophy work - with a beginning, middle and end - or in an off-beat style like a novel or a play. These days you could even fashion it as an illustrated comic.

Courses in Philosophy

Feeling the itch to study philosophy formally? Ensure that you include in your study of philosophy the branch called 'moral philosophy' or 'ethics' - different names for the same thing.

There are various types of courses: online learning, distance learning, part-time evening courses, full-time college, and university level routes. You might find a few animal rights courses online, at a relatively lightweight level. Some college and university philosophy courses offer modules dealing with animal rights as part of their overall course. But you are unlikely to find a comprehensive, full-time course in animal ethics and certainly not one devoted entirely to animal rights. However, the situation is changing so keep a look out.

In view of the dearth of animal rights courses, do not be afraid of being self-taught. You can be a good philosopher without taking a formal course in philosophy; after all, many famous philosophers never followed an authorised course themselves and obviously the first philosophers could not. Books on philosophy are plentiful. Read some about philosophy in general to get an overall grasp of the subject. After that do the same for ethics. Then read up on animal ethics in particular and finally zero in on animal rights.

References

(1)   Garner, Robert. An*imals, Politics and Morality.* Manchester University: Manchester. 1993:4.
(2)   Derbyshire, Stuart. In Gilland T et al. Animal *Experimentation: good or bad?* Hodder & Stoughton. 2002:47.
(3)   Bentham, Jeremy. *An Introduction to the Principles of Morals and Legislation.* 1789. xvii:311.

Chapter	Activities for Animal Rights
4	*12. Flyer*

How about looking down on your opponents to observe them and learn what they are up to? You could take videos of what they are doing and radio instructions to a ground team to close in on them. Your opponents could be shooters, trappers, rustlers, diggers for animals to bait, and anyone holding an illegal event in the open air.

Flying their paramotors, Johnny Coyote and friends decided to teach the coyote hunters a lesson once and for all.

You do not need an aeroplane, quite an expense to buy and maintain. You just need a paramotor (see cartoon, below). A paramotor is the same as a paraglider but with an engine driving a propeller for ease of take-off and long-distance steering. It is the simplest and cheapest form of powered flight - a new paramotor costs about the same as a motorbike - and is easy to learn to fly. Although some bodies have classified paramotoring as a dangerous sport, it is said to be the safest way of flying, safer than riding a motorbike. Should your motor go dead, all that happens is that you glide and sink slowly to the ground, because your parachute is already fully deployed.

The Paramotor

A paramotor is a parachute, more technically a wing, attached to a harness with a little seat at the bottom bearing a small two-stroke motor. You lay out the wing behind you on the ground, strap the harness on to your back, start the motor and run a few steps. The wing inflates and gently carries you off the ground. Then you slip onto your seat and away you fly. Take-off distance is three to eight metres (10 to 25 feet) with a comparable landing distance. With experience you can even make a standing landing: land in zero feet.

You do not need a runway for take-off, just a big clear field (with a paraglider you would need a suitable hill for take-off). So if you live on the edge of town you need only carry your paramotor to a suitable field where you can launch yourself into the air. Otherwise, a paramotor is small enough to put in the back of a car and you can drive it somewhere else to get aloft.

Once airborne you can fly to all points of the compass travelling at up to 40 kph (25 mph). You can fly on long cross-country powered-flights or turn the motor off and glide silently in thermals, restarting the motor in the air any time you like. Increasing the motor's speed makes you climb, decreasing it makes you sink. You steer by pulling on special lines attached to the wing; pull on the left lines to go left, pull on the right lines to go right, pull on both sides to slow down. An alternative way of steering, for when you really need both hands free for filming, is to fit a tricycle undercarriage to the paramotor and press against its foot bars using your feet. You can buy a tricycle undercarriage from a small number of devotee paramotor-makers.

A tandem paramotor may be more suitable than a solo paramotor if you need to concentrate entirely on flying, in which case you will take an observer/camera operator with you. Of course, a tandem is more expensive and less manoeuvrable than the solo craft. But then when flying your paramotor as an observation platform you want one that is stable and easy to handle, not one that is made for performing aerobatics.

Learning to Fly a Paramotor

Some paramotoring enthusiasts organise themselves into clubs and offer to teach novices the ways of the paramotor. They may give you a minimum of 25 hours coaching spread over several days and offer you the hire of one of their paramotors plus flying equipment. Their syllabus should cover groundwork and airwork. Groundwork is what you must know before taking to the air, including knowledge about equipment, motors, safety, flying theory, weather and air law. The airwork is what you need to know to get airborne, fly around and land. On successfully completing a course they may give you a certificate that might be validated by a national or international body. The cost of the course could work out as equivalent to the price of a new paramotor.

However, paramotoring is a sport that so far has gone largely unregulated by the aviation authorities in most states, including the United States and Britain. Thus you will probably have no need for a licence to fly a paramotor and a certificate from a club may not be necessary. Indeed, there is nothing stopping you from learning to fly a paramotor without doing a course at all (but see What You Need, below). Another way to learn to fly a paramotor is by teaming up with an already experienced paramotor flyer. Or you could learn to fly a paramotor alone, like the early pioneers of flight; they had no one to instruct them. Whether or not you take a taught course or learn by yourself, in the end you still have to go solo - fly alone on your first flight - because no one else can fly the machine for you. There are a few dual machines about but they are not in much use.

Should you opt to learn to fly a paramotor alone you must be confident you can do it. Do not be in such a rush to get off the ground that you make potentially disastrous errors. Perhaps the most common mishap you can make as a novice paramotor pilot is during launching. Inexperienced paramotor pilots running along the ground may try to get into their seat too soon, before the wing has time to lift them properly off the ground. They lose their balance and fall over, and there follows embarrassment and injured pride. The really unlucky ones get their propeller bent as it bites the dust. This is about the most serious practical blunder you can make when learning to fly a paramotor, even with instruction from a club.

Read all you can about paramotoring, especially if you intend to master by yourself the art of how to fly a paramotor. Work through one of the syllabuses for learning to fly a paramotor. You can pick up a syllabus on the Web or get one from a club. There is a fair bit about paramotoring online, including video clips of paramotor pilots taking off, flying about and landing. Two good books are by Whittall (1) and Goin (2).

What You Need
What are the prerequisites for flying a paramotor?

- Enthusiasm for flying and pioneering aerial animal rights.
- A budget that will buy and maintain the equivalent of a motorbike.

- Be able to transport your paramotor by foot or by car to where you will launch yourself.
- Be in reasonably good health, ie able to run a few steps during take-off with about 30 kilos (60 pounds) of motor and harness on your back. A disability may not be a problem provided you can do this, and control the paramotor in flight. Some machines are of relatively lighter weight and you could opt to fit a tricycle undercarriage for a wheeled take-off.
- You may also want insurance against personal or third party injury. This could be where gaining a certificate from a paramotoring club can be handy if the insurers insist on evidence of worthiness.

Advantages of a Paramotor

1. Flying a paramotor is cheap compared with all other means of flying: a paramotor is easy to maintain, portable and you do not need a licence to fly it.
2. You can pilot your paramotor almost anywhere (but see Disadvantages, below) to make observations and take photos that you cannot do when flying a remote controlled helicopter. (As an aerial snooper your helicopter must be in your field of vision the whole time, otherwise you cannot know where it is, which way it is pointing or even which way up it is - see Aerial Snooper, Chapter 4. You always know where your paramotor is and what it is doing because you are strapped to it.)
3. Flying time for a paramotor is one to two hours, depending on your weight and flying conditions. (Much longer than the 30 minutes or so for a remote controlled helicopter.) And you can increase your flying time by taking a bit of spare fuel with you - simply land and top-up.
4. Fuel is ordinary gasoline (petrol) that you can buy at any filling (petrol) station. However, you must mix it first with a small amount of oil. The 'gasoil" ('petroil") mixture lubricates the moving parts; without it the engine will seize up.
5. You could easily fly up to 5,000 metres (15,000 ft) altitude - the world record is over 6,000 metres (18,000 ft). But civil aviation regulations will restrict you in most places to a much lower altitude of a few hundred metres above ground; however, this is no draw back when flying a paramotor for animal rights or for fun.
6. In addition to animal rights work you could use your paramotor for wildlife surveys and aerial photography. In some countries you cannot legally do this for commercial gain from a foot launched paramotor. However, by fitting a tricycle undercarriage for take-off and landing you miraculously convert your paramotor to a different class of machine to which this rule does not necessarily apply. Check the aviation regulations of your state.

Disadvantages of a Paramotor

1. Paramotors are basically fine weather machines. Given a paramotor's speed it is unsafe to use a paramotor when winds blow at 25 kph (15 mph) and over or in poor weather.
2. With no cockpit to shield you from the wind in a cold climate you will be chilled in the cold months.
3. Civil aviation rules forbid flying paramotors over built-up areas and close to airports (check the regulations for your state).
4. Animal abusing opponents will not think you are spying on them, until perhaps they get to know what you are up to and listen for you coming; a paramotor is as noisy as some lawnmowers. But you can always turn off the motor to glide silently and then turn it on again in mid-flight when you need it. Quiet electric paramotors are being developed.

Also see the section Fly Drones/UAVs for Animal Rights, in Chapter 4.

Bibliography

- Whittall, Noel. Paramotoring From the Ground Up: a comprehensive guide. Airlife Publishing: England. 2001.
- Goin, Jeff. Powered Paragliding Bible. Airhead Creations. 2006.

Chapter	*Activities for Animal Rights*
4	*13. Personal Activist*

In this section are some simple personal activisms that most people can do. But we start with a bit of a difficult one. As an animal rights activist you cannot do any better activity for animal rights than the one below. All other activities are far less effective than this one.

Here is the Single Most Effective Thing You Can Do for Animal Life

Stop making babies (or at most make only one).

Seventy thousand years ago there were some 15,000 people on Earth. Now we are over seven billion people.

The more people, the greater the destruction to animal life and Nature.

Being a veggie or vegan is not sufficient.

Some More Self Activism for Individuals

Other activities, should you not be up to the one above, come at different levels of convenience and if there is a secret for successful personal activism it is that you should do what you feel comfortable with and are good at doing.

1. Let's Stop *It!*

Most people call an animal an 'it', as if animals are unfeeling sticks or stones. They compound the offence by calling inanimate human creations, such as a car, ship or country, 'she'. So let's stop calling an animal an 'it'. Make a contribution to animal rights by calling animals always him or her, he or she. You are conveying that animals are beings, with needs of their own. Calling an animal an *it* makes him an inanimate depersonalised object; as the philosopher Jeremy Bentham said: "animals...stand degraded into the class of things." (1)

Once a being is depersonalised down to the level of an it, we feel we can do anything we like to him without considering his moral rights. Kicking a stone or throwing away a stick has no moral consequences.

But where do we draw the line? Should we stop at invertebrates? There is no logical reason to draw the line anywhere in the animal kingdom in that invertebrates are also males and females. Of course, some animals, like the workers of social ants and wasps, are sterile and some animals are hermaphrodites, like slugs and snails. But you can still call them him or her generally speaking.

What do you do if you do not know the sex of an animal? The rule in the English language is to assume the masculine until proven otherwise. Feminists will probably object to this rule and might demand political correctness instead. They may try to give equal weight to both sexes by saying "he or she". But this is clumsy. However, the Finnish language solves this awkwardness with a neat han. Han in Finnish means he and also means she: one word for both genders. Let's extend this idea. If we adopt han in English than we could go one step further to make han additionally mean 'it'. Thus, han in English would mean he, she or it and would:

- Avoid belittling animals by calling them it.
- Avoid saying only 'he' when we mean both genders.
- Avoid unwieldy repetition of 'he or she' all the time.

Examples of han:
- Han (he) sat down to tea with scones.
- Han (she) is a thoughtful and independent cat.
- The whale yawned, rolled over then han (he) swam away.
- I gave a banana to a monkey and han (he) ate it.

Political analysts have wondered whether the equivalence of the sexes in Finnish has some connection with Finnish women getting the right to vote long before other women in Europe. So if we stop calling animals it, might we not start treating them better too? Another two other good Finnish words are hanet meaning him or her and hanen meaning his or hers.

If we adopted all these words in English:
- Han would mean he or she or it.
- Hanet would mean him or her or it.
- Hanen would mean his or hers or its.

Alternatively, if these Finnish words are too much to accept into English, we could recast the English he, him and his respectively as het, hit and hits (that is, combine them with it or its). The big question is how to make these words catch on permanently.

2. Speak Plainly
Should we be lulled and sweetened by euphemisms when faced with decisions about what to do with animals who get in people's way? Or should we speak openly and honestly about what is happening and not hide behind word substitutions to cover up what we are doing? People adopt euphemisms when they want their actions to sound impartial, necessary, professional and reasonable, so that consciences are saved and nobody objects to what they are doing. Some euphemisms:

Meat for Animal: strictly speaking, meat is muscle, but this does not stop supermarkets selling processed products which they describe as 'meat' but which can be from any part of an animal, such as lungs and brains.
Veal for Calf: Calves for veal are raised in inhumane conditions, solo in tiny crates. **Infested** meaning 'has some': Beaches may be 'shark infested' but never 'human infested'. A few sharks (or rats) becomes an infestation.
Road kill for Motorist kill: Roads do not kill anyone; it is the motorists who kill. **Cull, Control, Harvest** mean kill: People do not kill wild animals; they 'cull' and 'control' them and 'harvest' their wild populations. Cull is a polite word whose action is somehow necessary and officially sanctioned. So we get:

> *"A cull of 5,000 hedgehogs is due to begin on North Uist in the Western Isles of Scotland on Monday. Scottish Natural Heritage wants to get rid of all the hedgehogs on the Uist islands because they have been destroying colonies of wading birds."*
> BBC News.

3. The Cute Factor & Invertebrate Harmony
The cute factor refers to supporting some animals, such as fluffy animals with big dark eyes, because they are more attractive than other animals. The opposite side of the coin is ignoring some animals, like rats, snakes and spiders, because they might seem repulsive. Many people would be outraged by a slaughter of baby seals but are silent about 'cull' of rats. Yet rats are as intelligent and as social as seals and moreover deserve equal moral consideration. People blame rats for spreading disease; but in the first place it is poor human living conditions with unsanitary habits that create the circumstances for rats to multiply and spread disease among people.

So let's practice animal rights at the lowest level, that of the invertebrate: insects, spiders and other animals without a backbone. Invertebrates make up over 99 per cent of animal species, are vital to the well-being of the biosphere, and we can learn to appreciate them and the many wonderful things they do. People often commit the number fallacy: because there are lots of them it does not matter if we kill them. But neither number nor body size determine the value of life. Invertebrates are small, but if we are aware of them and practice invertebrate harmony even on a small scale, then we will be more compassionate beings.

Here is a couple of things you can do to practice invertebrate harmony. Instead of squashing invertebrates to get rid of them, pick them up carefully and gently and release them outdoors in a place that is suitable for them. It is said that no one is ever more than a metre from a spider. There is at least one spider sitting next to you now without you knowing it. But the odd spider will not harm you and if you get rid of one, another will soon take his place (a house is like a cave, their natural habitat). So unless they are causing a real nuisance leave them where they are.

4. Let's Be Vegan or Veggie

Humans eat vast numbers of animals. In the United States alone every week people slaughter 175 million poultry, 2 million pigs, 700,000 cattle, 60,000 sheep, plus a host of other animals (2). But vegetarians and vegans opt out of the killing system. If you become a vegan or vegetarian you might save a pig or two annually, at least theoretically.

That animals have rights is one of the most basic reason people have for giving up eating animals. Specifically, animals have the right to live their own lives and not have humans kill them for food. In a more practical vein, vegetarians and vegans say their diet is healthier than a meat-based diet. Veggies and vegans like to claim they have lower blood pressure and fewer heart and bowel disorders than meat-eaters. People in the dietary business used to assert that your health would fail and you might die if you did not eat meat. But generations of healthy vegetarians and vegans are ample proof that they were wrong. Eating animals is dispensable and largely a matter of taste.

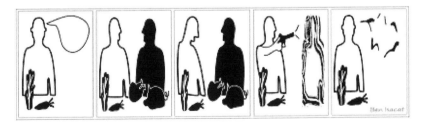

As a veggie or vegan you might help slow climate change - provided the veggie habit leads to farmers rearing fewer livestock. Methane is a potent greenhouse gas that traps more heat than carbon dioxide and the methane belched by the world's livestock is widely questioned as a factor contributing to global warming. It is generally claimed that 90 per cent of New Zealand's greenhouse gas emissions come from the country's 40 million sheep (eight sheep to every human).

Vegetarianism is a personal commitment to animal life by setting an example to other people. If you are not already a vegetarian or vegan do not be put off joining them by thinking you have to give up eating animals overnight. There are degrees of vegetarianism, like a freegan does not generally eat meat but might if other people discard it as waste, and a flexitarian eats meat only rarely. Simply cutting back on meat-eating is a good start. You do not need to eat special fancy foods; just eat a more extensive diet of everything else and more of it. Veganism is just a step removed from vegetarianism; just give up eggs and dairy products, phase out using leather, feather pillows and other animal products, and you are there!

More Activisms
Here are suggestions to get into the swing of more active activisms for animal rights.

- Read Labels

Ask the people who serve you where the ingredients of your food, cosmetics or medicine come from. Unless they are really knowledgeable they will probably not know, but you could patronise alternative products if you find out that any ingredients are derived from animals. Look for up-to-date cruelty-free product guides on the Web to help you. Some ingredients to look out for are:

- o Musk: oil from the scent glands of certain wild animals, in particular the musk deer. The deer are killed in traps or confined all their lives to cages hardly bigger than themselves. However, quite a lot of the musk in perfumes today is synthetic.
- o Rennet: a protein taken from the stomachs of slaughtered calves, lambs and kid goats. Rennet in the living young converts their ingested mother's milk into solids for digestion. Rennet is the chief means for making cheese hard. Some hard cheeses, though, are made with artificially cultured rennet and may be suitable for vegetarians.
- o Collagen: another protein taken from animals. It is used in cosmetics.
- o Gelatin (American English) or gelatine (British English) is derived from collagen and used in cosmetics and many foods.
- o Lactose: a sugar that comes from milk. It is added to various foods, lotions and medicines.
- o Cochineal: extracted from the ground up bodies of insects and used to add a red colour to foods and lipsticks.

- Watch News

Speak up to defend animals when opportunities arise. Write to the news media when you think they are acting against the interests of animals. See Media Watcher, Chapter 4, for details.

- Spurn Animal Products

Eschew fur items, not only fur clothing but also cosmetic and artists' fur brushes. These brushes are sometimes made from synthetic material but they are also made of animal hair. You can also find brushes with a mixture of synthetic material and fur. The labelling is often obscure and misleading.

191

- Study Animal Ethics

Ask for animal ethics to be taught at your school, college or university. Animal ethics is a bona fide scholarly pursuit that incorporates animal rights but has broader scope (see Chapter 2: Animal Ethics.)

- Dissection

Urge your school or college if they are into cutting up real animals to 'dissect' animals virtually by computer program instead.

- School Pets

Ask your school not to keep animals at the premises for educating the children/students.

- Make Menus

Ask for more animal-friendly (or at least less animal-unfriendly) food at your college or work refectory. For instance, get management to ban eggs from caged hens and offer eggs from genuine free-range hens and generally to shun factory farmed animals. Persuade management to provide simple information about the food they offer so that diners know what they are eating and have a proper choice of alternatives - free-range and organic.

- Suggest Books to Buy

Suggest good animal ethical books (books on animal ethics, animal rights and animal welfare) that your public or college library can buy for their shelves. Ask your library to put up a display of these books.

- Stimulate Ethical Policies

As far as you can, trade with companies that have publicly published ethical policies. For example, use banks with a stated code of ethics. Pressure companies that have no ethical policies regarding animals to embrace a code of ethics incorporating animals. Become a shareholder in animal abusing companies in order to criticise them more effectively as a shareholder. Publicise their response or lack of one.

- Stir Up Ethical Purchasing

Get your company to make its purchases from animal-friendly companies. If your company is not animal-friendly, ask them why they are not - with the intention of putting ideas into their head. Has your company a code of animal ethics spelling out how the company should act regarding animals and animal products? Get management or colleagues to compose a code.

Are Goldfish Bowls Cute

A goldfish BOWL is an ornament
with interesting symmetry
but many problems

Fish cannot hide from fellow fish
or the outside world
or search for food
or explore

Artificial life support is tough
Fish excretion pollutes
Sufficient oxygen cannot dissolve
Sunshine drives out oxygen in the water

Fish face a life
of distress and
tedium
and endless
numbers die slowly

Bowled fish cannot
tell us their needs- so wake up to them!

Ben Isacat
Human Animal Relations

- Act for the Little Animals on Your Doorstep

The common goldfish brings this home to us that animal rights is not just for big animals. Every year endless goldfish and other ornamental fish are sold and countless die. Many people stick their fish in glass bowls. The bowls are symmetrical and interesting but cause their inhabitants serious problems:

o The water becomes deadly because the fish release liquid and solid waste into it.

o The bowl has a small surface area, so not enough oxygen dissolves into it from the atmosphere for the fish to breathe.

o Left close to sunshine the water gets too warm and what little oxygen it has defuses out.

o The water has no vegetation to act as cover; the fish cannot conceal themselves from staring eyes outside the bowl nor shelter from each other within it.

- The fish cannot satisfy their natural instinct to search for food or swim into crevices and explore; monotony extends for them 360 degrees all around.
- Artificial life-support systems in bowls are weak, difficult to maintain and are no substitute for a better home.

Goldfish cannot shout and wave placards telling their people what they want. So it is up to us to point out to our fish-keeping neighbours the demerits of bowling fish. Point out to them how they can keep their fish happy, that fish do best in a roomy tank or, if they are outdoor fish, in a well-positioned garden pond with lots of vegetation for aeration and cover. And what about birds in cages and animals in tiny garden hutches...?

References

(1) Bentham, Jeremy. *An Introduction to the Principles of Morals and Legislation.* 1789. xvii:311.
(2) *Statistics of Cattle, Hogs and Sheep and Poultry Slaughter.* Annual Summaries. National Agricultural Statistics Service, United States Department of Agriculture.

Chapter	*Activities for Animal Rights*
4	*14. Author - Playwright*

"Writing is difficult, of course, and it takes time. Lots and lots of time...I'll write total rubbish for a long time, but as long as something's coming out I don't mind." From Working Writers: Evie Wyld Interview. Evie Wyld, prize winning storywriter and Booktrust's 2009 'Writer in Residence'.

The Importance of Fiction

A huge portion of the literature people consume is fiction. Bookshops and public libraries, knowing this, devote considerable floor space to fiction stories. Fiction storywriters are respected the world over and outstanding writers are honoured. But you do not have to be a literary marvel to write good stories. What you need is ambition, grit and a bit of knowhow. So give people a good read with a subtle underlying animal rights message to influence their opinions and discussions. Remember: Subtle Stories Sway Sentiments.

Is there an animal rights genre? Yes, some works of fiction are clearly animal rights oriented. Two examples are the animal rights novel *Elizabeth Costello* and the animal rights play *Every Breath*, below, and the other examples are also strongly into animal rights.

Elizabeth Costello by J M Coetzee

In Coetzee's (b 1940) novel the protagonist, Elizabeth Costello, is a frail, grey haired woman, a distinguished novelist, delivering lectures at institutions. Her talks include raising questions about the moral status of animals.

At a dinner given for her after a lecture, discussion turns to isolating a quality that raises humanity above animals. Someone declares that animals live in "a vacuum of consciousness". Costello replies, "What I mind is what tends to come next. They have no consciousness therefore. Therefore what? Therefore we are free to use them for our own ends? Therefore we are free to kill them?"

One of the most celebrated animal rights storywriters, Coetzee sets a tough trail for writers to emulate: he is a professional writer, received the Nobel Prize in Literature in 2003 ("for his riveting portrayals of racial repression, sexual politics, the guises of reason, and the hypocrisy of human beings toward animals and nature"), and is the first author to win the Booker Prize twice.

Every Breath by Judith Johnson

Johnson (b 1962) wrote the play *Every Breath* to fit into the school curriculum. The play is a family drama that even-handedly probes dilemmas of the animal-rights vs medical-research gulf. A primary theme revolves around a teen vegetarian, concerned with animal rights and nature, and his older sister, a meat-eating scientist, committed to using animals for research. The two other characters in the play are their mother and her boyfriend and the tensions between the characters threaten to disrupt the family's unity.

The play received financial backing from both sides of the animal experimentation divide. Actors of the Y-Touring Company, a travelling theatre outfit, performed the play at the annual Edinburgh Festival in 2006 and at schools around Britain. After every performance, the actors retain their stage characters and debate with their audience the meaning of the play. Oberon Books published the play in 2007.

For more see Activities for Animal Rights in Chapter 4, under Street Theatre Actor.

War Horse by Michael Morpurgo

This story points out the power of storytelling, emphasizing that bare statistics (millions of horses dying in the First World War) hardly make a dent on people but that everyone is roused and inspired by the story of a single individual.

The war horse is Joey, bought by the cavalry and transported with other horses from Britain to France for the First World War. Joey's rider is killed. Joey drifts around no-man's-land and is captured by the enemy. Eventually, Joey's original owner finds him and takes him home across the sea. Uplifting ending, though not for the masses of horses, who died of infections, exhaustion and injuries; Britain alone lost nearly half a million horses, one horse for every two men (R Holmes. *The Oxford Companion to Military History*. 2001:417).

Morpurgo (b 1943) originally wrote *War Horse* as a short story for children, published in 1982. It has been translated into several languages and made into radio and stage plays and a film.

Doctor Rat by William Kotzwinkle

Dr Rat is insane, he has been a laboratory rat for so long, and tells of the

196

appalling medical experiments on the animal inmates, rats to monkeys. "Death is freedom", he shouts and stresses the need for more funding, "We've got to continue verifying facts that were established a hundred years ago." A revolt breaks out; the rats take over the premises. Dr Rat fights to protect the laboratory and restore order, but the animal revolution against human tyranny spreads worldwide...

Kotzwinkle (b 1938) wrote his short book as a reflection on inhumanity to animals and the use of animals in medical research. First published in 1976, the story has been described as clever, sickening, touching and written with brutal wit.

The Jungle by Upton Sinclair
Published as a serial in a journal, then as a novel in 1906, the story's characters are immigrants labouring in the Chicago stockyards meatpacking industry. The stockyards were abysmal for the workers and worse for the animals, the backdrop. The slaughterhouses were the origin of some of the earliest international corporations dealing in animals and the story gives insight into how the slaughterhouses were run. The novel stimulated labour reform, but did little for the animals.

> "...and as for the other men, who worked in tank rooms full of steam, and in some of which there were open vats near the level of the floor, their peculiar trouble was that they fell into the vats; and when they were fished out, there was never enough of them left to be worth exhibiting, sometimes they would be overlooked for days, till all but the bones of them had gone out to the world as Durham's Pure Leaf Lard!"

Published in 2003 by Sharp Press. It is also free online from The Project Gutenberg: www.gutenberg.org.

Eva by Peter Dickinson
Dickinson (b 1927) wrote this sharp and humorous novel for young people. Eva is a teenager injured in a severe accident. She wakes up in hospital materialized into the body of a young chimpanzee from her dad's research laboratory and has to adapt to her new position...

Gollancz published the novel in 1988 and Macmillan Children's Books published it in 2001. The story stimulates discussion on issues like animal rights, medical ethics and euthanasia.

Etre the Cow by Sean Kenniff
Etre (French for 'to be' or 'to exist') is a simple bull who spends his life in a

197

pasture. He tries to grasp his seemingly inescapable predicament: he is fenced in, powerless, but aware. He despairs, yet recognizes he must defy his bovine condition and decides to confront life...

You can interpret Kenniff's (b 1969) short novel, published in 2010, in many ways: as a story about animal life, animal rights, what it means to be alive, or as a straight allegory of the human condition.

Short Stories Online
There are many online sources dedicated to the short story and just three are:

Booktrust. Short stories and advice on writing for aspiring writers of all ages and backgrounds: www.booktrust.org.uk.
World Stories. Stories from around the world: www.worldstories.org.uk.
Carve Magazine. Superior short fiction: www.carvezine.com.

Write Your Short Story
Try a quick fun trial. Write a short story now of up to 7,000 words. Think about it for a few minutes. Always start with a simple idea (simple things tend to get complex; therefore, if you start with a complex idea it will likely get out of hand). You will want the ingredients of a good story:

- **Characters** - the personalities in your story.
  The fox, his lady-fox and her cubs, the fur farmer and his dog.
- **Plot** - what happens in your story.
  The easy-going fox has been living at the fur farm making love to lady foxes, not realising why they and their cubs go missing. He finds out from the farmer's dog that he and his latest love are in imminent danger of being skinned. The fox decides to breakout.
- **Conflict** - obstructions that hinder the main character's fulfilment: the heart of the story.
  The fox cannot abandon his lady-friend or her cubs and they seem doomed.
- **Climax** - the highpoint of the story.
  The fox, his lady friend and their cubs manage to flee but run straight into the pursuing farmer.
- **Resolution** - how the conflict is resolved.
  The foxes bonk the farmer on the head and reach the shelter of the forest.
- **Twist** - a sudden new development at the end of your story.
  The foxes crash into a bloody trapper who decides to use them as

bait. But the foxes push him onto one of his traps and make their way to freedom and a new life.

•

Write the story quickly, even before it is all set out in your mind, and see where it takes you. Put your story aside and reappraise it after some weeks. It may be better (or worse) than you first thought and reveal faults from which you can improve.

Write Your Play

What is your play's genre: mystery comedy, drama, romance, science fiction, fantasy? You can mould any genre to animal rights. The play may be any length and divided into one or several scenes (each scene portrays an event) and larger acts (they have intermissions between them).

- **Plot**
  The best plays have simple plots; kick off with something intricate and your task will become impossible. Write an outline of the plot in a single paragraph. Your scribble is a basic plan of the play so that you do not get side-tracked.

- **Characters**
  Make up a list of characters. Aim to make each character a different personality. What drives them? What threatens them? What happens to them?

- **Drafting**
  Sketch a rough draft of the dialogue (the key to a good play) and scenes as they come into your head. Just get your basic ideas down.

- **Editing**
  Edit your draft several times. Get the characters and dialogue right: are they interesting? Cut out everything that does not contribute to driving the action forward.

- **Criticism**
  Hand out copies of your play to anyone who will give you their honest opinion about it. Consider their advice and rewrite as necessary.

Your Future?

Might you have the qualities of a storywriter or playwright? To find out you must keep writing and keep learning. Check bookshops and the Web on how to write stories and plays. Get feedback on your works and improve your skills via online writers' forums, such as WritingForums.org, WritingForums.com and Writing.com.

People must read your stories, so disseminate them widely. As a new author or playwright:

- Try non-paying markets: writers' magazines and web sites pay little or nothing, but display your work.
- Try paying markets when confident (and check the books Writer's Market and Writers' & Artists' Yearbook).
- Display your stories on your blog or website (see the chapter Activities for Animal Rights, under Blogger).
- Submit your play to your local school or community amateur theatrical society to stage.

You might turn your stories or plays into books. A number of online companies use Print on Demand (PoD) technology to print books one at a time for anyone who makes an order, unlike the bulk printing and mass distribution of typical publishers. Lulu (www.lulu.com) and CafePress (www.cafepress.com) offer PoD at no cost to you as an author, and you can set a profit margin, like a dollar or something per book. Basically, you write and upload your manuscript with a cover design, and when someone makes an order, they print and dispatch the book and pay you your earnings.

Finally, when you are really hammering out those words, you might try a regular commercial publisher - but that is another story!

Chapter	*Activities for Animal Rights*
4	*15. Animal Friendly Traveller*

What's the Problem?

Animal abusers earn money by displaying animals to travellers and tourists, especially in Asia, Africa and South America. The animals or their parents, often taken from the wild, are frequently poorly kept, neglected or over-worked. They eventually die or their owners kill them when they are past their usefulness. The final betrayal is selling their body parts as souvenirs. Untold numbers of animals suffer like this for the tourist trade and you could witness it anywhere in the world.

Many travellers would not tolerate similar cruelties in their own country. Nor should we accept as an excuse for cruelty the assumed sanctity of another country's customs and culture. Each of us is responsible for ensuring as far as we can that our behaviour does not contribute to animal suffering, even when we are abroad. We can go native in foreign lands but must keep our compassion.

What You Can Do: The Five Freedoms

It is normal to wonder just when you should step in to try to prevent cruelty. Mistreatment may not be clearly apparent when you are just a temporary visitor to a country with strange customs. But we can bear in mind a minimum standard for animal welfare. Animals must have access to their proper food, to water and shelter, should look healthy generally and not have physical wounds or obviously be mistreated, such as whipped or punched.

When judging whether to intervene you can apply The Five Freedoms as your standard criteria. The Five Freedoms are applicable worldwide but were first proposed in Britain in the 1960's and subsequently endorsed by the Farm Animal Welfare Council, set up by the British government to advise it (see Chapter 8: The Five Freedoms). The Five Freedoms are so basic and applicable to animals used in trade that they serve for any animal, not just farm animals.

The Five Freedoms are:
1. Freedom from Hunger and Thirst
2. Freedom from Discomfort

3. Freedom from Pain, Injury or Disease
4. Freedom to Express Normal Behaviour
5. Freedom from Fear and Distress

Examples of Animal Attractions
Some schemes to look out for are these.

- Bear dancing: wild bear cubs are caught and trained to stand on their hind legs to dance and do tricks for onlookers.
- Animal photography: young animals like monkeys, chimpanzees and lion cubs, are made to let tourists fondle them while a photo is taken. Tourists are photographed standing next to large exotic animals, like an adult lions or bears.
- Traditional medicine: for example, bears are kept in tiny cages and farmed for their bile sold as 'medicine' for ailments; tigers are killed for their penis for people in Asia to eat as an aphrodisiac.
- Cats and dogs: across Asia cats are cooked and skinned alive; dogs are hung slowly by the neck to die, reputedly to make them taste better.
- Souvenirs and trinkets: these are made from animal body parts, like bones, ivory, shells and coral reefs; many come from species that are 'protected' by law.
- Selling animals as pets: many pets are taken from the wild all over the world and die during shipment by traders.
- Circuses and aquariums: for fish, sharks, turtles, dolphins, orcas and all sorts of animals, where their basic needs are not met.
- Roadside Zoos: animals are tethered or caged to attract customers to buy goods on display.

So what can you do when you discover abuses like these? You prepare yourself before you travel, take action when you travel, and do some follow-up when you return home.

Before You Travel
You may be using tour operators. Ensure they do not encourage or advocate activities that exploit animals or that they deal with hotels that do. Tell them at the outset, preferably in writing, that you want animal-friendly services. Many operators may not be familiar with animal-friendly travel, so tell them what animal-friendly travel means: non-patronisation of animal cruelty - including being able to obtain vegetarian or vegan food. If an operator really cannot accommodate your wishes then think twice about using them.

Prepare before you go on your trip. Being prepared will make you feel more confident and take a lot of worry off your mind. Aim to get a good idea of what you could do should you encounter animal cruelty where you intend to travel. You can do much by searching the Web:

- Find out what animal mistreatment you might expect to come across. You can count on certain abuses in particular countries, such as serving tortured cats and dogs in restaurants in China and south-east Asia and bear dancing in India and the Balkans.
- List potential helpers in the region where you will be travelling, especially humane societies and bodies that enforce animal welfare.
- Try to find out animal friendly laws where you are going. You will then have a measure of control over abusers by quoting to them the law in their country as a stimulus for them to stop their abuse.

While You Travel

The simplest thing is to ensure as far as possible that you patronise only cruelty-free attractions. Avoid paying for entertainment, goods or food that you think may contravene humane behaviour to animals.

However, a stronger response is to object and complain about abuse. Take immediate action while travelling if you see animals being mistreated or you may lose the opportunity to help them. The least you can do is find who is in charge, outline your position and ask them to stop what they are doing. You have made a stand, however they react, and communicated to them that not all tourists approve of their activity.

A stronger step is also to complain to the local authorities. Legal protection is so varied that in some countries you may not easily be able to persuade the authorities to take action. But even in foreign countries you have a right to complain. Use your right for the animals you see abused. Remind the authorities that the money tourists spend is an important means of revenue for their country and that animal abuse turns tourists away and gives their country a bad name.

In serious cases, where you really have to get in touch with the authorities, collect as much evidence as you can for them. This would be best before you tackle the abusers themselves about their behaviour.

- Note the date and the place. Record how many animals are involved, whether young or old, and their species. Take photos or video and keep any freely available documents (like leaflets). Try to collect written and signed statements from other witnesses with their addresses. Finally, get the names of the abusers concerned.

- Lodge a complaint with the local police if you think anything is illegal. Inform local animal welfare organisations that may be able to help and request they send an officer immediately to check the situation. The testimony of an expert witness, such as a vet, can be invaluable.
- Tackle your hotel, tour operator and local tourist office if they have any involvement. Ask your local consulate or embassy for guidance on what can be done.
- Ask other witness of the abuse to follow your example; the more people who protest, the more seriously you will be taken. Give witnesses full details of who to contact.

Prompt and continuing action is crucial; the more you dawdle the greater the chance that all the evidence will fade and the authorities will do nothing. Try to keep the originals of any documents, but first make copies of them if you have to hand them over as evidence. Stay in the area as long as possible until the problem is in hand or return later. Keep a record of everyone you contact and decisions made.

Be persistent. If you are not satisfied by enforcement officers tell them you will speak to their superiors, and do so if need be. If the authority is reluctance to act and you still cannot get anywhere, try the local dignitaries, such as the local mayor and councillors. You may find that persuading people to act is easier if they know you have alerted the local news media about your story; officials want to keep their jobs and often do not want a bad press.

When You Return Home

If you could not contact local animal welfare organisations where you saw the abuse, write to them on your return home to say what happened and ask if there is anything they can do. Also give your tour operator the full story, even if they were only remotely implicated. Say that as an animal friendly traveller you can only support and recommend tour operators if they take positive action to recognise animal abuse and, if not suppress it, then at least not to patronise its perpetrators.

Don't feel that you are powerless to help animals on your travels. Being an animal friendly traveller you also help local communities, because in the long-run they will gain from a healthier respect for animals. A better life for animals will not come about overnight, but a continual flow of Western ideas about animal ethics and complaints from disaffected travellers will count.

Chapter	*Activities for Animal Rights*
4	*16. Politician*

Animal Politicians

Politically minded? Then start your own animal political party. Think again if you presume that advocating for animals is not a hot political issue. Members of the most successful animal rights party in the world sit in the Dutch parliament. The party leader, Marianne Thieme (b 1972), said, "We want a constitutional amendment, guaranteeing animals the right to freedom from pain, fear and stress caused by humans." (1) The party's manifesto lists over 200 actions to protect animals and nature from human exploitation.

The Dutch animal rights party began in 2002 when two women set up Partij voor de dieren (Party for Animals). Inevitably, few people took them seriously at first. But the news media gave them wide coverage, drawing in valuable supporters and attracting candidates to stand in all but one of Holland's electoral districts. The party's activists fought the elections with a tiny budget and minimal political experience, and had to struggle with their non-political full-time jobs. The outcome was that the Party for Animals won two seats in the 150 member legislature, almost two per cent of total votes in 2006. Nine of their representatives also won sits in Holland's provincial states.

Elsewhere other animal activists have also founded animal rights political parties: in Canada (Animal Alliance Environment Voters Party), Germany (Partei Mensch Umwelt Tierschutz - or Tierschutzpartei for short), Spain (Partido Antitaurino Contra el Maltrato Animal) and Britain (more below).

Animals Count

Forming new political parties is common in countries like Holland with proportional representation. But it is not altogether uncommon in countries with a first-past-the-post electoral system, such as the United States and Britain. Indeed, the neatly named Animals Count is one of the latest parties to emerge on the British political arena. Animals Count is chaired by co-founder Jasmijn de Boo (b 1975) who was an active member of the Dutch Party for Animals and one of their candidates for the 2004 elections to the Parliament of the European Union.

The overriding factor in the constitution of Animals Count is respect for living beings. This respect is based on recognising that animals have an interest in fulfilling their lives and avoiding suffering. The Party's constitution states that humans have a moral obligation to protect the interests of animals and that by doing so will live in a more worthy human society. The aims of Animals Count can be summed up as:

- Promote animal rights.
- Advance the moral and legal status of animals.
- Encourage animal welfare education.
- Protect nature.
- Advocate healthy living.

Starting a Political Party

So what must you do to start a political party? First, get together with other people who share your politics and commitments. Second, follow the rules for starting a new political party in your country. The rules will likely include registering your party with the appropriate authority, opening a bank account in the party's name, and making a formal public declaration of intent that you are forming a new political party. Your formal declaration would include:

- The name of your party.
- The address of your party headquarters.
- The names of the party leader and main post holders, such as chair and treasurer.
- The party's manifesto, along with the party's mission, aims and constitution.

As well as supporting animal rights you will have to give thought to your mainstream policy: taxation, health, education, law and order, defence, foreign policy, and so on. You must also deliberate on how your party will be funded, happily by a high profile patron - with an open cheque book. Not least you should inform the news media with a press release (see Chapter 3: News Media) to win supporters.

Your Political Prognosis

Your chances for gaining power are best if you live in a multi-party state with a proportional representation electoral system. Proportional representation favours many small parties getting seats in the legislature. However, in this system you would almost certainly have to form a coalition with one or more other parties, in order to dominate other groupings. Therefore you would have to jiggle your policies a bit to make your policies acceptable to your coalition partners.

It is unlikely you will be elected to govern in a state with a strong two-party first-past-the-post system. Nevertheless, in a two-party system the party in power might conceivably invite you one day to join them in a coalition should they become weak and desperate for your support to bolster their administration.

However, you could nevertheless have a positive influence for animals even if you never get to wield power, and even if only a minority of the electorate supports you. Your mere presence could make the main parties moderately revise their policies in your direction in order to capture the vote that would otherwise go to your party. This is what happened in Holland in the run up to the elections to the European Parliament in 2004. Political commentators stated that the Party for Animals would do well, consequently mainstream parties added animal issues to their own policies to seize the animal vote. In fact, Canada's Animal Alliance Environment Voters Party see themselves as deliberately playing this role. Rather than develop as a strong independent party in their own right, they lend their endorsement to animal-friendly candidates standing for the major parties, which is strategy you could try.

Your Colour
Political parties often identify themselves with a colour for easy recognition. Colours in Europe are traditionally red for left wing, blue for right wing, and green for parties that strongly support nature. Yellow and pink tend to be associated with centre parties. Orange tends to be for nationalistic parties, black for the far right and purple for royalist parties. Buff could be your appropriate political colour - the colour of animal disguise and camouflage. Failing that, why not a green-buff union!

References
(1)   Animals Count. www.animalscount.org (accessed May 2008).

Chapter	*Activities for Animal Rights*
4	*17. Prisoner Supporter*

Animal Rights Prisoners

The animal rights movement attracts all sorts of people and a few have broken the law in 'acts of conscience' and landed in jail. Among the first animal rights activists to feel the weight of the law were Robin Howard, convicted of damaging two boats used for hunting seals, and Ronnie Lee and Cliff Goodman, jailed for three years for damaging animal research equipment, in 1970's Britain, according to the Animal Liberation Front.

Sentences of up to twelve years for some convicted animal rights activists are startlingly disproportionately lengthy when measured against convictions for crimes such as homicide and rape. (For more about offences see Chapter 5: Law & Order.) The worst conception of animal rights prisoners is that they are dangerous extremists and terrorists who must be locked away to protect the public. Another view is that they are caring individuals who risked their liberty to help animals. Either way, you may want to support animal rights prisoners and there are a number of good reasons for doing so.

- Befriending prisoners is not necessarily endorsing their crime (befriending a fine dodger does not necessarily mean you endorse fine dodging).
- Anyone who risks jail for a cause, no matter whether you think their actions were right or wrong, clear or confused, is worthy of support.
- Anyone in jail deserves help and sustenance on humanitarian grounds. Prisoners, like other people, desire compassion and respect.
- Befriending animal rights prisoners is a form of activism, provided you openly declare that it is. In this case you are providing camaraderie to animal rights prisoners, assuring them that they are not abandoned.

Finding Prisoners to Support

A few animal rights web sites, like the Animal Liberation Front, list prisoners for support or have links to web sites that list prisoners. Pick out a prisoner and make sure they are still doing time (information on web pages gets stale and the prisoners may be out and about). If you intend to visit make sure your prisoner is not too far from where you live.

Three ways of supporting prisoners are letter writing, visiting and fundraising.

Letter Writing

Writing a letter will be the easiest first step for you to take to support a prisoner. Even when writing to a complete stranger and never getting beyond sending only the one letter, receiving it can be a pleasant distraction from a tedious existence for the prisoner. However, do not expect your prisoner to reply quickly, if at all, and do not feel obligated to correspond for the whole of their jail sentence. Should they reply, write only as many letters that you feel like sending. It is also better to cultivate a letter writing relationship with just one prisoner than to write cursorily to several prisoners and then give up because of the inconvenience of writing so many letters.

Your first letter could amount to just a few lines. Writing it might be difficult so here are some suggestions:

- Write where you found your prisoner's details.
- Say why you are writing, eg because you wish to be active in animal rights by engaging in prisoner support or that you are merely seeking a pen pal.
- Describe some generalities about your life.
- Ask them what life is like in prison and if they have plans for the future.
- Ask if you can offer some assistance, eg by sending them articles they lack.
- Close by writing that you hope your prisoner will reply but that you will not be offended if they do not respond.

Some letter writing do's:

- Write your name and address on your envelopes in case your letters are rejected.
- Date all of your letters to keep track of them.
- Give a friend's address if you do not want to reveal your own. (PO box numbers do not necessarily protect you because in some cases anyone can find out the address by walking into a main post office and simply requesting it.)
- Send photos or drawings, but keep them impersonal and without sexual implications.
- List all the objects you enclose in your letters. Do the same if you reach the stage of sending parcels, such as toiletries. This is a check that your prisoner receives everything you send them.
- Be frank with your prisoner about what you are and are not ready to do (like write indefinitely or send a hacksaw blade).

- Know your prison's rules about letter writing. Ask the prison for a copy of the guidelines for visitors and prisoners.

And some letter writing don'ts:

- Do not be critical (your prisoner has already been condemned by the law) but give your support helpfully and unconditionally, even if your prisoner is cynical or hostile.
- Do not let your prisoner impose on you or be manipulative. Tell them you will break off relations if they are.
- Do not build false hopes with your prisoner, such as by making promises you might not keep.
- Do not write anything compromising. Escape plans and details of the prison's security are out, as is writing racially offensive or obscene messages; the jailers may read your letters routinely and can stop them. Much the same applies to phone calls you may make to your prisoner; prison staff can listen in.

Visiting

There might come a time when you may want to visit your prisoner. Never just turn up; always ask your prisoner in advance if they would like a visit. Notify the prison that you wish to visit and be sure to get a copy of their regulations for visitors. Find out the prison's visiting rules, such as if they permit handing prisoners anything, and stick to them. Take identification with you to show the jailers you are who you claim to be. Make sure you arrive well before time to avoid disappointing your prisoner with a non-visit because of some unexpected mishap. Expect that you might be searched.

Fundraising

A prison does not necessarily cater for all the needs of its prisoners. Your prisoner might lack commodities like food, stationery, magazines, books, compact disks, or the travel costs for their family and friends to visit them. So you could ask them if they would like you to fundraise for them. Of course, you are under no obligation to raise funds, but if you are into fundraising then you might consider it. Or, instead, you might chip in now and then and buy them the odd item from your own pocket.

Life in prison for months or years can be grim, but a befriender from the outside world can bring a prisoner a measure of relief and encouragement for better days ahead. However, once you have begun to support a prisoner and get worried about the writing/visiting system, do not keep things to yourself but tell your prisoner and sort them out with the prison authorities.

Chapter	***Activities for Animal Rights***
4	*18. Public & School Speaker*

As an animal activist you may be called someday to speak for animals. You could also give talks about animal rights to schools and community groups, professional associations and to any society that wants an interesting speaker at their meeting. There is scope for you to be an independent speaker. Alternatively, you could speak on behalf of an animal rights organisation; some organisations even give you training. Once you get into your stride you may find that you are a naturally gifted public speaker and that giving talks is a bracing and worthwhile craft.

Titles for Talks
As a public speaker you could ask patrons whether they would like you to tailor a talk to their particular activities. You may also want to develop a few talks on specific stock-in-trade titles. Your own titles for talks could be something like:

- What are rights and what do people gain from animal rights?
- Is animal rights based on inane thinking or critical reasoning?
- Is vegetarianism immoral?
- Why did philosophers from ancient times to the Renaissance condemn animals?
- Are animal rightists anti-human?
- Is factory farming moral farming?
- What is animal testing and is it good for people?
- Why promote animal rights?
- How does property status affect animals?
- Is wearing fur good for us?

Shaping the titles of your talks in the form of a question, like the ones above, will help you focus on what exactly to speak about and will give your talk a direction. By posing a question you give your audience an augment with a conclusion that may be controversial and that they can agree with or dispute. It makes your talk more interesting than merely describing a situation or rolling out a list of facts with no clear finale. So begin your talk with a question and end it with a conclusive answer. Do not just tell your listeners but convince your listeners of the rightness of your case.

What You Need to Be a Speaker

You will need certain personal qualities for giving talks to audiences. You should:

- Enjoy speaking in front of a group of people.
- Have a good knowledge of animal rights issues and/or specialist knowledge in your particular field of animal rights.
- Have good presentation skills.
- Be able to empathise with diverse kinds of audiences.
- Have the ability to deal with questions from your audiences.

Should you think you do not have these qualities then you may be able to develop them. While some people are naturally accomplished speakers, the art of public speaking can be learned and improved with experience and there are many clubs, books, web sites and courses on the subject. The key requirements are enthusiasm, persistence and - preparation.

Preparation

You must plan your presentation to carry it through effectively; you cannot just turn up hoping for the best. (A presentation is a talk plus anything else that goes with it, such as showing a video or hosting a question and answer session at the end of your talk.)

Depending on who you are addressing, talks could last 15 - 20 minutes for school children or 30 - 45 minutes for adults. It is useful to bear in mind that the more you pack in to your talk the more your listeners will forget, even by the time they walk out the door. Your most important point might simply be to make a good overall impression and you do not need to prattle on overly long to achieve that.

At the composition stage of writing your talk think about the characteristics of your audience. What is their age group? How much might they already know about animal rights? And whether they might be inclined for or against rights? A class of young school children, a meeting of farmers or medical students pose different challenges. Seeing things from their perspective will help you prepare.

Research the topic for your talk, use reliable sources of information and look out for specific illustrations that strengthen your argument. What about displaying statistics? Detail will probably bore your audience and they will forget it quicker than you can spill it out. Instead, they will remember best an understandable, clear and striking visual graphic. For example, when talking about vegetarianism or factory farming you could display a very basic diagram of the annual number of animals people consume against the increasing human population. Draw everything simple - and extra big so that people at the back of a hall can see clearly.

Anticipate questions that your listeners might ask at the end of your talk and devise reasonable and impartial answers. Finding good answers to potential questions will further your understanding of your subject. Your knowledge will also help keep you calm and unflustered during your talks because you know you will be able to cope with questions. Your confidence will enhance your credibility with your audience as well as the standing of animal rights with them.

Learn a talk as thoroughly as you can. Knowing it back to front will fortify your composure when presenting it. It is said that Winston Churchill spent one hour rehearsing important speeches for every minute he spent delivering them. This will be too much of a chore for most speakers. But try to deliver without reading from notes, although an occasional glance is in order to remind you of major points and changes in direction. Give most of your attention to the audience.

Presentational Tips
1. Arrive early and chat with some of the audience. Get to know them a little. It will help improve your nerves and limber you up. Speaking to people you met and spoken to can be easier than addressing an audience of complete strangers.
2. Make sure any equipment you use, like visual aids, works properly. While checking equipment go over in your mind the important points you are going to make and imagine delivering your opening remarks.
3. The ultimate aim of your talk is to change or strengthen the attitude of members of your audience in favour of animal rights. So speak from your heart and try to inspire your audience without putting on an overblown act.
4. Concentrate everything on getting your key message (one or two points) across to the audience. That is the reason for giving your talk.
5. Do not be alarmed if you see blank faces. Do not waffle on but interact with your audience. Ask if they understood what you have just been going over and restate or rephrase again if necessary.
6. Strive to grab your listeners' attention by enlivening your subject. One formula is to develop a dialogue; look at individuals and ask them

rhetorical questions, like "What do you think happened?" or "How would you react if...?"

7. Displaying a PowerPoint presentation will provide added interest to your talk and act as a prompt for points you wish to make.

8. Keep an eye on the clock and do not ramble on past your allotted time or you will risk annoying people.

9. Leave time for a discussion or a question-and-answer session at the end of your talk.

10. Answer questions fully and with respect, irrespective of whether you think the questioner is hostile or stupid. You could also encourage questions throughout your talk.

11. Someone asks you a question and you are stumped for a reply. No one knows all the answers and if you do not know say so. If appropriate say you will find out and get back to the questioner with an answer.

12. Complete silence on closing your talk? Activate blank faces by asking if they agree with such-and-such a point; pick out individuals and ask for their opinion.

13. Made a mistake or forgot a line? Backed into the blackboard and brought it crashing down? Everyone goofs-up occasionally. Carry on and learn from your blunders so that you make a better show next time.

14. At the end of your presentation get feedback by asking people what they thought about it so that you can improve on it. Talk to the organisers or circulate a questionnaire.

15. Given the nature of the human onslaught on animals it is easy to fall into the habit of being negative or emotionally charged. However, be upbeat and positive. Emphasise solutions to problems, not just the problems or atrocities themselves.

16. Diplomatic tact is an asset; remain calm, factual and professional, especially when confronted by an aggressive individual or a disruptive audience (see Chapter 4: Teacher, under Disruptive Students)

Approaching Institutions

The most direct way for getting engagements is by looking up institutions, schools and colleges, societies and clubs. Phone them and ask if they would like a speaker. Make sure they clearly know that you speak for animal rights and not about animal welfare, environment, or some related field. When you have given a talk at these places ask for referrals to other parties.

In addition promote your own web site or blog specialised for animal rights outreach speaking (see Chapter 3: Internet). On your web site tell readers:

• About yourself and why you speak for animals.

- Your lecturing experience, relevant qualifications.
- Age ranges you address and duration of talks.
- Typical themes of your talks, examples of their content, and duration.
- Tools you use: videos, booklets, activity sheets, etc.
- Your catchment area or how far you are prepared to travel to an engagement.
- That your talks are free but reimbursement for travelling expenses is appreciated.
- You may also want to say if and how your talks are adapted to school curricula.

Make it really easy for readers to contact you by including an online form they can fill in. It would have fields for a school's name, its address, the name of anyone you should contact, and their phone number and email address.

Alternatively you could give talks by volunteering through one or more non-profit organisations that offer animal rights presentations to schools and elsewhere and are looking for speakers. A non-profit organisation might require that you are well versed on animal rights issues and have some experience delivering lectures and presentations. A few non-profits give training and material to their would-be speakers. Better still, you can work through non-profits as well as promote your own web site for giving talks.

When a school or institution is interested in engaging you, confirm the time and date with them in writing. At the same time you could also find out:

- The theme(s) they would like you to cover.
- The number of students in the class.
- The students' age group.
- The students' level of knowledge of animal rights.
- How long your presentation is expected to last.
- Any special areas that you should cover or avoid.
- Whether you can show videos, illustration, etc and what facilities are available, like visual aids or video equipment.

It may be an idea to put most of this in a booking form to send them when confirming your presentation.

Getting Material for Talks
Ask established animal rights organisations for relevant material to hand out at your talks: videos, DVD's, leaflets, posters and any merchandise. Many

organisations would be happy to recruit you to distribute their stuff and you could also offer to fundraise for them through your talks.

Further Development

Perhaps you do not want to give talks yourself. Then an alternative approach is to develop a list of experienced people who would like to give talks and market them to schools and societies. Send out letters of introduction with brochures outlining your service and your speakers. If you can afford it consider a full-size four page colour brochure with pictures; it stands the best chance over any other kind of literature of being filed for future action if they cannot use you immediately. Send out newsletters with the brochures when you are established.

Chapter	*Activities for Animal Rights*
4	*19. Fly Drones/UAVs*

Drones / UAVs

How can you observe animal abuse in inaccessible or prohibited outdoor areas? Remote low altitude aerial surveillance using drones (also called UAV's) is a bourgeoning market. So fly a miniature drone which while flying overhead records action on the ground with stills or video. Supply animal protection organisations with footage and document animal abuse for them as evidence for litigation. Abuses include illegal sporting, hunting and poaching, and activities normally out of sight, such as at abattoirs and factory farms.

Check the work of ShadowView (see Useful Links, below), a drone specialist animal protection group.

In the jargon, drones are sometimes described with long-winded names like unmanned aerial vehicles (UAV), unmanned aerial systems (UAS) and remotely piloted aircraft (RPA), all shortened to important-sounding initials. Some people call a miniature UAV an MAV.

The *Predator*, a large military drone with a camera
at front under fuselage and rockets the under wings.
Photo: WikiCommons.

What are Drones/UAV's?

Civilian drones are miniature aircraft piloted by someone on the ground instead of in the aircraft; they are flying robots. Drones are either fixed wing

217

or rotary (that is helicopters). A fixed wing plane could be ideal for surveying large areas over land or sea. Helicopters can speed along too, but in addition they can hover and dodge about a small area to keep a continuous record of what is happening on the ground.

Hitherto, drones have been expensive, large, high-flying and long-range aircraft. Possibly the most well-known drone/UAV is the Predator, a multi-million dollar reconnaissance machine and rocket firing assassin that the US military use for killing missions.

But advances in camera, flight and battery technology since the 1990's are making possible cheap miniature drones for civilian purposes. A mini-drone may cost you anything from a few hundred dollars to a few thousand dollars. Add to this the cost of cameras and miscellaneous items.

Mini-drones are up to about a metre long (three feet) and weigh around two kilograms (eleven pounds). Flight endurance of drones is about 30 minutes depending on payload weight and you need a clear patch of land for take-off and landing. Helicopter drones are variously multi-rotored: tricopter, quadcopter, hexacopter and even octocopter.

Applying Mini-Drones/UAV's
Animal protection organisations are employing or considering drones to document poaching of big game in Africa, the killing of seals in Namibia, illegal hunting of hares, badgers and foxes and badger baiting in Britain, and driftnet fishing in the Mediterranean involving whales, dolphins, sharks, turtles and birds as well as fish. These organisations include the World Wildlife Fund, PETA, Sea Shepherd Conservation Society, League Against Cruel Sports, and Ulster SPCA.

It is said that drones/UAV's will transform society in many ways. Just a few uses of civilian drones are:

- **Wildlife conservation**: assessing deforestation, distribution and density of populations and species, and poaching (eg illegal trade in horns and ivory).
- **Industry**: inspecting integrity of structures, such as buildings, bridges, power lines and pipelines.
- **Search and rescue**: in difficult terrain, for instance mountains and deserts, take images through cloud, rain or fog, day or night using thermal imagery

- **Police**: examining traffic and crowd size, scanning motor vehicle license plates, patrolling borders.
- **Agriculture**: monitoring free-ranging livestock, evaluating crops such as for moisture or fertilizer content.
- **Archaeology**: discovering and mapping new sites for excavation.
- **Cinema & television**: soaring and hovering shots of actors and scenes.
- **Leisure**: flying drones, either solo or with a club, as a hobby for enjoyment.

Flying Your Drone/UAV

You could be a team of one to fly your drone but it is easier to be a team of two members: the pilot and the camera operator. The pilot remotely controls the aircraft and the camera operator, standing next to him, is responsible for observing and recording pictures. Their jobs are separate because drones are as demanding to fly as full scale aircraft carrying a crew.

The drone pilot must concentrate all the time on keeping his craft in the air. He can set an irregular course using GPS (geographical positioning system), controlled via satellites, that the drone will fly by itself automatically. Or he can manipulate a small console or transmitter which includes controls for the ailerons for rolling, elevators for pitching, rudder for yawing, and throttle for speed. Piloting a helicopter, whether a full size one you can sit in or a drone that you can tuck under your arm, takes more patience and skill than controlling a fixed wing aircraft. You have to make the drone helicopter hover, fly up and down and go forward and backwards.

The camera operator controls where the camera points, the mode the camera is in and what it records. The camera transmits images of everything it sees, displaying them on a laptop monitor for the camera operator to see and save if useful. Fixed wing drones often carry a camera within their fuselage. But an external payload can be attached to the bottom of the airframe of helicopter drones (see pictures). Cameras should be easily interchangeable, if you wish, for example, to use thermal imaging. Selecting the right cameras for the right jobs takes as much consideration as selecting the right drone.

What Kind of Drone/UAV?

For animal rights work, depending on your objective, a helicopter drone may be more suitable than a fixed wing drone. With a helicopter the camera operator can see what is happening by flying the drone backwards or turning it in its own length. However, if you need to cover a lot of ground quickly, rather than observe a small patch for a while, you might swap your rotary drone for a fixed wing drone.

Some drones, just like the larger people-carrying aircraft, have aerobatics capabilities (like fighters). These are for hobbyists who want to fly loops and roles with their drones. You will want a model that is a stable platform (more like an airliner) for taking pictures without blurring images.

The more equipment your drone carries (the greater the 'payload'), and the more windy and adverse weather your operating area is prone to, the heavier your drone should be for strength and stability. Generally, the size of your drone will dictate the camera payload. Flight time shortens as the camera weight increases.

You can design and build your own mini-drone but you will find it a lot easier to buy one complete or as a kit to assemble at home. Assembling a drone as a kit could take you five to twenty or so hours and you should not need any specialist knowledge or tools.

The Law for Drones/UAV's

Flying drones is a serious enterprise. It is regulated by law, so do an online search to find out what the law in your country says about flying commercial drones (whether you fly them for profit or not). In the United States, for example, the Federal Aviation Administration restricts flying drones to below 130 metres (400 feet); this is no handicap for animal welfare work. And the Civil Aviation Authority in Britain reminds you that when flying your drone you must be careful to keep your aircraft a safe distance from people, vehicles and structures, and only fly it in suitable weather.

As more commercial drones take to the air worldwide, so the law of each country is adapting itself and changing to accommodate this new industry. Be careful to stay within the law and keep up to date with it as it changes.

Flying drones seriously, you will need public liability insurance and you might insure cameras separately.

Beware Drone/UAV Pitfalls

A drawback when flying a miniature drone is that usually you cannot let the machine out of your sight, so you have to stay close to it. Presently, this is demanded by law in some countries. Furthermore, you may not know which way it is facing or even whether it is upside down unless you can see it. Monitors are developing, however, to the point where you can track some drones however and wherever they fly and the law may change accordingly. Until then you cannot spy behind far off hills and other blind spots where you cannot see your drone. If you need to fly over obscured terrain, consider piloting a paramotor and going up in person (see Flyer in Chapter 4).

The weather can be another problem. All aircraft, manned or unmanned, are affected by it. Some drones will cope better than others in wind and rain, but even if your drone can speed along at a spanking rate of, say 50 k/hour (30 mph), and the wind is gusting more than this, then it would be rash to fly it. It is likely to crash. You just have to wait for better conditions.

Beginning Drones/UAV's

Flying drones is a serious activity. But for a complete beginner, possibly the best way into it, to fathom whether you like it and gain basic experience, is to start at hobby level. A concise outline is Craig Issod's eBook Getting Started with Hobby Quadcopters and Drones. Search the Web for information and guides on miniature drones (...and UAV's, UAS's, RPA's, and of course MAV's!) and literally work your way upwards.

Useful Links

- ShadowView: www.shadowview.org - a non-profit drone/UAV group.
- Quadcopters: www. quadcopters.co.uk - an example of one of the growing number of online multi-rotor specialists.
- Dragonfly: www.draganfly.com - an American online drone business.

Chapter	*Activities for Animal Rights*
4	*20. Scientific Investigator*

The Scientific Investigator

A scientific investigator researches and reports evidence for publication so that campaigners acting on the information can reform harmful practices. This is a bit like doing investigative reporting (see Investigative Reporter, Chapter 4) in that you try to find answers that would be difficult to obtain if people knew you were investigating them. Doing scientific investigative research might appeal to you for similar reasons but has more of a scientific bearing, making use of statistical techniques and scientific report writing. A science or social science degree could be of value here; however, anyone with a strong ability and fondness for investigating and writing can educate themselves on how to go about doing it. In recent years much has been written about scientific investigative research (1) and proficiency comes with action and practice.

An Example Investigation

Pet shops are fairly easy to identify, open to the public for perusal and, looking innocent, you can question the shop assistants. These factors may be some of the reasons why pet shops have come under the scrutiny of investigative researchers. The aim of these researchers is to protect animals from the pet trade by identifying illegal practices and ill-treatments that could then be acted on. Jordi Casamitjana, an independent animal welfare consultant and investigator, has carried out a number of investigations and one was on pet shops in Scotland (2), outlined below.

Scientific work for an investigation comes in at the very beginning. You must take utmost care to design your investigation so that your prospective findings can stand up to thorough questioning by anyone wanting to shoot them down. For example, to investigate pet shops you must first clearly define and state what a pet shop is. One way of doing this is to find out what the law says that constitutes a pet shop. If there were no laws relating to this and nothing else acting as a guide then you would have to write down your own definition, such as 'a premise that sells animals as pets as a commercial business, excluding breeders who handle or raise pedigree pets for sale'.

You could concentrate on a few of the really bad pet shops in your area. However, you may want your investigation to be applicable to all pet shops generally in your region to stand the best chance of your work being acted on by animal rights organisations. In this case you must obtain a representative sample of pet shops that can be said to be characteristic of all pet shops in your region. A simple way of doing this, as Casamitjana did, is by digging up and listing all the shops and selecting at random a number of them for investigation. 'Random' means that every shop has an equal chance of being selected for a visit. If the sample of pet shops you visit is not random it will not be representative of all pet shops in the region and make your findings and conclusions doubtful and unreliable. Of course you could visit all the pet shops, but this will be overly costly and time consuming.

You also need an adequate number of pet shops to visit because the more shops you check, the more your findings will be reliable. How many pet shops to choose? This is somewhat subjective but at least a quarter to a third of total pet shops in the region seems reasonable, which is how Casamitjana chose.

There were various other problems Casamitjana had to address before he could set foot inside his first pet shop. One was that he was going to look for abnormal behaviour among the shops' animals. So what constitutes abnormal animal behaviour? Casamitjana defined abnormal animal behaviour as actions not normally seen in animals living in the wild and he concentrated on stereotypies. A stereotypy is behaviour, seen in humans as well as animals, that is repetitious and appears not to have an obvious function. Pet shop stereotypies include pacing up and down, rocking back and forth, pacing round in circles, head bobbing, and bar-biting (of a cage). You can see stereotypical behaviour in animals at zoos and factory farms. Animal behaviourists think that animals living in unstimulating conditions in captivity perform stereotypies to help them cope with the frustration, boredom and stress of their living conditions. A stereotypical behaviour by an animal indicates a problem of well-being.

Casamitjana identified other conditions indicative of potentially poor welfare in pet shops. He considered the animals' housing (which might be barren and cramped) and compared it with officially approved standards. He also noted animals trying to escape, animals vocalising, customers teasing or handling the animals, shop assistant proficiency - judged by the shop assistants' standard of advice - and shop compliance with legal regulations, such as not selling animals to minors. Finally, after detailed preparation, Casamitjana posing as a customer was ready to visit the pet shops.

Among Casamitjana's findings was that over half the pet shops he visited had animals who showed abnormal behaviour and were clearly distressed, possibly because of inadequate housing. Several shops had poor customer-animal interactions. Shop assistants often failed to give adequate advice and often gave poor advice. Some shops did not have a valid pet shop licence to operate and others were in breach of their licence. Casamitjana wrote his report and it was published by Advocates for Animals as an indictment on pet shop standards. Campaigners working for pet shop animals are now better armed to help these animals. Knowledge is power!

Define Your Subject

A subject for your investigation may not immediately occur to you. Choosing one will then be your first task; read Investigation Ideas in Investigative Reporter, Chapter 4. Three tips are:

- Select an investigation that deeply interests you, for should your interest wane while on the job you may never complete it.
- Always keep your research plan simple. Plans that are initially simple often grow complicated and if you start with an already complicated plan it is likely to get out of hand.
- Try to discuss your chosen subject of investigation and work out some details with an established investigator if you can find one (search the Web).

Your Report

Like Casamitjana you will have to know how to write a report. The aim of writing one is to convince readers that what you did is important and that action should be taken about your findings. Your research report will be the only concrete evidence of your research. If you do not write a report or have no other documentary evidence, like video, to show what you found then no one will know what you have done and no action can be taken. Furthermore, the quality of your research will be judged directly by the quality of your writing (succinct, clear, logical and strictly relevant) and how well you convey the importance of your findings.

The best way to know how to write a report is to study reports by other researchers. To find them check books, journals and the Web. You will see that there are four basic sections to a written report:

- Introduction: the problem and why you are investigating it.
- Methods: what you did to investigate the problem.
- Results: the specific findings of your investigation.
- Discussion: your interpretation of your findings and if there are other authors how your findings fit in with their work.

You will want a pithy descriptive title for your report and may wish to include other sections in it, like:

- Abstract: a brief statement of what you did, what you found and your conclusions. This goes at the top of your report under the title.
- Acknowledgements: to people who helped you. This could go at the end of the report.
- Appendix: stuff that might be added, like raw data, that does not fit in the body of your report. The Appendix goes at the back of the report.
- References: a list of the authors with their published works that you cite in your report. This goes at the very back of the report.

A strong move is to write a literature review and mix it in with the Introduction. A literature review is a summary of the findings and conclusions of other researchers (if any) on your subject of investigation. For example, you can state in one sentence that so and so, investigating such and such, found this and that and concluded whatever. You should try to build on the findings of other researchers to:

- Add substance to your report.
- Give your report more context, breadth and greater credence.
- Establish yourself as knowledgeable about your subject.

Another good move is to design your study from the outset from the best techniques of other researchers while avoiding their faults. Even if no one has published anything on your subject for investigation you should mention it. If there are no publications on your subject then you will be a trailblazer and researchers following in your steps will cite you in their report!

References

(1) Forbes, Derek. *A Watchdog's Guide to Investigative Reporting: a simple introduction to principles and practice in investigative reporting.* Johannesburg: Konrad Adenauer Stiftung. 2005. (Accessed online May 2007.)
(2) Casamitjana, Jordi J. *Caged to Sell: a study of animal related problems in Scottish pet shops in the year 2003.* Advocates for Animals. 2003.

Chapter	***Activities for Animal Rights***
4	*21. Solo Information Worker*

The Work

Assemble and display to the public the information and eye-catching material from the larger animal activist organisations. Obtain a foldable table on which to arrange your goods and pick a site where you can pitch it, your portable information centre. Try street markets, fairs and festivals, wherever you can lay out your shop and lots of people pass by. Collect booklets, brochures, CD's, videos, pamphlets, posters, newsletters, stickers, badges and petitions for people to sign and many organisations will give you their donation collection tins.

Practical items to take with you are a tablecloth, a transparent waterproof cloth for when wet weather threatens, paperweights for windy days and victuals to sustain you. Get a portable chair unless you intend standing all day. Ask the appropriate authorities beforehand if you need permission to set up where you intend, there may be restrictions, and get the official's name in case you have to refer back to them because of any problem.

Chit Chat With the Public

Engage in polite conversation with people who approach your information centre. Should they be particularly interested in animal rights, you might convince them to take on a practical role of some sort (with you at your centre or with an animal rights organisation). In this case do not let them go without getting their contact address or phone number and soon get in touch with them again or their initial willingness may cool. Do not waste time disputing issues with convinced detractors or by converting the already converted when you might miss other people standing nearby who may be sympathetic. Be friendly, helpful and patient to win 'hearts and minds'.

The Portable Display

Portable display boards bearing pictures, text and documents will make an attractive background to your centre. Arrange your display boards around the back and sides of the table. The boards could treble the working area of your information shop. They could be single or double width, hinged together with plastic or tape, and be single or double tiered (one on top of the other) and be made of laminated plywood for lightness and strength. Suitable dimensions are in the region of 0.5 thick x 65 wide x 100 high in centimetres (about 0.25 x

25 x 40 in inches) that you are able to carry comfortably and that your art or hardware shop can supply.

Cover the boards with coloured cardboard and pin or stick your material to them. Place a heading in large letters over the top of each board, like 'Factory Farming Tortures Animals', or 'Veal Calf Outrage', or 'Animals Made Into Fur Brushes'. Add pictures with simple and concise text next to them for the passing people to read. Passers-by may not want to hang around long to read much, so 'bear-bones' text is best. The less text you write, the more people will remember! Let the pictures carry the impact and it is the pictures that people will recall most vividly.

Would This Be Your Motto?

At times it is appropriate to offer a payment or donation to your suppliers for your stock of information, especially if your suppliers are among the smaller organisations. Their material can be expensive to produce so work hard to distribute it to best advantage. *Persuade to Convert* could be your information centre's motto!

Chapter	*Activities for Animal Rights*
4	*22. Voluntary Worker Abroad*

Volunteer to work abroad - for your gap year, career break, change of direction, early retirement or just a vacation. Organisations around the world engaged in animal, wildlife and conservation projects need volunteers to work with them for at least a month to a year or more and you might find a niche working in animal rights. You travel about, live in a new-to-you environment, plunge into the local population and culture, pick up a foreign tongue; altogether an unforgettable experience.

Although many opportunities exist for working with animal welfare and conservation organisations, at present few bona fide openings currently exist for purely animal rights work. So you could mix animal rights with animal welfare and conservation. An example of a good project that combines all three, would be one that effectively rehabilitates animals stolen from the wild, say for the pet or zoo trade, back to the wild.

Search for Animal Rights Openings

So how do you find animal rights volunteer positions? Search the Web. One web site for example states, "Experience the magic of India while helping to promote animal rights." Then goes on to say, "Working for an animal welfare NGO with a strong track record, you'll have plenty of chances to roll up your sleeves and get involved in spreading awareness about the care, management and nutrition of pets and homeless animals to all sections of Indian society." This NGO, however, is only one per cent into animal rights. Still, this is a good start.

Animal welfare and conservation are not the same as animal rights (Chapter 3: Comparing Animal Philosophies). Therefore, when volunteering for an animal welfare or conservation organisation be careful that you will actually be active in some way for animal rights. Some bodies involved in animal welfare and conservation may oppose animal rights. Conversely, some people in animal rights oppose and disparage animal welfare, taking the view that "Animal 'welfare' laws do little but regulate the details of exploitation." (1)

Check Bona Fides

How do you check the honesty of an organisation? The only way is to ask them for a list of all (or at least twenty) of their recent volunteers with contact details so that you can check their experiences. A good organisation ought to be able to give you a list. They must send you a reasonably full list because if you get only half a dozen or fewer names they may be in the hand of the organisation to say good things and there is no point contacting them for an opinion. If the organisation has 'no time' to send you a full list, or 'does not do that sort of thing', or makes up some other excuse, tell them why you want the list. If they still refuse then seriously consider dropping them flat.

What You Need
To be successful on your voluntary work abroad you:

- Need energy, enthusiasm and a real commitment to work hard to meet the mental and physical challenge.
- Should be able to adapt to circumstances if you find yourself working in isolated surroundings, possibly living in conditions you might consider sub-standard or primitive, out of touch with your family and friends, and experiencing many strange cultural differences.
- Should be able to commit yourself for several months, offer certain skills or expertise if a particular project demands it, and meet travelling costs, living costs and other expenses like administration, insurance and taxes.

Home Thoughts
Alternatively, instead of going abroad, you could opt for volunteering at an animal rights organisation in your neighbourhood. An example is People for the Ethical Treatment of Animals who advertise on their web sites for volunteers in their American and European offices. An organisation like this needs volunteers to assist in administration office work, participate in demonstrations and photo calls, to carry out research for campaigns, pack parcels, distribute leaflets and undertake other duties as necessary. Choose your days and hours of work.

Finally
While travelling as a voluntary worker in any kind of job, whether related to animals or not, keep an eye open for animal abuses that you can do something about on your own initiative. Read Animal-Friendly Traveller, Chapter 4.

References
(1) Best S & Nocella A J. *Reflections on the liberation of animals.* p12. In: Best S & Nocella A J (eds.). *Terrorist or Freedom Fighter?* Lantern Books. 2002.

Chapter	*The Law & Animal Rights*
5	*1. Terrorism*

Snappy Page Essence
Terrorism is the use of intimidation and violence, often against innocent people, to impel change in society. Some terrorists remain shady; society honours others. For animal rights, the most practical way to advance is on a broad front, everyone doing what they do best.

"Their number is not important, but their thought."
Leo Tolstoy (1)

A Definition of Terrorism

Terrorism is the systematic use by people of intimidation and violence, often against innocent people, to impel change in society. Through terrorism a small number of people can exert a disproportionate influence on society. Massive security forces are often ineffectual when combating a few dedicated terrorists who strike anywhere then vanish to fight another day.

Terrorist organisations are small, typically with around a dozen to a few hundred individuals, occasionally a few thousand. Violent animal rights extremists are often referred to as terrorists by some politicians and news media. Since the 1970's the number of violent animal rights extremists has been growing in Britain and their approach has spread abroad, especially to countries like Australia and the United States. However, despite the news reportage they stimulate, British violent animal rights extremists are thought to total only 300 to 400 people and draw on less active backing from 3,000 to 4,000 supporters.

Background to Terrorism

Terrorism is as old as history, but the expression terrorism originated in 18th century revolutionary France. The state ordered the arrest, torture and execution of thousands of citizens during the French revolution (1789), in the period known as the Reign of Terror, to murder political enemies and impose order on society. Robespierre (1753 - 1794), French lawyer and radical political leader, is quoted as saying, "Terror is nothing but justice, prompt, severe and inflexible." Robespierre personally ordered dozens of executions and himself fell prey to the terror when he was imprisoned and guillotined.

Many people turned to terrorism after the Second World War when their nations sought independence from colonialism. Once they gained independence, however, several erstwhile terrorists became respected leaders of their country. Menachem Begin (1913 - 1992) led the Irgun, a terrorist group fighting British rule in 1940's Palestine. One of the Irgun's acts was the bombing of the King David Hotel in Jerusalem, the central British administrative offices, killing over 90 people. In 1977 Israel elected Begin as Prime Minister. Ironically, Israel then had to deal with Yasir Arafat (1929 - 2004), himself a one-time terrorist, fighting Israel for Palestinian independence, who subsequently became President of the Palestinian Authority and a Nobel Prize winner for peace.

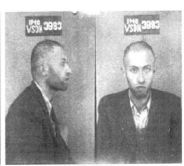

Left Photo: Menachem Begin (left) as Prime Minister of Israel in 1978 with the President of the United States, Jimmy Carter, and the President of Egypt, Anwar Sadat (right). (Jimmy Carter Library / Wikimedia Commons.) Right Photo: Menachem Begin as a young aspiring terrorist in 1940. Photo taken by the Soviet secret police (the NKVD) and found in the secret police (KGB) archives. (Wikimedia Commons.)

So terrorists do not necessarily remain contemptible shadowy figures, even though terrorism is rejected with horror and aversion by most people most of the time. A well-known phrase is 'someone's terrorist is someone else's freedom-fighter'; somebody is or is not a terrorist depending on where your political sympathies lie. You can always justify your terrorist inclinations by appealing to philosophy. With a utilitarian attitude your doctrine would be 'better a few people die for the majority of people'. Under a deontology viewpoint your doctrine would be 'do your duty irrespective of the consequences, be they good or bad'. (See under Ethical Theories, in Animal Ethics, Chapter 2.)

But What Really is Terrorism?
Terrorism causes widespread public anxiety because anyone may be injured or killed. But for national governments to fight terrorism effectively they first need to know what they are fighting. Exactly what terrorism is, however, and

who is and who is not a terrorist, have always eluded clear definition. What happens in actuality is that both sides in a dispute convincingly employ words like terrorism and terrorist to bring discredit on the opposing side.

So you must be careful when politicians and national bodies define terrorism. Who are these politicians and national bodies, what are their political interests and how exactly do they propose to tackle terrorism? If you are not careful they may fool and manipulate you, ostensibly against terrorism, but in reality to further their own questionable political aims. You may find yourself sanctioning laws and actions that buttress their powers but conflict with democratic society and work against your personal liberty.

Animal Extremism & Terrorism

Politicians, the news media and people with vested interests in animals sometimes accuse animal rights extremists of terrorism. Violent animal rights extremism is largely confined to Europe and North America. It began in Britain in the mid-1970's where animal rights extremists began using violent methods (for examples see Chapter 3: Direct Action, under Examples of Animal Rights Direct Action) to make their point or intimidate people such as livestock exporters, fur traders, animal breeders and animal laboratory workers.

It is fair to say that these animal extremist activities should not be taken lightly. Some of them, like arson, carry a jail sentence and others, like setting up letter bombs and booby-traps, can cause serious injury. However, although there have been narrow escapes, violent animal rights extremists have not intentionally killed anyone with such conduct. On the other hand some animal rights activists have died while on actions (a case is Jill Phipps, in Chapter 6).

But should we label violent animal rights extremists as terrorists? It makes sense to distinguish terrorist from violent extremist in order to maintain the right level of response to their acts. Terrorists, like the Irgun and today's Al Qa'eda, do not hesitate to kill people deliberately. Al Qa'eda terrorists in 2001 hijacked four airliners in the US and used them as guided missiles to kill 3,000 innocent people. It would be an overreaction, but one often found in the news media, to lump violent animal rights extremists with terrorists.

Does AR Extremism Work in Practice?

No one can say with certainty whether direct action (see Direct Action, Chapter 3) or extremism for any cause is efficacious. Discussing animal rights, Richard Ryder sums it up:

"Yet any historian knows that in some earlier reform movements little progress was made until illegal and sometimes violent acts occurred. Whether reforms would have been achieved without the direct action of the suffragists, for example, or whether they would have been achieved more slowly, are matters for conjecture." (2)

Most people might agree that extreme actions can sometimes lead to big effects. The Boston tea-party is an often cited case. Angered at having to pay taxes to the British crown without Parliamentary representation, Colonialists in Massachusetts in 1773 flung the consignment of tea, on which tax had to be paid, off merchant ships into Boston harbour. Their act developed into the American War of Independence, radically changed American society and led in 1776 to the world's first major declaration of human rights (see Animal Rights, in Chapter 2).

One ingredient of the Boston tea-party was the publicity the action created. People delight in reading about excessive and exceptional human behaviour - and the modern news media deluge us with extremisms. Violence gets noticed; quiet initiatives are seldom trumpeted. Whether publicity caused by animal rights extremism is good or bad there is no doubt that it thrusts animal rights into the public conscience. Extreme direct action stirs up controversy, stimulates debate and keeps it alive. When it comes to animal rights you might therefore argue that extremism is good for animals (that is it gets publicity).

The flip side of extreme action is quietly and politely improving attitudes by education and argument, by appealing to rationality, compassion and a sense of justice, and by changes in the law (for example Chapter 4: Teacher, Animal Lawyer, and Philosopher). This is slow work but effective in that it makes for a great and long-lasting change in people's attitudes and in most wars it is attitudes that must be won.

Conclusion
In conclusion, it is impossible to know the single best way to bring about a revolution in society. The most sensible means is probably to advance on a broad front, everyone doing the best they can in their own way.

References
(1) Tolstoy, Leo. *Pima (Letters):* 8 - 15 March, 1881, 63, 45 - 52.
(2) Ryder, Richard. In Peter Singer (editor): *In Defense of Animals.* 1985:77 - 88.

Chapter	*The Law & Animal Rights*
5	*2. Violence or Nonviolence?*

Snappy Page Essence

No one has succeeded in weighing the efficacy of violence versus nonviolence to the satisfaction of all. People argue as their opinions take them. Possibly the best overall course is to remain true to basic humane principles.

"In moral terms, the granting of rights to animals leads to the conclusion that direct action in their defence is not only permissible but also a moral duty, although whether this justifies some of the more extreme actions involving violence is an open question." Robert Garner (1)

Scope of AR Extremism

Animal rights extremists caused £2.6m of damage to property in 1,200 actions during 2000 and are the prime cause of violence in Britain since violence in Northern Ireland eased, according to BBC News (2). Animal rights extremists have harassed their opponents, carried out arson attacks, planted and sent bombs and other devices through the post and issued death threats to individuals, animal laboratories, shops, factories, farms and other targets. The police fear that sooner or later someone will be gravely injured if not killed.

Many analysts maintain that the Animal Liberation Front (ALF) is an extremist group, an instigator and leader of animal rights violence. Set up in 1976 by Ronnie Lee, ALF claims it is not a violent organisation. But this may depend on what you call violent. Kinds of actions typically carried out by groups claiming inspiration from ALF are outlined in Chapter 4, Direct Action, under Examples of Animal Rights Direct Action. Analysts say ALF promotes 'leaderless resistance' groups, each group consisting of one or a handful of individuals, autonomous and completely detached from their instigating body, yet acting towards the same ultimate goal.

Another two extreme animal rights groups were the Animal Rights Militia, first active in the 1980's, and the Justice Department, created in 1993. Both groups claimed to be unrelated to the ALF although many critics saw the same few people behind all three groups. The Animal Rights Militia claimed they were behind the grave robbing in 2004 of a woman involved with animal abuse; two years later three animal activists in their thirties were tried for the theft of her body and sentenced from four to twelve years jail.

The ALF now has a branch in the United States, where they are a horror to the Federal Bureau of Investigation (FBI). The FBI classifies some political and economic opponents as 'terrorists' and lumps ALF members in with them. Other US agencies classify terrorists only as political groups who cause people bodily injury or death, so are not concerned with ALF.

Can We Justify Violence?

A few people utterly reject reacting violently. Even if seriously physically attacked they would rather die than fight back. But most people would hit back sufficiently motivated and with violence if necessary. But whether you are for or against violence there is a good pragmatic question to ask about it. Is violence efficacious?

Kinds of Violence

First, a little digression. What sort of violence are we talking about? Violence is not possible to define definitively, but for the purpose of the following discussion let's make out four kinds of violence. This is an imperfect definition but covers a lot of ground. It includes zero violence, that is, nonviolence. It also includes violence to property, that is, property damage.

1. Gandhi nonviolence

This is peaceful resistance by masses of people in the style of Mohandas Gandhi (1869 - 1948) and Martin Luther King Jr (1929 - 1968). Analysts of violence often quote these men as the prime exponents of nonviolence for Indian independence and black American civil rights, respectively. Gandhi called his style of nonviolence satyagraha. Although satyagraha is never violent under any circumstances, it is not necessarily always legal. For example, Gandhi incited people not to pay salt tax and he called for mass trespasses. The British imprisoned Gandhi several times for his intransigence.

2. Physical violence to people

Physical violence, like brute assault or murder, is rare in animal rights campaigning and not representative of the animal rights movement, although the news media make much of it given an opportunity.

3. Mental violence to people

Harassment or torment, for instance by a noisy crowd screaming insults while picketing someone's home, is a mental torture for the occupant. Mental violence like this clearly overlaps with violence to property (below) in that you will likely suffer mental trauma if your home is burnt down in an arson attack.

4. Violence to property (property damage)
Some people claim that you cannot be violent to property because property cannot feel pain. They call property damage sabotage, to set it off from violence. Eco-activists in the United States call property damage ecotage or monkeywrenching. Destroying equipment, say at an animal laboratory or slaughterhouse (when no one is around to be injured) may be absorbed by insurance and cause little personal bother to the owners. However, violence to property could conceivably end up as violence to people if care is not taken; someone trapped in a burning building might die or be injured or someone might be run over accidentally in a subsequent high speed car escape.

Views For & Against Violence
Physical violence to people (under 2, above) is pretty straight forward. As for the other three kinds of violence (1,3 & 4, above), people voice assertions for and against them and their effect on powerholders (the people in society who hold power). The table below is a summary that compares and contrasts some important views of what people say for and against violence.

Is Violence Efficacious?
No one has been able to weigh the practical efficacy of nonviolence versus violence and come up with a ultimate conclusion that everyone can agree upon. The reckoning is too complicated. Instead, people argue for violence or nonviolence as their opinions take them.

The American philosopher Tom Regan outlines how we might hypothetically justify violence against people to save animals (3). In his opinion you could use violence against people provided you have tried all nonviolent means first, that you have adequate time and conditions, that you are rescuing animals from extreme or mortal harm and that you do not use violence excessively. However, Regan thinks that in actuality we can never justify violence to people even when these conditions are met. Nonviolent methods, he says, are never sufficiently exhausted. He holds this view even though he acknowledges that animals are harmed and dying all the time and that the violence some animal rights activists do is like nothing compared with the huge harm people do to animals, often backed by the law and social respectability. Applying nonviolent methods, for Regan, is the only way to advance, even though they are laborious, strain our patience and the results are often ambiguous.

What about the effectiveness of mental violence to people and property damage? Partly by using these means some animal rights activists in Britain have succeeded in closing down companies breeding cats and dogs for experimentation (Hillgrove Farm and Consort Kennels) and are on the road to closing down Huntingdon Life Sciences, a much bigger breeder. (See Chapter

3: Direct Action, under Stop Huntingdon Animal Cruelty.) Such determined campaigns show that these methods can be effective, at least in the short-run.

These methods contribute to save some animals and create publicity, public debate and new converts for animal rights.

Views For & Against Nonviolence vs Violence	
Nonviolence	**Mental Violence & Property Damage**
1. Anyone can do it; no need for special training or physical fitness.	1. Animal activists cannot muster the full force of nonviolent action (eg mass marches and mass arrests) so must rely on violence.
2. Appeals to the majority of people.	2. Appeals to relatively few people (especially the young).
3. Must use nonviolent methods because there are too few activists ready to break the law.	3. Breaking the law is an effective weapon because you need only a few activists ready to do it.
4. You are not likely to be hurt or go to jail for doing it.	4. There is a chance you could go to jail.
5. The possibility of hurting innocent people is very low.	5. The possibility of hurting innocent people is low - provided you take adequate and well thought out precautions against mishaps.
6. Makes the news media focus on the issues, not on the violence which then eclipse the issues.	6. Brings an issue to public notice and if the violence is continuous keeps it there.
7. Is slow and low key but can be effective in the long-run. Makes political change come about by steady progress (eg Britain slowly development from absolute monarchy to liberal democracy without a revolution).	7. Sometimes has an obvious and agreeable link between a violent action and its result. Is necessary for political change (eg France and Russia overthrew their absolute rulers by bloody revolution).

8. Takes a long time but is more effective in the end. We must be patient.

8. Must advance however we can; time has run out; cannot be concerned about principles.

9. In democracies we should use democratic methods within the democratic system to pursue goals.

9. We must shatter laws that protect injustice, regardless of democracy or public opinion, especially when powerholders refuse to respond.

10. We should be open and accountable and therefore should cultivate a good relationship with the powerholders and police.

10. We must confront powerholders and police because they are repressive agents of the state.

11. Less likely to provoke violent counter measures by the powerholders against you and avoids futile cycles of violence and counter-violence.

11. Provokes retaliation by the powerholders (showing that violence is a serious threat to them).

12. More likely to win over public sympathy, particularly if powerholders retaliate with violence against you that you do not resist.

12. Can win public sympathy, provided people are not injured (eg Sea Shepherd ramming whaling ships, Chapter 3: Direct Action).

13. Weakens powerholders because they cannot justify repressive measures to retain their authority.

13. Makes powerholders see nonviolent activists as less unreasonable and therefore more ready for compromise.

14. In our moral relationship with others we are guided by the Golden Rule: 'treat others how you would like them to treat you'.

14. In our moral relationship with others we are guided only by desired results: 'the end justifies the means' (ie the result justifies the methods we use to get there).

Property damage can also work on another level, for example, through apparently unjustifiable, pointless destruction or defacement of property - what people call vandalism. Karen Dawn, American writer and journalist, tracks controversial animal related stories in the news media (see the entry Media Watcher). Through her web site (DawnWatch.com) she alerts her subscribers to send rational, animal-supportive responses for publication to the news editors where the stories appear. In Dawn's opinion there is no unfavourable or adverse animal rights publicity. She says any publicity keeps the issue of animal rights alive and enables members of the public to send intelligent and enlightening comments to the press to influence the reading public for the better.

Critics of violence, however, say that rescuing a few animals and closing down some animal-using companies are only fleeting victories. They say that what we need is to create lasting change and for that we must transform the views of the majority of people in society. For example, Bill Moyer (1933 - 2002) was an American activist who fought for civil rights and the environment for nearly 40 years. In his Practical Strategist (4) he summarises his discoveries about how successful nonviolent campaigns develop and describes a nonviolent method for activists to develop their strategies.

Moyer's argument is that ultimate power lies with the people, not with the powerholders (in Moyer's case nuclear power companies and official state authorities and in our case politicians, animal experimenters, factory farmers and other upholders of animal exploitation). Powerholders, says Moyer, can only prevail as long as the majority of people believe the powerholders are working in the interests of society. Changes in the opinion of the majority of people, says Moyer, can force new conditions, such as fresh social policy and legislation that powerholders are forced to accept in order to retain power. Moyer says that activists must target the majority of people by nonviolent activities to "alert, educate, win over, inspire and involve" them through upholding society's values, traditions and sympathies; a social movement on the violent fringe will only alienate the majority of people and so be ineffective.

Can Moyer's campaigning style really help in the case of animal rights? His outlook is based on mass nonviolent resistance. Bruce Friedrich, a vegan who has worked for animal rights in the US and specialised in 'confrontational' animal activism, voices an alternative opinion (5). Friedrich considers Gandhi nonviolence and warns that animal rights activists cannot follow the example of Gandhi and King. Gandhi and King, two giants of activism, could muster millions of people to march for their cause and rouse world public opinion behind them. But in contrast, says Friedrich, there are too few animal activists to hold massive demonstrations and world public opinion is presently not on their side. Consequently Friedrich believes we have nothing much to learn from Gandhi nonviolence.

Friedrich's models for action are the underground slave railroad in America and the resistance to Nazism in Europe: small numbers of people using intrigue, deception and sabotage fought for the interests of others. Friedrich acts where he puts his mouth. In Washington DC he assaulted the visiting mayor of London by throwing water in the mayor's face (6). He did a year in jail for 'destroying government property' - battering a jet fighter with a hammer (6). And he was arrested by the British police for streaking Buckingham Palace with "go vegan" painted across his backside, just as President George W Bush was meeting the monarch (6, 7).

Indeed, you could argue that the campaigns of Gandhi and King, along with other social change campaigns, are not strictly comparable with animal liberation. As animal liberation philosophers have stated, the objects for freedom are not humans but the liberation of species not our own. Campaigning for social change directly affecting humans has human self-interest at its heart, something that campaigning on behalf of other species lacks. Campaigning for animal liberation, philosophers point out, is therefore more difficult.

Going back to Moyer, you could argue that it is not necessary to engage in extremism for animal rights. We could win over more people to animal rights by making rational arguments for rights and by showing evidence beyond a reasonable doubt that issues harming animals also harm human society. An example is Ray Greek and co-workers who make a scientific case that animal experimentation harms humanity (8). Another example is the many activists who argue about the effects of factory farming on human society, such as chemicals in human food, contamination of water and the spread of disease to people.

At the same time as sharpening our rational skills and appealing to reason, we must limit as far as possible the mechanisms for harming animals. Harms must be countered with technology to make effective, inexpensive alternatives, like:

- Animal eating: invent synthetic but realistically satisfying meat.
- Animal experimenting: devise superior non-animal procedures.
- Animal wearing: produce attractive, durable, synthetic fibres to replace wool, fur and leather.

When people see that animal abuse does not benefit them, but corrupts or exhausts human society, more people will favour animal rights.

Conclusion
Many actions must be won to win a war, whether world war, war on terrorism, or war on animals. Each action is just a small part leading to overall victory. We cannot know which actions contribute significantly to the final victory so we have to fight them all. Therefore until we know what kind of actions

actually work, activists should contribute what they can, whether raucously demonstrating in the street or quietly philosophising in books.

"We are all working toward the same goal and we should support one another - as long as basic humane principles are not violated." Bruce Friedrich (5)

References

(1) Garner, Robert. *Animals, Politics and Morality.* 1993:239.
(2) BBC News. *Animal Rights, Terror Tactics.* 30 August 2000. www.news.bbc.co.uk. (Accessed online July 2007.)
(3) Regan, Tom. *How to Justify Violence.* In Best A & Nocella A J Jr (editors). Terrorists or Freedom Fighters? New York: Lantern Books. 2004.
(4) Moyer, Bill. *The Practical Strategist: movement action plan (MAP) strategic theories for evaluating, planning and conducting social movements.* Social Movement Empowerment Project, San Francisco. 1990. (Accessed online July 2007.)
(5) Friedrich, Bruce. *Strategic Nonviolence in Perspective.* No Compromise: the militant, direct action newspaper of animal liberationists and their supporters. Issue 11. (Accessed online on July 2007.)
(6) News Releases. People for the Ethical Treatment of Animals. (Accessed online July 2007.)
(7) Telegraph.co.uk. 19 July 2001. (Accessed online July 2007.)
(8) Greek, Ray & Greek, Jean S. *Sacred Cows and Golden Geese: the human cost of animal experiments.* Continuum: New York, London. 2000.

Chapter	*The Law & Animal Rights*
5	*3. The Law - US & Britain*

Snappy Page Essence

When doing animal rights you may wish to know a bit about what law enforcement agents might come down on you. However, virtually all animal rights activists have nothing to worry about.

Might you run foul of the law? When doing practical animal rights you would do well to know a bit about what you may be up against.

United States

One of the Federal Bureau of Investigation's (FBI) ten top priorities is to "protect the United States from terrorist attack." You would think this applies to Al Qa'eda, Hamas and Hezbollah. It does, but the FBI apply it equally to investigating and preventing animal rights extremists and 'eco-terrorists' from operating in the US.

The deputy assistant director of the Counter Terrorism Division of the FBI said in testimony before the Senate Committee on Environment and Public Works in 2005 that 'animal rights extremists' and 'eco-terrorists' are "one of today's most serious domestic terrorism threats" (1). A threat is posed in particular, they say, by the Animal Liberation Front (ALF), the Earth Liberation Front (ELF) and Stop Huntingdon Animal Cruelty (SHAC). The FBI sees these groups as 'special interest extremist movements'. The FBI say that from January 1990 to June 2004 these extremists claimed over 1,200 events causing the loss of millions of dollars.

You might, however, be sceptical about the FBI matching animal rights and eco extremists with callous and fanatical international terrorist killers. But the FBI say that extremists such as these use direct action (see Chapter 3: Direct Action) against individuals and companies and define direct action as "often criminal activity" that damages property or causes economic loss to business interests or other concerns. The FBI say they only get involved when "volatile talk turns into criminal activity" and have no interest in activists who debate issues and labour to change policies by peaceful means. The FBI stand alone, however, as the only US law enforcing agency to classify animal activists as terrorists.

FBI vs Extremists

This is how the FBI sees animal rights extremists. Animal rights extremists are organised as small groups of one or more individuals who carry out actions. They keep rigid security procedures and generally act entirely independently and separately from each other so that discovering them and planting informers is difficult. Common targets of extremists range from fur farms to restaurants and include research institutions and the pharmaceutical and cosmetics industries. Their methods of attack include animal releases, phone call harassment, making personal threats to individuals, paint spraying and damaging property, theft, arson, bomb attacks and occupation of premises. They incite illegal activities on their web sites and post targets and instructions for making incendiaries on the Internet. None of this has endangered human life, but the FBI believes this may change and their web site quotes a threat from an extremist threatening to kill people.

The FBI try to "detect, disrupt and dismantle" animal rights and eco activists engaged in illegal pursuits. They bring together intelligence analysts, program managers, agents in the field, locally and federally, engage over a hundred 'Joint Terrorism Task Forces' and liase with law enforcement agencies internationally. The FBI offered a reward of up to $30,000 for information leading to the arrest of animal rights extremists for attempted arson in Los Angeles. Some prosecutions of extremists in recent years have been for releasing fur farm animals, attempted firebombing and arson. The FBI arrested a number of SHAC activists for attacking the New Jersey branch of Huntingdon Life Sciences and in 2006 a federal judge sentenced six activists from four to six years imprisonment.

Why has the FBI come down so heavily on animal rights and eco extremists? Part of the reason is because the Bush administration strengthened American law with various Acts relating to domestic extremism (ie 'terrorism'). One law in particular is the Patriot Act. The Patriot Act became law in 2001 and provides US law enforcement agencies with greatly strengthened powers for countering terrorism. By broadening the official interpretation of terrorism to include 'domestic terrorism' the Act managed to ensnare animal rights extremists. For such an important Act, it was rushed through the normal law making procedures in record time in the wake of the 9/11 attack on America and an increasing number of people are criticising it as an attack on American civil liberties.

Britain

The National Extremism Tactical Coordination Unit (NETCU) was set up by the British Government in 2004 and is staffed by police officers to deal with domestic extremism, specifically to protect research and business. NETCU define extremists as the "small minority of campaigners who seek to further their cause by committing criminal offences" and are often associated with single issue campaigns, like animal rights, anti-war protestation, anti-globalisation and anti-genetically modified crop production.

NETCU essentially focus on animal rights extremists and define this extremism as "Any unlawful or, if not actually unlawful, recognisably anti-social act, motivated by an intention to disrupt lawful business or to intimidate, perceived by any party involved to be rooted in opposition to the perceived exploitation of animals." Examples include abusive language, threatening behaviour, mass trespass, and damage to property. (2)

NETCU is headed by a National Co-ordinator for Domestic Extremism and is one of a number of bodies policing domestic extremism in Britain. The organisation advises and operates with other national law enforcement bodies and with counterparts in Europe and the US (especially the FBI), working with them on investigations and exchanging intelligence and expertise. NETCU also liase with industry, business companies, academic institutions and the Government, providing them with advice and information about countering domestic extremism and associated illegal activities.

Extremist Tactics
NETCU say there is a pattern of animal rights extremist tactics that intensifies over time. The tactics themselves reach out beyond their 'primary targets', such as animal experimenters and their institutions, to strike at confederate companies or 'secondary targets', such as their suppliers, industry contractors and other service providers, and even shareholders of these companies. They also picket the employees and families of confederate companies, even their friends and neighbours. (See Direct Action, Chapter 3, under Stop Huntingdon Animal Cruelty.)

• Stage One
Extremists may politely write, phone and visit their primary targets asking them to stop their activity. They do the same with their secondary targets, asking them to stop trading with the primary target. They may also publish the names of their targets on the Web and demonstrate outside their homes.

• Stage Two
Contact is the same but this time abusive or threatening. Extremists trespass on the company's property to disrupt the company's work. They gather information about the company's clients (such as by bribing staff or stealing documents) to identify secondary targets. They photograph the company's

staff and staff cars, demonstrate outside staff homes and make threats against staff on their web site.

- Stage Three

Extremists damage and vandalise property at their target company's staff homes. They harass and are abusive to staff members, their families, friends and neighbours. And they try to harm the reputation of individual members of staff.

Establishment Fights Back

One of the primary weapons directed against animal rights extremists in Britain is judicial injunctions or anti-social behaviour orders issued by a court of law. These state specific places activists must not enter or defined activities that individuals or groups must not do. Activists breaching an injunction served on them may be arrested and land up in prison.

At times in their zeal the police have over-acted. A case in point was in 2006 when the Law Lords ruled that the police had violated the right of citizens the freedom to protest when they blocked a group of people from travelling by coach to an anti-war demonstration. But most often it is not the police but activists who get into trouble. Through 2006 and 2007 a number of animal rights activists were:

- Found guilty of mailing indecent articles by post.
- Convicted of sending dead animals to companies.
- Jailed for conspiring to damage an animal research company.
- Jailed for trying to firebomb a house.
- Charged relating to improvised postal bombs.
- Charged with blackmail.
- Jailed for intimidation.
- Jailed for sending threatening letters.
- Sentenced for burglary.
- Fined for breaching an injunction.
- Jailed for breaching an anti-social behaviour order.
- Sentenced after an activist's DNA matched threatening letters sent more than two years earlier.
- Jailed (three activists) from four to twelve year for desecrating a grave and kidnapping its corpse.

Thus the law does not favour illegal (or even 'anti-social') animal rights activists. But nor does it favour anti-animal rights activists. In 2006 the police cautioned an Oxford University student for sending a malicious email to animal rights activists.

For a discussion about breaking the law, see Violence or Nonviolence? in Chapter 5.

References
(1)   Federal Bureau of Investigation. www.fbi.gov. (Accessed May 2007.)
(2)   NETCU. www.nectu.org.uk. (Accessed May 2007.)

Chapter	*The Law & Animal Rights*
5	*4. Police Arrest*

Snappy Page Essence
Almost all animal rights activists are never arrested by the police. However, if the police do arrest you it is well to know what to expect and what you can do. Gen up here.

Be Prepared

Most people do not want to be arrested by the police and by far the majority of animal rights activists never are. But people who try to change society by using direct action run the risk of arrest. You may even want to be arrested as part of your strategy, if you carry out an open rescue or similar action, to challenge the establishment and send your message to the public with greater impact (see Chapter 4: Animal Rescuer). One way or the other, the prospect of arrest can be emotionally disagreeable, so prepare yourself by knowing what to expect.

The following account is generalised for English speaking countries. But laws vary locally and from one country to another; they also change from time to time. So before going animal-active you may wish to find out which laws you might conceivably breach that are applicable to you and in what circumstances you could be arrested. Some common charges brought by police against animal rights activists concern offensive behaviour, intimidation, affray, obstructing public access, obstructing the police, trespass and property damage, and you might brush up against any of these charges at some point in a civil rights or animal rights campaign.

Should you think that you could be arrested you must get professional advice for your location. Remember that in the criminal justice system of the English speaking countries you are innocent until proven guilty.

In the Street & At Your Door

The police can detain you when you are out and about. They might search your clothing and bags if they suspect you of breaking the law. Should you be in a car when they stop you they might search that too. On finding nothing some police will let you go and give you a receipt with their identification number and the circumstances of the encounter. If they do not give you a receipt make a note of their identity numbers and the circumstances in case you need the information later; you may want to make a complaint if the police were unreasonable and will need the information. After the police have searched you, ask them whether you are free to go and leave if you are. If you are not free to go, they might continue to detain you for a while or arrest you. In a serious incident you would do well to find witnesses. After the incident find a lawyer and see a doctor for a physical examination if you were injured.

Perhaps the police have been given information about you, think you may be dangerous, and intend to arrest you. They might then arrive at your home in the early hours of the morning. That is the most likely place to find and nab you, while you are sleepy before you can run, assuming you might do a quick departure. The police may search you, but they do not have the right to search your house unless they first obtain a search warrant.

At the Police Station

At the police station the police should tell you the reason for your arrest, if they had not already done so when they arrested you. Depending on the country you are in, you may be obliged to give your name and address, they may remove your personal belonging, and take your fingerprints, saliva swab and photograph. You may then be shown to a cell where you have to wait.

You may have to wait a long time in the cell but the police cannot detain you for more than a certain period without charging you with an offence. Being charged with an offence means that you will have to appear in court. The period of waiting in the cell could be 24 hours or longer (some say the police make you wait to 'soften you up'). Eventually they will get round to interviewing you. After the interview they will charge you with an offence or say you can leave without you being charged. Either way you should soon be out of the police station and home again.

Your Tactics

Go along with the police when arrested. Use force and they will subdue you. Resisting arrest can be a crime and look bad for you, even if you are innocent and wrongly arrested. Your best tactic is to be civil and co-operative as far as possible.

At the police station, phone a dependable family member, friend or colleague who can help you. Let them know the police have arrested you and tell them the name of the police station where you are being held. The police should allow you to do this. Keep the phone call to the point as they will not let you talk for long.

You may be emotionally upset so calm down and try to relax. Speak to the officer assigned to look after your welfare (you should have one). Ask for a drink, the toilet, medication or anything else you need. Do not rush. You will probably not feel up to it but ask for pen and paper and make notes of what is happening and the identities of the officers involved with you. Do not rely on memory alone; details can fade and blur in the confusion of your situation and with the passage of time.

Know Your Rights

While being interviewed at the police station bear in mind that the police may not have enough evidence against you and might rely on you to incriminate yourself. Do not allow your situation to frighten you into admitting anything. You can best do this by knowing your legal rights. You always have legal rights although they may vary from one country to another. Among your rights at the police station you may be able to:

- Know why you have been arrested and the charge against you.
- Inform someone you know about your arrest.
- Have a lawyer present and to consult with privately.
- Speak to the officer in charge of your welfare.
- Be treated respectfully and humanely by the police.

Two of your most important legal rights are to remain silent and to have a lawyer present.

Remaining Silent

You have the right in some countries not to answer questions put by the police. In the United States, under the Fifth Amendment of the US Constitution, citizens and non-citizens have the right to remain silent whether questioned by the police or other government agency (eg FBI). However, in certain US states you have to give your name and address, although not anything else.

After arrest by the police in Britain you used to have a right to silence, but not anymore. You must state your name and address. However, refusing to answer other questions is not a crime as such and the police cannot force you to speak. So do not be intimidated that your silence might be held against you if you have the prospect of going to court.

Be careful when you do say something, even if you are innocent and think you have nothing to fear. Do not let any deception or apparent friendliness by the police loosen your tongue. It is always better to remain silent rather than lie, which can go against you, innocent or not.

During the interview the police may take written notes or use a tape recorder. You may be able to see these notes or a transcript of the recording. But do not sign anything unless they describe your situation correctly and if your lawyer says you should sign. The same applies to signing anything, written by you or provided by the police. The exception is a receipt for your possessions and whatever your lawyer okays.

Having a Lawyer Present

You have the right to have a lawyer present in person at the police station and should be allowed to phone one. Tell the police you will say nothing unless you are advised by your lawyer and then only answer through him. Be honest and straightforward with your lawyer. Having a lawyer present is not an indication of guilt. A lawyer is for you to use to protect your legal rights.

Your lawyer should advise you on what to answer and when to stay quiet. Even if you have nothing to hide, what you say could be misinterpreted, even distorted by someone and held against you. When you reply to questions only state what you are certain about.

Do not worry about taking a long time to find a lawyer. You might try finding one through an animal rights organisation, your trade union or professional association, or a Citizens Advice Bureau. If you cannot fix yourself up with one you might get a lawyer on duty at the police station to represent you. In some circumstances your lawyer could be free.

Suing the Police

The police sometimes act outside their legal powers and if this happens with you then you could sue them. A common claim people bring against the police is wrongful arrest and detention for an act they did not commit. Assault by the police is another common claim. You will likely need evidence and witnesses to support your claim. Perhaps you can get free legal aid if you are unemployed or on a low income. On winning your case you will get financial compensation. Lose your case and you may have to pay the costs of your legal suite including the costs the police bore.

Bear in mind that law courts do not dispense justice; they dish out the law! Sometimes justice and the law coincide, but not always. So you must seek advice about your *legal* standing from a good lawyer - no matter how just you think your case!

Chapter	*Assorted Animal Rights Activists*
6	*1. Steven Best (b 1955)*

Steven Best's critics brand him as an American militant animal rights activist on the extreme fringe and a spokesman for terrorists. More sympathetic people describe him as an associate professor of philosophy at the University of Texas, El Paso, and a scholarly, although outspoken, voice on animal rights.

After leaving school Best drove trucks and worked in factories for some years. Then after studying film and theatre he took degrees in philosophy and joined the staff at Texas University. In 2002 his colleagues recognised his talents by appointing him to the chair of the philosophy department. But after three years of ups and downs they unseated him after a vote of no confidence. Best claims this academic reversal was because of his animal rights activism, an assertion his colleagues reject.

The road to animal liberation began for Best one day in his mid-twenties. While eating a burger at a fast food restaurant he was smitten by a revelation. He made the connection between what he was eating and animals; he converted to veganism. Revelation struck again a few years later while reading Peter Singer's book Animal Liberation. Best was already a human rights activist and now he became an animal rights activist. By working for animals, he says, he is also working for humans.

Best is a controversial figure partly because of his involvement with the British originated Animal Liberation Front (ALF). ALF, for its hundreds of actions to rescue animals and destroy the property of companies that harm animals, is often denounced as a terrorist group by the news media and government bodies (such as the FBI and the US Department of Homeland Security). So when Best co-founded the North American Animal Liberation Press Office in 2004 he was a marked man. As for his academic career, he accepts that in a conservative, conformist academic world his open support for ALF will retard his prospects. But he insists that academics must speak out and that it is time to show support for ALF.

Best says he supports ALF because of their effective and fair methods of the real terrorists - the people who violate and kill animals. Best professes he is not an ALF activist and that his ALF press office simply gives information on ALF activities. But he believes that educating the public and legislating for animal friendly laws cannot by themselves succeed in abolishing animal abuse. Animal activists, he says, must attack the animal abusers directly. For justification he cites the human slavery abolitionists' attacks on slave traders in the 18th and 19th centuries.

So Best was surprised one day in 2005 by a Home Office notification that he was banned from entering Britain. Best had been arranging a trip to Britain to address an animal rights meeting marking the effective campaign to shut down a farm that had been breeding guinea pigs for experiments on animals. Apparently, the Secretary of State, on the strength of newspaper reports, had listed Best as an advocate of violence and terrorism and therefore as a threat to 'public order'. The ban was part of the British government's action to control extremists and terrorists as a result of the 9/11 terrorist attack on the US. After considering an appeal by Best, however, the Home Office rescinded and let him in - but still banned his fellow animal activist colleagues from entering Britain. To Best's knowledge this was the first time anyone from the US had been prevented from entering another country for advocating animal rights.

Steven Best is a philosophy professor who lives with his rescued cats, but his objective is revolutionary politics. He intends to annihilate social injustice and humanity's lethal control over animals and nature that are, Best says, intrinsic to capitalism and civilization. He wants to wake people to action and motivate them to transform the world into a true democratic, libertarian and socialist society. Best says:

> "I always prefer a conversation to a war, but we are in a battlefield not at a bargaining table." (1)

However, one critic replies:

"What makes Best a caricature rather than a serious dissident is not his intellectual vapidity, colossal as it may be, but his unwillingness to distinguish between the life of a human and that of a rodent." (2)

Some of Best's animal liberation books are: Terrorists or Freedom Fighters? (editor, with Anthony J Nocella Jr), 2004; Animal Rights and Moral Progress, 2006; and Igniting a Revolution, (editor, with Anthony J Nocella Jr), 2006.

Reference

(1) *The Epiphanies of Dr Steven Best.* Claudette Vaughn. Vegan Voice. 2004. (Accessed February 2007.)
(2) Staff Editorial, *The Daily Iowan*, January 2005. (Accessed February 2007.)

Other Sources

- *Igniting a Revolution: Voices in Defense of Mother Earth.* Claudette Vaughan. Abolitionist Online. 2005. (Accessed February 2007.)

Chapter	*Assorted Animal Rights Activists*
6	*2. John Lawrence (1753 - 1839)*

Lawrence is one of the earliest writers in modern times on animal rights and welfare. His book published in 1796, *A Philosophical and Practical Treatise on Horses, and on the Moral Duties of Man Towards the Brute Creation* (1), is a detailed account on horsemanship and the horse. It is remarkable for its day for a chapter entitled *On the Right of Beasts*, in which Lawrence implores us to treat animals kindly and with consideration because they are rational, sensible and have souls. Lawrence argued that animals have rights, a basic right of care, which should be endorse by the state.

Lawrence recounts wanton cruelty he saw around him - horses thrashed with whips, cattle with tongues cut out and sheep with feet cut off (all alive) - and says,

> "I therefore propose, that the Rights of Beasts be formally acknowledged by the state, and that a law be framed upon that principle, to guard and protect them from acts of flagrant and wanton cruelty, whether committed by their owners or others." (2)

Lawrence also expresses that the state should enact laws to protect livestock during transportation and slaughter - anticipating Martin's Act passed by Parliament in 1822 and the first law by a state to give a measure of protection to domesticated animals (see Richard Martin, in Chapter 6).

Lawrence declared that wilful cruelty, as well as vivisection, should be outlawed and he opposed animal baiting. Yet he favoured killing animals for sport - as long as they were subsequently eaten. He also supported fox hunting, in the belief that foxes are vermin, and deserve as predators to be hunted and killed in turn. (But then who should hunt and kill the human predators, or are humans exempt from this logic?) His acquisition of a small farm and his interest in poultry might have influenced his attitude to hunting.

Very little is known about his life, but he was born in England where he lived and was descended from a line of brewers. For more about Lawrence see the entry Lawrence, John in the Oxford Dictionary of National Biography (3).

References

(1) Lawrence, John. *A Philosophical and Practical Treatise on Horses, and on the Moral Duties of Man Towards the Brute Creation.* T Longman: London. 1796.

(2) Op cit. volume 1, chapter 3, page 123.

(3) Mitchell, Sebastian: *Lawrence, John.* Oxford Dictionary of National Biography. Oxford University Press: Oxford.

Chapter	*Assorted Animal Rights Activists*
6	*3. Richard Martin (1754 - 1834)*

Martin was an Irish politician and an animal and human rights activist. Animal welfarists remember him especially for pioneering legislation through the United Kingdom parliament to outlaw cruelty to animals. They also honour him as a leading founder of the Royal Society for the Prevention of Cruelty to Animals (RSPCA). Founded in 1824 the RSPCA was the modern world's first animal welfare organisation. The RSPCA inspired other countries to establish similar societies, such as the American Society for the Prevention of Cruelty to Animals, set up in 1866.

Martin had a reputation for being extraordinarily kind hearted to people and animals, earning the nickname Humanity Dick. He was a keen duellist and considered as one of the best exponents of duelling in Ireland. When an unbalanced bully, George Robert FitzGerald, killed a dog, Martin challenged him to a shoot-out and they wounded each other. When asked why he defended animals so utterly, Martin is said to have encapsulated his passion for duelling and his concern for animals with the explanation: "Sir, an ox cannot hold a pistol!" The law later hanged FitzGerald for another offence.

When aged 22 Martin became a member of the Irish Parliament. But when the Act of Union dissolved the Irish Parliament about 1800 he took a seat as a member in the United Kingdom parliament, representing County Galway, where he was born.

Martin fought for social reform on many fronts, including emancipation for Catholics, abolition of the death penalty for convicted forgers and freedom for slaves. But he is remembered in particular for the legislation, popularly called Martin's Act, or the Cruel Treatment of Cattle Act, that, with the help of others, he drove through Parliament. Martin's Act banned the ill treatment of equines, cattle and sheep. Martin's Act was the first parliamentary law by any country to proscribe cruelty to animals.

Extract from the Cruel Treatment of Cattle Act 1822, also known as Martin's Act:

> "...if any person or persons shall wantonly and cruelly beat, abuse, or ill-treat any Horse, Mare, Gelding, Mule, Ass, Ox, Cow, Heifer, Steer, Sheep, or other Cattle...and if the party or parties accused shall be convicted of any such Offence...he, she, or they so convicted shall forfeit and pay any Sum not exceeding Five Pounds, not less than Ten Shillings, to His Majesty...and if the person or persons so convicted shall refuse or not be able forthwith to pay the Sum forfeited, every such Offender shall...be committed to the House of Correction or some other Prison...for any Time not exceeding Three Months."

None of Martin's further attempts to introduce laws to protect animals succeeded, including bans on dog-fighting, cock-fighting and bull-baiting. Instead, people took to mocking his energetic prosecution of anyone ill-treating an animal. Alongside this, Martin was a sport hunter, hunting his estate of 9,000 ha (22,000 acres), a third of County Galway, that he inherited from his father. Many influential people who supported the RSPCA were also sport hunters or farmers, which is why the organisation floundered by largely excluding wild animals and farmed animals from its remit. The RSPCA did not begin to become a less ineffective humane society until over a 170 years later in the 1990's.

When Martin was 72 he fled Britain to Boulogne because of political intrigue and inheritance debts on his estate. The town was a busy French port and a popular resort for British expatriates and he died there a few years later. However, a year after his death, Martin's Act was finally enlarged to ban the fighting and baiting of animals. Martin's grave in Boulogne was bombed during the Second World War, so his bones were re-interred in the cemetery's ossuary. A marble plaque was erected there from RSPCA funds and in English and French it reads: "...he piloted...the first act to protect animals."

Chapter	*Assorted Animal Rights Activists*
6	*4. The McLibel Two*

The name McLibel epitomises the six year libel trial fought by two ordinary Londoners, Helen Steel (b 1965) and Dave Morris (b 1954), against the international, multi-billion dollar fast food giant McDonald's. The legal conflict exposed dubious practices of unrestrained big business and demonstrated the interconnectedness of animals, green issues and social justice.

London Greenpeace was a small group in 1980's London, Britain, campaigning for social justice (and no relation to Greenpeace). McDonald's, symbol of globalisation and the American lifestyle, epitomised for them much of what they were fighting to change. In 1986 they produced a leaflet accusing McDonald's of corrupt practices, including cruelty to animals, destruction of rainforests, exploitation of their staff and selling unhealthy food. Many groups worldwide were demonstrating against McDonald's but London Greenpeace brought all the issues together in the one leaflet: *What's Wrong With McDonald's* and distributed copies outside McDonald's restaurants in London.

McDonald's was spending millions of advertising dollars every year convincing people to eat their junk food. They threatened or sued everyone who criticised them, no matter who they were, whether national corporations, the press or individuals, and almost everyone backed down from this giant. McDonald's could not sue London Greenpeace as it was only an association of individuals, so they pick five activists and told them to apologise or appear in court.

Three activists recanted but Helen Steel, sometime gardener and nightclub bar worker, and Dave Morris, sometime London postman, stood firm.

Consequently in 1990 McDonald's served libel writs on them - even though both denied distributing the offending leaflet. Steel and Morris were unwaged at the time of the trial and could not afford a lawyer. But despite being naive of libel law and court procedures they decided to fight the case themselves. Their moral claim was to defend the right to criticise and scrutinise multinational companies. Fortunately, pre-trial hearings gave Steel and Morris valuable experience with court procedures and they had free but sporadic advice from sympathetic lawyers. McDonald's engaged the best professional team of lawyers they could buy.

The trial proper began in 1994 at the Royal Courts of Justice in London. A witty reporter called the case the McLibel Trial, a nickname that stuck, and Steel and Morris were dabbed the *McLibel Two*. Keeping everything going was an ordeal for the Two. A typical day started at seven or earlier in the morning to get ready for the day's proceedings, such as preparing questions to put to witnesses. Once home from court, preparations continued up to midnight for the following day. All this was on top of looking after their mundane domestic affairs, whereas the McDonald's team of lawyers had partners at home and office staff to help them.

What gave the McLibel Two the strength to keep going was the thought that the case was not a personal struggle between them and McDonald's, but a campaign for justice against a multinational company trampling over people, animals and nature. Encouraging letters from a well-wishing public and £40,000 in donations and other support lifted their spirits. The 'McLibel Support Campaign' held a march for free speech and questions were asked in Parliament opposing the use of libel writs by big companies to silence critics.

In one of the several legal machinations, McDonald's council succeeded in discharging the jury, which might have proved hostile to McDonald's, on grounds that its members were ordinary people who would not understand the scientific evidence. But Steel and Morris petitioned the House of Lords, the highest court in Britain, and the jury was reinstated. After all, the McLibel Two were ordinary people and if they could understand the evidence then a jury should be able to understand it as well.

Everyone thought the trial would take only a few months, but it ran for six years turning into the longest trail in British legal history (and subsequent legal battles continued for several more years until 2005). Finally, the judge reached a verdict. Steel and Morris were guilty of libelling McDonald's and had to pay them £60,000 in damages (later cut by a third). Damages were relatively light because the judge upheld some of the allegations against McDonald's, such as causing animal suffering, exploiting children through advertising, and misleading the public about their food's goodness. Steel and Morris swore never to pay McDonald's. McDonald's chose not to force them to pay - possibly with public relations in mind.

The McLibel Trial was a moral victory for the McLibel Two and the biggest public relations blunder in the history of business for McDonald's. McDonald's became a symbol of corporate badness using animals, nature and people merely as means to make a profit. The McLibel Trial received worldwide coverage in the news media for the right of ordinary people to freedom of speech against powerful multi-nationals. As Dave Morris said:

> "The reality is that McDonald's itself is a completely nondescript, money-making organisation, full of hot air - without advertising it would be nothing." (1)

References
(1) *Dave Morris.* One-Off Productions. 1996. (Accessed online February 2007.)

Other Sources
Helen Steel. One-Off Productions. 1997. (Accessed online February 2007.)

Chapter	*Assorted Animal Rights Activists*
6	*5. Andrew Linzey (b 1952)*

Andrew Linzey is an Anglican priest, theologian, Oxford academic, and a rare champion for animal rights within the Christian Church. He and his work are described in Chapter 4: Preacher, under the heading *Animal Preachers Past & Present*.

Chapter	*Assorted Animal Rights Activists*
6	*6. Ingrid Newkirk (b 1949)*

Newkirk is an animal rights activist - sometimes militantly, arrested over 20 times - and co-founder and president of People for the Ethical Treatment of Animals (PETA), said to be the world's largest and most prominent animal rights organisation.

Born in Britain, schooled and brought up in India an only child, insatiable animal eater, by age 19 she owned her own fur coat (squirrel). Her adult life was spent in the eastern United States where she became aware of animal suffering after taking some cats to a shelter thinking they would be cared for. They were killed instead. A career change led her to become a deputy sheriff handling cases of animal cruelty. After sliding towards vegetarianism for some years she finally committed herself one day when (with a pork chop scheduled for supper) she saved a starving pig, the only survivor of animals abandoned at a farm. But Newkirk is no namby-pamby; she was also a poundmaster, which means she had to kill hundreds of stray animals.

Then she met Alex Pacheco, a volunteer at the animal shelter where Newkirk was working. Pacheco was a university student and already an established animal rights activist (see Undercover Investigator, Chapter 4). He gave her a copy of Peter Singer's book Animal Liberation. Singer's book and Newkirk's work with animals coalesced and she and Pacheco founded PETA in 1980 working from her home in suburban Maryland. Dedicated to establishing and defending animal rights, their goal was to influence as many people they could about animal suffering. That is still PETA's goal today, now based in Norfolk, Virginia, with over a million members, hundreds of staff and affiliates abroad. After many years of dedicated work, Pacheco left PETA to explore new areas of animal rights.

PETA and the personality of Newkirk become synonymous. As president of PETA Newkirk speaks internationally on animal rights issues. She believes that animals are sentient, have intrinsic value and deserve equal consideration of interests with humans. Controversially, Newkirk compares humanity's treatment of animals with the Holocaust (see The Animal Holocaust, Chapter 1).

PETA focuses on a number of areas but primarily on factory farms, laboratory animals, animals in the clothing trade and in the entertainment industry, because, as Newkirk says, these areas have the greatest numbers of animals who suffer the most for the longest time. Newkirk herself is a board member or supporter of a number of animal rights organisations, such as EarthSave International and United Poultry Concerns. She also openly supports the Animal Liberation Front (ALF), often branded by detractors and news media reports as a 'terrorist' group (see Terrorism, Chapter 5). This and other activities have brought her to the attention of the FBI.

Newkirk's method is to outrage and repel people. She says PETA is the biggest animal rights group because it succeeds in getting attention by doing outrageous things. As an outrage directed to herself, and to remind us of what humanity is doing to animals, she directed in her will for some of her skin to be barbecued and eaten, other parts of her skin to be made into leather goods, and her feet should be scooped out and turned into umbrella stands (after elephants).

Critics of Newkirk claim she made PETA a lean radical abolitionist group but then let it degenerate into welfare. Newkirk responds by saying that PETA is abolitionist but on the way to abolition if you can ease the suffering of animals then you should not turn your back on them (see new welfarism in Comparing Animal Philosophies, Chapter 3). Newkirk says:

> "The opportunities for activism are all there and I believe every single part is vital, because all the spokes in the wheel are needed in order for the wheel to go around." (1)

Newkirk has written Kids Can Save the Animals: 101 easy things to do (1991); You Can Save the Animals: 251 simple ways to stop thoughtless cruelty (1999); 250 Things You Can Do to Make Your Cat Adore You (1998); Free the Animals: the story of the animal liberation front (2000); Making Kind Choices: everyday ways to enhance your life through earth and animal friendly living (2005).

References
(1)   Ingrid Newkirk by Catherine Clyne. Satya. 2000. (Feb 2007).

Other Sources
* *Ingrid Newkirk - taking on the critics.* Animal Liberation NSW, 2001
* *We're stunt queens. We have to be.* Gary Younge. Guardian. 24 Feb 2006.

Chapter	*Assorted Animal Rights Activists*
6	*7. Jill Phipps (1964 - 1995)*

Jill Phipps was a British animal rights activist and veteran campaigner for animals. She was crushed under the wheels of a truck during a protest to stop the live export of calves. The calves were being transported to Coventry Airport in England for export to Amsterdam and thence to farms across Europe to make veal. Protesters gathered outside the airport. Phipps and a few protesters broke through a police cordon with the intention of slowing one of the trucks by chaining themselves to it. Phipps was caught under a truck and her spine snapped.

Protesters had frequently burst through police lines on earlier days, but this day something went wrong. For lack of evidence the truck driver was not charged with manslaughter. Jill Phipps' family blame the police for keeping the transporters moving. Her mother said, "Whatever happened they were determined to keep the convoys going. They had no contingency plan for people running into the road." (*The Guardian.* 5 February 2005.)

Phipps' death evoked widespread public sympathy and stirred fellow activists' resolve to keep up their protest against live animal exports. The exports from the airport eventually stopped when the aviation freight company went bankrupt.

The plaque on Jill Phipps' grave reads 'Died as she lived fearlessly fighting for animals.' Her memorial web site states "Jill is not a martyr, she is a hero and her actions will inspire and give courage to everyone who knew her and to many thousands of people who never met her."

For more about live animal exports, see The Battle of Brightlingsea, in Direct Action, Chapter 6.

Chapter	Assorted Animal Rights Activists
6	8. Henry Salt (1851 - 1939)

Henry Stephens Salt wrote the first book entirely devoted to animal rights, published in 1892: *Animals' Rights: considered in relation to social progress* (1). He sought to impress people not to kill or eat animals and submitted that such behaviour is the distinction of a civilised society:

> "...it is ourselves, our own vital instincts, that we wrong, when we trample on the rights of the fellow-beings, human or animal, over whom we chance to hold jurisdiction."

Salt was a British social campaigner, writer, naturalist, prominent anti-vivisectionist and vegetarian. He was born in India and educated in England. After attending Cambridge University he taught classics at Eton preparatory school but left to adopt a vegetarian life-style growing vegetables at a remote country cottage while writing for a living.

Salt believed animals should be free to live their own lives and that humanity has a responsibility to treat them compassionately and justly. His animal rights book influenced Gandhi (1869 - 1948), political and spiritual leader of India and advocate of vegetarianism and of non-violent protest.

Salt's social reform interests included schools, prisons, criminal law, flogging in the Royal Navy, vivisection and food-animal slaughter. In 1891 he founded and was general secretary of the Humanitarian League that opposed, on grounds of ethics and good social science, the infliction of avoidable suffering on any sentient being whether man or beast. Among the League's aims was better protection for wild and domesticated animals, abolition of corporal punishment and the death penalty, and opposition to vivisection, the fur and feather trade and hunting for sport (such as fox hunting with hounds).

Among his books are A Plea for Vegetarianism (1886), The New Charter, a Discussion of the Rights of Men and the Rights of Animals (1896), The Logic of Vegetarianism (1899) and Our Vanishing Wildflowers (1928).

References

(1) Salt, Henry Stephens. *Animals' Rights: considered in relation to social progress.* Macmillan: New York. 1892. Reprinted 1980.

Chapter	*Assorted Animal Rights Activists*
6	*9. Henry Spira (1927 - 1998)*

"Their suffering is intense, widespread, expanding, systematic and socially sanctioned. And the victims are unable to organize in defence of their own interests." Henry Spira (1)

Henry Spira is celebrated for his animal liberation campaigns and winning strategies. His friend and colleague Peter Singer (see Chapter 6, Peter Singer) said of him, "Henry Spira was the most effective activist of the modern animal rights movement" and wrote his biography as a tribute and to show people how to action animal liberation: *Ethics into Action: Henry Spira and the animal rights movement*. (2)

Spira was born in Belgium and his family settled in New York City when he was 13 to escape Nazi persecution of Jews. He served in the American army, worked on a car assembly line, and taught at a New York college. But his main occupation from age 16 was seafaring in the American merchant marine. As a seaman he fought for human rights against the then crooked and ruthless American maritime union and was thrown out of the navy for his troubles. While active in civil rights he even crossed the FBI, who put him under surveillance.

Only when Spira reached his forties did he become animal-oriented after someone gave him a cat to look after. Contemplating his feline companion Spira asked himself why people took care of some animals while sticking a fork in others. Just then he happened on an article, *Animal Liberation*, in the New York Review of Books (1973). It was written by Peter Singer - a philosopher and animal rights writer Spira had never heard of - but the article inspired him to attend Singer's lectures. As Spira later wrote, "Singer made an enormous impression on me because his concern for other animals was rational and defensible in public debate. It did not depend on sentimentality..." (1)

Spira was more pragmatic than philosophical, as getting things done was foremost to him. His tactics were to set a relatively small feasible goal, assemble activists with diverse contributing expertise, study the problem from all angles, especially from his opponent's point of view, and enter into constructive discussion with his adversary whenever possible. Then, when Spira was prepared, he submitted his target to a sustained campaign until he won.

Spira was a highly effective animal liberation activist yet he was personally modest. He did not seek status or money for himself and worked for animals from his cluttered New York City flat. He elected to go without the staffing and financing of the big regular animal protection organisations. Although honoured by prestigious organisations he shut away all his awards in a cupboard.

Spira's first big battle for animals started in 1976 with New York City's Museum of Natural History. The Museum's laboratory was experimenting on cats, apparently to learn about sexual behaviour, but according to Spira it was simply mutilating them. His group kept up a campaign of pressure on the Museum to stop the research. Finally, a year later and after much publicity, the laboratory closed. The campaign was acclaimed as the first American victory for animals against vivisection.

Building on that experience he took on Revlon, the cosmetic industry giant, and their Draize test. The test supposedly evaluates the safety of commercial preparations for humans by dripping drops of the substances onto the eyes of rabbits who are held down in racks. A highlight of the campaign was a full-page newspaper advert, one of many in Spira's animal liberation career, placed in the New York Times exclaiming "How Many Rabbits Does Revlon Blind for Beauty's Sake?" Eventually Revlon admitted their error and opened a fund of hundreds of thousands of dollars to explore alternatives to the Draize test. Other cosmetics companies chipped in so as to look good. Thanks to Spira, the better cosmetics companies now print "not tested on animals" on their products.

Spira took on other seemingly inflexible corporations, including Avon, Procter & Gamble, and the poultry and fast food industries. He also attacked the United States Department of Agriculture, exposing their branding of cattle's faces with red hot irons; the Department dropped its branding soon afterwards. And he took on the slaughterhouses, ending the practice of hoisting conscious cattle into the air by a leg to await slaughter.

Spira's campaigns put on the political agenda cosmetics testing and cruelty to food-animals. His victories were the first big successes of the American animal rights movement to reduce the suffering that humans inflict on animals.

References

(1) Spira, Henry. Fighting to Win. In: *In Defense of Animals*. Peter Singer (editor). 1985:194 - 208.
(2) Singer, Peter. *Ethics into Action: Henry Spira and the animal rights movement*. Rowman and Littlefield. 1998.

Chapter	*Assorted Animal Rights Activists*
6	*10. Three Philosophers:* *Tom Regan (b 1938)* *Richard Ryder (b 1940)* *Peter Singer (b 1946)*

"All animals are somebody - someone with a life of their own." Tom Regan (1)

Tom Regan

Among Tom Regan many books is *The Case for Animal Rights* (1983). Translated into several languages it made him a public name. Regan, an American advocate for animal rights and an emeritus professor of philosophy, asserts that animals have intrinsic value (a value in themselves without reference to human needs) because they have feelings, beliefs, preferences, memories, expectations, and so on. He calls animals with such features "subjects of a life" because "what happens to them matters to them." He says "All animals are somebody - someone with a life of their own. Behind those eyes is a story, the story of their life in their world as they experience it." (1) Regan sees the animal rights movement as part of the human rights movement and maintains that animals who are a subject of a life should have the same rights to life as humans.

Regan's position clashes with his contemporary, Peter Singer (see below). Singer argues that subjective human preferences can occasionally outweigh the interests of animals. To avoid this, Regan counters that it is better that animal rights are based on intrinsic value. Regan says this will thwart people putting their own interests before animals whenever it suits them, prevent exploitation of individual animals for the greater good (of humans), and stop morality being an exclusively human club.

Among Regan's books on animal ethics are: All That Dwell Therein: essays on animal Rights and environmental ethics (1982); The Case for Animal Rights (1983); Defending Animal Rights (2001); and Empty Cages: facing the challenge of animal rights (2004).

Richard Ryder

Richard Dudley Ryder, British animal ethics philosopher and animal welfare campaigner, was a psychologist who experimented on animals but now speaks out for animal rights.

Ryder denounces Utilitarianism because it justifies the exploitation of some animals if there is a net gain in happiness for the majority of other animals (that is humans). Instead, he advocates his philosophy of Painism: that all animals who feel pain should be worthy of rights and that moral worth should be based on reducing the pain of individuals (for more see Painism, Chapter 8).

Ryder coined the term speciesism in the 1970's, popularised by Singer (below) in his book Animal Liberation, and coined painism in the 1990's to describe his ethical philosophy.

Ryder's books include Victims of Science (1975), on the use of animals in research; Animal Revolution (1989), on the recent history and development of animal rights; Painism (2001), on the moral theory of painism; and Putting Morality Back Into Politics (2006).

Peter Singer

Australian ethicist and professor of philosophy, Peter Albert David Singer, first took part in a public demonstration for animals in his twenties while at Oxford University. The protest was held in the street against factory farming and featured caged paper-mache hens and a stuffed calf in an imitation stall.

Peter Singer is widely credited with inaugurating the modern animal rights movement with his book, *Animal Liberation* (1975), which questions the human treatment of animals. It is the book for which he is most well-known to the public - its second edition was translated into over 17 languages, including Chinese, Korean and Hebrew. The book gave the animal rights movement a philosophical basis and, along with Singer's status as a reputable philosopher, awoke interest in academic circles setting off a chain reaction of thought and publications about animal ethics and animal liberation.

Singer believes that our treatment of animals is one of the foremost ethical issues of today. He says toleration for the mistreatment of animals is a prejudice that, like sexism and racism, does not have a rational basis, and failure to take into account animal suffering is to be guilty of speciesism.

Singer's ethical philosophy is practical, following Utilitarian principles: the best solution to a moral problem is the one with the best likely consequences for the majority concerned. Hence, you may be morally justified if you cause relatively little harm to a few beings to minimise a greater harm to more beings. Thus, you might experiment on (but not kill) some humans or animals to save the lives of many more humans or animals; but it would be wrong to kill or cause severe pain to the many to save a little distress to the few.

Although Singer argues in Animal Liberation that we should not give greater preference to the interests of humans over animals, he also argues that some individuals are more valuable than others and deserve higher priority in moral disputes. In Singer's view, a sentient animal, a subject of a life, like a rat, has a higher priority to life as he has more to lose than a non-sentient being, like a worm. Similarly, a being who is more sentient, like a chimpanzee, has more to lose than a being who is less sentient, like a rat.

Among his many activities, Singer is a founder member of the Great Ape Project that is trying to influence people to confer on the great apes the same basic rights as humans. And Singer sets an example to us all: he does not just lecture about ethics, he gives away a fifth of his income to good causes.

Singer's many books include: Practical Ethics (1979); Animal Factories, with James Mason (1980); The Expanding Circle (1981); In Defence of Animals, editor (1985); Applied Ethics, editor (1986); Ethics into Action: Henry Spira and the animal rights movement (1998); One World: ethics and globalization (22002); In Defense of Animals: the second wave, editor (2005); The Way We Eat: why our food choices matter, with Jim Mason (2006); and over 300 articles on ethics.

References
(1) *Giving Voice to Animal Rights*. The Satya Interview with Tom Regan, Kymberlie Adams Matthews. (Accessed February 2007.)

Chapter	*Numbers of Animals Raised*
7	*& Killed*

1. Summary

Here are estimates of the numbers of animals people eat, wear and experiment on worldwide. This is a limited selection because the kind of animals people use and their numbers people kill are vast and estimates are not always available.

Estimates of Some of the Consumption by Humans of Animals Annually Worldwide.	
	Annual Number or Mass
Chickens	50,000,000,000
Pigs	1,200,000,000
Sheep & Goats	500,000,000
Beef Cattle	300,000,000
Fish	132,000,000 tonnes
Meat Consumption	250,000,000 tonnes 40 kg per human
Fur-bearers	Farmed mink: 30,000,000+ Farmed fox: 5,000,000+ Wild fur-bearers: millions
Experimental Animals	41,000,000 to 100,000,000

Interpreting Statistics
Statistics always need interpreting with care. If you are not wary you may easily make mistakes and get a distorted view of what you are trying to find out, as the following two problems show.

- Total Counts vs Spot Counts

When interpreting animal statistics ask yourself whether they are about all the animals alive in the year or a count of all the animals alive on just one day of the year (for instance on 1st of January or 30th June). The latter kind of count is sometimes called a 'spot count' and often yields far fewer numbers. Sources of statistics do not always make clear which kind of figure they are using.

- Commercially Viable Numbers vs Absolute Numbers

Bear in mind when reading animal statistics whether they include only commercially viable adult animals or all animals - living and dead, young and old. A good example of this is chicken statistics. Half the number of egg-laying chickens is not recorded on official statistics because male chicks are eliminated soon after hatching (they are minced up to make fertiliser and pet food). To get the real number of chickens in the egg-laying industry (as opposed to just egg-laying hens) you must double the number to include the missing thrown-out males.

<table>
<tr><td>

Chapter

7
</td><td>

Numbers of Animals Raised & Killed

2. Meat Consumption
</td></tr>
</table>

Summary
- People eat about 250,000,000 tonnes of meat annually worldwide (Table 1).
- China consumes more meat than any other country (Table 1), but not on average per person (Table 2).
- People in China, United States and Brazil combined eat half the world's meat (Table 1).
- Worldwide each human eats on average 40 kg of meat (Table 2).
- New Zealanders eat more meat per person on average than any other country (Table 2).
- The amount of meat people eat is growing by about five million tonnes per year (Table 1).

This entry summarises the amount of meat people eat worldwide and is based on official statistics from the Food and Agriculture Organization of the United Nations (FAO). Animals and meat herein mean livestock and poultry and exclude seafood. For seafood see Chapter 7: Fish.

More & More Meat

The figures for meat consumption in the tables below are based on statistics from the Food and Agriculture Organization of the United Nations (FAO). FAO started collecting records in 1961. Their statistics show that the average amount of meat consumed per person has doubled over the last 40 years, increasing steadily from 21 kilograms per person in 1961 to 40 kilograms per person in 2002. Most of this growth is in the developing countries as their populations and incomes increase. China, for example, eats over 20 times its 1961 tonnage. However, although China is the biggest meat eating country (Table 1) the average consumption per Chinese is 52 kg per year, way below America at 125 kg of meat per human per year (Table 2) and western European counties, such as Britain at 80 kg of meat per human annually.

According to the UN, the average meat consumption of livestock (cattle, sheep, etc and not including sea food) per human in 2005 was 41 kilograms, and will reach 54 kilograms per person in 2050 (*The State of Food and Agriculture, 2009*. Food and Agriculture Organization of the United Nations).

In addition to meat, people are consuming more eggs and milk and this increased consumption has been called the 'Livestock Revolution'.

Minimum Human Meat Consumption

These FAO statistics exclude fish. To include fish in human meat consumption you might add about an extra third to the tables below (which are for livestock and poultry only). However, the results will still be minimum figures of human meat consumption. It is not possible to collect totally accurate statistics about millions of animals from all over the world. As FAO admits, "Data is reported by individual countries, which may have varying capacities for data collection." Therefore the statistics on this page are only a rough guide to consumed animal tonnage and should be look upon as minimum figures.

Conclusion

For the foreseeable future, perhaps for as long as humanity persists, billions of animals will continue their cataclysmic fall down the abyssal human throat.

Notes for the Tables

Figures from both tables are based on statistics collected by the Food and Agriculture Organization of the United Nations (FAO), FAOSTAT on-line statistical service (FAO: Rome, 2005). Earth Trends, World Resources

Institute, displays FAO statistics online as the Agriculture and Food Searchable Database. Table 1 is from Meat Consumption: Total and Table 2 is from Meat Consumption per Capita (both accessed online February 2008). FAO define meat consumption as "...the total meat retained for use in country for each country per year. Total meat includes meat from animals slaughtered in countries, irrespective of their origin, and comprises horsemeat, poultry, and meat from all other domestic or wild animals such as camels, rabbits, reindeer, and game animals."

Table 1. Meat Consumption per Country.
Top Ten Countries & Worldwide, 1998 - 2002.
Meat here means livestock and poultry only.
Millions of metric tonnes.

	1998	1999	2000	2001	2002
China	59	60	64	65	68
United States	33	35	35	35	36
Brazil	12	13	14	14	15
Germany	7	7	7	7	7
Russian Federation	7	6	6	7	7
France	6	6	6	6	6
Japan	5	6	6	6	6
Mexico	5	5	6	6	6
India	5	5	5	5	6
Italy	5	5	5	5	5
World	224	228	234	238	247

Source: see Notes for Tables.

Table 2. Average Annual Meat Consumption per Human. Top Ten Countries & Worldwide, 1998 - 2002. Meat here means livestock and poultry only. Kilograms of meat per human.					
	1998	**1999**	**2000**	**2001**	**2002**
New Zealand	140	138	122	147	142
Luxembourg	NA	NA	147	134	142
Bahamas	123	141	152	135	124
Denmark	126	130	130	139	146
Cyprus	126	132	134	132	131
United States	120	124	122	120	125
Spain	115	114	112	115	119
French Polynesia	105	103	107	109	112
Canada	103	107	107	108	108
France	102	100	100	103	101
World	38	38	39	39	40

Source: see Notes for Tables.

Chapter	*Numbers of Animals Raised*
7	*& Killed*

3. Chickens

Summary

Factory farms keep almost all chickens worldwide and every year they:

- Raise and kill over 40 billion broilers (Table 2).
- Keep over 6 billion egg-laying hens, killed after a year, who lay over a trillion eggs (Table 3).
- Kill over 6 billion male chicks soon after hatching in the egg-laying industry (Table 1).
- In total over 50 billion chickens are killed annually (Table 1).

Types of Chicken

Almost all chickens in the world are factory farmed. The four categories of factory farmed chicken are:

- Broiler
  Male and female chickens packed into huge sheds and slaughtered after a few weeks to eat.
- Egg-layer
  Hens are crammed into cages and made to lay up to 300 eggs in a year. After one year they are sent for slaughter.
- Male chicks in the egg-laying industry
  A male chick hatches for every female chick. They are killed soon after hatching and sold as fertiliser and pet food.
- Breeder
  Breeders are mainly females and breed more broilers and egg-layers. They are slaughtered after about a year.

Breakdown of Chicken Numbers Worldwide

Table 1 shows that there are over 50 billion chickens worldwide: broilers, egg-layers, male chicks and breeders. All the chickens are killed within or after about a year.

Table 1. Breakdown of Chicken Numbers Worldwide	
Broilers	40 billion (see Table 2)
Egg-layers	Over 6 billion (see Table 3)
Male chicks in the egg-laying industry	Over 6 billion
Breeders	Several millions (60 million in the US alone)
World Total	Over 50 billion

Numbers of Broilers Produced Annually

About 40 billion broilers are alive in any one year (Table 2). Just three countries produce over half of them: US, China and Brazil. Worldwide the number of broilers is increasing by about a billion per year.

Table 2. Numbers of Broilers Produced Annually. Top ten countries & Worldwide 2008 to 2012. Figures are in billions.					
	2008	2009	2010	2011	2012
United States	8.3	8.0	8.3	8.4	8.3
China	5.9	6.1	6.3	6.6	6.9
Brazil	5.5	5.5	6.2	6.5	6.8
European Union (27)	4.3	4.3	4.6	4.8	4.8
Mexico	1.5	1.4	1.4	1.5	1.5
India	1.3	1.3	1.4	1.4	1.4
Russia	0.8	1.0	1.2	1.3	1.4
Argentina	0.7	0.8	0.8	0.9	0.9
Iran	0.7	0.8	0.8	0.8	0.8
Turkey	0.6	0.6	0.7	0.8	0.8
Others	7.2	7.4	7.6	7.8	7.9
World Total	36.8	37.2	39.2	40.5	41.5

Source: see Notes for Tables.

Numbers of Egg-laying Hens and Eggs

The figures in Table 3 are an example of the worldwide numbers of egg-laying hens and the number of eggs they produce, in this case for the year 2011. For this year, there were about 6.4 billion egg-laying hens producing one trillion three hundred billion eggs. China is the biggest producer (2.5 billion hens and 1.3 trillion eggs), the US is the second largest producer (340 million hens and 90 billion eggs).

Table 3. Numbers of Egg-laying Hens. The top ten egg production countries & worldwide for 2011.		
Countries	Numbers of Hens	Numbers of Eggs Produced
China	2,500,000,000	474,000,000,000
United States	340,000,000	90,000,000,000
Brazil	280,000,000	38,000,000,000
India	240,000,000	58,000,000,000
Indonesia	240,000,000	24,000,000,000
Mexico	190,000,000	47,000,000,000
Japan	140,000,000	42,000,000,000
Russia	140,000,000	39,000,000,000
Ukraine	110,000,000	16,000,000,000
France	50,000,000	15,000,000,000
World Total	6,400,000,000	1,300,000,000,000

Source: see Notes for Tables.

Notes for the Tables

A precise count of the number of chickens worldwide is impossible and therefore figures in all these tables are rounded to avoid spurious accuracy and totals do not necessarily add up.

The source for the figures in Table 2 is Livestock and Poultry: World Markets and Trade. United States Department of Agriculture. (Web site

accessed July 2012.) Figures for 2012 are forecasts. Figures are in billions; thus the total number of broilers produced for 2011 was about 40 billion.

The original USDA data for Table 2 included only the countries which are the major animal producers, thus the World Total in this Table is a minimum figure. The data were in tonnes of ready to cook chickens (that is minus heads, feet and internal organs). The live slaughter weight of US broilers, according to USDA information, averages around 2.5 kg (5.5 lbs). Therefore, I made the assumption that each ready to cook chicken weighs about 2 kg (4.4 lbs) and gives a conservative estimate of broiler numbers worldwide. USDA state that their data are based on "USDA-FAS attaché reports, official statistics, and results of office research."

The figures for Table 3 are based on The Statistical Reference for Poultry Executives, by Watt Executive Guide to World Poultry Trends, 2011 (www.WATTAgNet.net). Their figures are rounded in Table 3 to avoid spurious accuracy and for ease of reading.

Chapter	Numbers of Animals Raised
7	& Killed

4. Pigs

Summary
- People keep about two billion pigs worldwide (Table 1).
- At least half the world's pigs live in China and 85 per cent of pigs live in three countries: China, European Union and United States (Table 1).
- People kill over one billion pigs annually worldwide, an average of 23 million pigs a week (Table 2).
- Three countries kill about 85 per cent of the world's pigs: China, European Union and United States, respectively about 12 million, five million and two million pigs per week (Table 2).

Their suffering is intense, widespread, expanding, systematic, and socially sanctioned. And the victims are unable to organize in defence of their own interests.*

* Henry Spira *Fighting to Win.*
(In Peter Singer: *In Defence of Animals.* 1985)

Ben Isacat

Notes for the Tables
The source for the figures in Table 1 and Table 2 is *Livestock and Poultry: World Markets and Trade.* United States Department of Agriculture. www.fas.usda.gov (web site accessed July 2012).

The USDA provide two sets of figures in their original data: 'Total Beginning Stocks' and 'Production Crop'. Beginning Stocks are the animals alive at the start of the year and breed the Production Crop. The number of Beginning Stocks remains roughly constant from year to year and it is largely the Production Crop that is slaughtered.

USDA state that their data are based on "USDA-FAS attaché reports, official statistics, and results of office research" and that their data include only those countries which are the major animal producers. World Totals, therefore, are minimum figure. Figures for 2012 are a projection.

Livestock are impossible to count accurately; therefore the figures in Table 1 and Table 2 are rounded to avoid spurious accuracy and totals may not necessarily add up exactly.

Table 1. Number of Pigs People Keep Worldwide.
Top ten countries & Worldwide 2008 to 2012.
Figures are in millions.

	2008	2009	2010	2011	2012
China	1,080	1,119	1,148	1,118	1,117
European Union 27 states	418	411	414	411	417
United States	183	182	179	180	183
Brazil	68	70	72	75	76
Russia	43	45	47	47	50
Canada	45	42	41	41	41
Japan	27	28	27	27	27
Mexico	25	25	25	25	25
Korea, South	23	23	24	20	22
Ukraine	14	14	16	16	16
Others	24	15	16	16	16
World Total	2,012	1,972	2,008	1,972	1,979

Source, see Notes for Tables.

Table 2. Number of Pigs People Kill Worldwide.
Top ten countries & Worldwide 2008 to 2012.
Figures are in millions.

	2008	2009	2010	2011	2012
China	637	656	678	641	658
European Union 27 states	258	258	262	260	258
United States	115	115	114	115	117
Brazil	35	36	37	38	38
Russia	27	29	30	30	32
Canada	31	30	29	28	28
Japan	17	18	18	17	17
Mexico	16	16	16	16	16
Korea, South	14	15	15	12	15
Ukraine	7	7	8	8	9
Others	15	8	10	10	10
World Total	1,171	1,187	1,125	1,175	1,196

Source, see Notes for Tables.

Chapter	*Numbers of Animals Raised*
7	*& Killed*

5. Sheep & Goats

Summary
- People keep about 1,000,000,000 sheep worldwide (Table 1).
- About half of the world's sheep live in seven countries (Table 1).
- People kill about half a billion sheep and goats a year worldwide (Table 2).
- About half the world's sheep and goats are killed in just two countries: China and India (Table 2).

Table 1. Number of Sheep Kept Worldwide.
Top ten countries & Worldwide for years 2002 to 2006.
Figures are rounded in millions.

	2002	2003	2004	2005	2006
China	136	144	157	171	174
Australia	106	99	101	101	100
India	61	62	62	62	63
Iran	52	52	52	52	52
Sudan	48	48	49	50	50
New Zealand	40	40	40	40	40
Britain	36	36	36	35	35
Turkey	27	25	25	25	25
South Africa	26	26	25	25	25
Pakistan	24	25	25	25	25
Others	469	477	490	505	512
World Total	1,025	1,034	1,064	1,091	1,101

Source: see Notes for Tables.

	1996	1997	1998	1999	2000
Table 2. Number of Sheep & Goats People Kill Worldwide. Top ten countries & Worldwide for 1996 to 2000. Figures are rounded in millions.					
China	181	155	177	193	200
India	85	85	89	92	94
New Zealand	32	33	32	31	31
Australia	28	31	31	31	31
Turkey	24	24	24	23	23
Spain	20	19	20	20	19
Britain	18	17	19	19	18
Saudi Arabia	10	11	10	11	11
France	9	9	9	8	8
Italy	8	8	8	9	9
Others	68	66	58	55	50
World Total	483	458	477	492	494

Source: see Notes for Tables.

Notes for the Tables

Figures in Tables 1 & 2 are rounded to avoid spurious accuracy. Entries do not therefore always exactly add up to the total.

Figures for Table 1 are from Earth Trends, World Resources Institute (www.wri.org, accessed March 2010), who get their data from the Food and Agriculture Organization of the United Nations.

Figures for Table 2 are from *Sheep and Goat Slaughter, selected Countries*. United States Agricultural Service (accessed online March 2010). They obtain their data from "counselor and attaché reports, official statistics, and results of office research".

Chapter	Numbers of Animals Raised
7	& Killed
	6. Beef Cattle

Summary
- People keep about 1,300,000,000 beef cattle worldwide (this excludes dairy cattle) (Table 1).
- Over half the world's beef cattle live in three countries: India, Brazil and China (Table 1).
- People kill nearly 300 million beef cattle annually worldwide (Table 2).
- Half the world's beef cattle are killed in three countries: India, Brazil and China (Table 2).

Table 1. Number of Beef Cattle People Keep Worldwide. Top ten countries & Worldwide, 2008 to 2012.
Figures are in millions.

	2008	2009	2010	2011	2012
India	364	371	378	383	387
Brazil	224	229	234	240	246
China	151	149	147	146	145
United States	124	131	130	129	126
European Union 27 states	120	119	117	116	115
Argentina	71	66	61	60	62
Colombia	36	36	36	36	37
Australia	37	37	36	37	38
Mexico	30	30	30	28	27
Russia	30	28	28	27	27
Others	100	89	70	69	68
World Total	1,325	1,309	1,287	1,291	1,298

Source: see Notes for Tables.

Table 2. Number of Beef Cattle People Kill. Top ten countries & Worldwide, 2008 to 2012. Figures are in millions.					
	2008	**2009**	**2010**	**2011**	**2012**
India	60	61	62	62	63
Brazil	49	49	49	49	50
China	45	43	42	41	41
United State	36	36	36	36	34
European Union 27 States	31	30	39	29	29
Argentina	15	12	12	12	13
Australia	9	10	8	10	10
Russia	8	7	7	7	7
Mexico	7	7	7	7	7
Colombia	6	5	5	5	5
Others	30	26	21	21	21
World Total	296	286	277	279	281

For the sources of these figures, see Notes for Tables.

Notes for the Tables

The source for Table 1 and Table 2 is based on 'Live Cattle Selected Countries Summary'. 'Total Cattle Beginning Stocks' plus 'Production (Calf Crop)' In *Livestock and Poultry: World Markets and Trade*. United States Department of Agriculture.www.fas.usda.gov (accessed July 2012).

USDA state that their data are based on "USDA-FAS attaché reports, official statistics, and results of office research." USDA say the cattle are adults and calves raised for meat and exclude dairy cattle but include buffalo in India. Their figures for 2012 are a forecast.

USDA data included two classes of cattle: *'Total Beginning Stocks'* and *'Production Crop'*. Total Beginning Stocks are the animals alive at the start of the year and most of these animals are used to breed the Production Crop for the year. Virtually all the Production Stock is killed for food (some would replace Beginning Stock and some Beginning Stock would be killed). The figures in

Table 1 include both categories. Cattle numbers in Table 2 are only the 'Production Crop'.

The World Total in both tables is a minimum figure. One reason for this is that the original USDA data do not include every country, although they do include the world's major animal producing countries. Furthermore, the USDA figures are based on cattle who are officially counted (for example, at farms and slaughterhouses); cattle slaughtered outside official premises may not be counted. For example, non-walking cattle (that is "non-ambulatory" cattle, too injured to walk) may be killed before they get to the slaughterhouse and are not counted. In the US alone, non-walking cattle totalled 465,000 in 2003, including 185,000 calves, and 450,000 in 2004, including 180,000 calves ('calves' in this case are cattle under 230 kg / 500 lbs).

Livestock are impossible to count accurately. Therefore the figures in both these tables are rounded to avoid spurious accuracy and totals do not necessarily add up exactly.

The World Total in both tables is a minimum figure. One reason for this is that the original USDA data do not include every country, although they do include the world's major animal producing countries. Furthermore, the USDA figures are based on cattle who are officially counted (for example, at farms and slaughterhouses); cattle slaughtered outside official premises may not be counted, for example, non-walking cattle (that is "non-ambulatory" cattle, too injured to walk) may be killed before they get to the slaughterhouse. In the US alone, non-walking cattle totalled 465,000 in 2003, including 185,000 calves, and 450,000 in 2004, including 180,000 calves ('calves' in this case are cattle under 230 kg / 500 lbs).

Livestock are impossible to count accurately. Therefore the data for these tables were are rounded to the nearest million to avoid spurious accuracy and totals do not necessarily add up exactly.

Chapter 7	*Numbers of Animals Raised & Killed*
	7. Fish

Summary

Generalising the data in the tables below for the year 2001 as representative for recent years:

- People catch about 92 million tonnes of wild (non-farmed) fish annually in Earth's oceans and seas (Table 1).
- People farm about 38 million tonnes of fish annually - about 22 kg of fish per person worldwide per year (Table 2).
- By weight of catch, China, Peru, United States, Japan and Indonesia are the biggest fishing countries, catching about a third of the world's total wild caught fish, with China the biggest, catching nearly a fifth of the world total (Table 1).
- China, India, Indonesia, Japan and Thailand combined produced about 80 per cent of the world's farmed fish, with China the biggest producer farming about two-thirds of the world's total farmed fish (Table 2).

Wild Caught Fish

People catch about 100 million tons of wild fish from the seas and oceans per year. This is nearly a five-fold increase over 1950 when people took about 20

Table 1. Tonnes of Wild Caught Fish for 2001. Top Five Producing Countries & Total World. 1 tonne = 1 ton. Data include shellfish.	
China	16.5 million tonnes
Peru	8.0 million tonnes
US	4.9 million tonnes
Japan	4.7 million tonnes
Indonesia	4.2 million tonnes
World Total	92 million tonnes

million tonnes of fish per year. Britain, once an imperial sea power, ranked 21st in 2001 with 0.7 million tonnes of wild caught fish. Nowadays, around 3.5 million boats fish the seas and oceans worldwide, with Russia and US owning the largest fleets of deepwater fishing boats.

The World's Three Most Wild Caught Fish (by weight. 1 tonne = 1 ton)

1. Peruvian anchovy (Engraulis ringens)
Also called the Peruvian anchoveta.
7.2 million tonnes in 2001.
Maximum length 20 cm (8 ins). Prefers sub-tropical waters, swims in massive shoals, particularly off Peru and Chile. A filter-feeder on plankton.

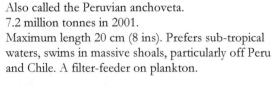

2. Walleye Pollock (Theragra chalcogramma)
Also called Alaska Pollock.
3.1 million tonnes in 2001.
Length up to 80 cm (2 ft 6 ins). Lives throughout the north Pacific. Can live up to 15 years.

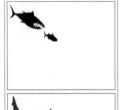

3. Chilean jack mackerel (Trachurus murphyi)
2.5 million tonnes in 2001.
Length up to 70 cm (2 ft 4 ins). Found in south Pacific and south-west Atlantic. Feeds mainly on fish larvas and small shellfish. Can live up to 16 years.

Ben Isacat

Farmed Fish
People farm about 38 million tonnes of fish per year. This is a 38-fold increase since 1950 when about one million tonnes was farmed. In 2001 the US ranked 10th at 0.5 million tonnes of farmed fish and Britain ranked 19th with 0.2 million tonnes of farmed fish.

The World's Three Most Farmed Fish/Shellfish
By weight. 1 tonne = 1 ton.

1. Pacific King Oyster (Crassostrea gigas).
Also called Japanese oyster.
4.2 million tonnes in 2001.
Usually 8 to 30 cm long (8 to 12 inch), a filter feeding oyster favouring shallow waters, introduced around the world from Japan. Reared primarily in estuaries.

2. Grass Carp (Ctenopharyngodon idellus).
3.4 million tonnes in 2001. Grows up to 1.5 m and 45 kg (5 ft and 90 lbs).
Lives in lakes and rivers. Original home was China and eastern Siberia and now introduced around the world. Feeds on plants and invertebrates.
Maximum reported age is 21 years.

3. Silver Carp (*Hypophthalmichthys molitrix*).
2.9 million tonnes in 2001.
Grows up to 1.0 m and 50 kg (3 ft 3 inch and 110 lbs). Prefers slow flowing waters of large rivers. Original home China and eastern Siberia but introduced around the world. Feeds on phytoplankton and zooplankton.

Table 2. Tonnes of Farmed Fish in 2001. Top Five Producing Countries & World Total. 1 tonne = 1 ton. Data include shellfish.	
China	26.1 million tonnes
India	2.2 million tonnes
Indonesia	0.9 million tonnes
Japan	0.8 million tonnes
Thailand	0.7 million tonnes
World Total	38 million tonnes

Notes for the Tables
Data for both tables are from S Vannuccini (2003): *Overview of Fish Production, Utilization, Consumption & Trade*. Food & Agriculture Organization of the United Nations, Fishery Information, Data & Statistics Unit.

Data for 'The World's Three Most Wild Caught Fish', for 'The World's Three Most Farmed Fish/Shellfish' and for fish elsewhere are from Food and Agriculture Organization of the United Nations (FAO), Fishery Information, Data and Statistics Unit.

Chapter	*Numbers of Animals Raised & Killed*
7	*8. Fur-bearers*

Summary
- Most farmed furs come from mink and foxes.
- About thirty million mink are farmed annually worldwide (Table 1).
- About five million fox pelts are marketed each year (Table 2).
- Over eight million wild fur-bearing animals are trapped per year in North America (Table 3 & Table 4).
- Racoons and muskrats are the most commonly trapped wild fur-bearing animals in North America (Table 3 & Table 4).

This section provides an impression of the numbers of animals killed for their fur by showing official statistics for farmed mink and foxes (Tables 1 & 2) and for trapped fur-bearing animals in North America (Tables 3 & 4).

Information about the worldwide trade in furs is incomplete because official statistics of farmed animals and trapped animals (eg Russia and China) are not always available. Even when statistics are published, not all fur-bearing animals and pelts (or 'furskins') are recorded. For instance, in addition to millions of foxes and mink killed for their pelts, millions more are kept as breeders to replenish stock, many animals die too young to produce marketable pelts, and many pelts are discarded as sub-standard before reaching market.

Statistics, therefore, tend to under estimate the numbers of animals killed for their fur. Treat the numbers below as estimated minimums.

Number of Farmed Mink Worldwide
About thirty million mink are farmed worldwide annually. Eight countries produce nearly 90 per cent of them. Denmark produces over a third. However, China's fur industry is growing fast and reached 8 million farmed mink in 2005 (*Dying For Fur*), second only to Denmark. See Table 1.

Number of Farmed Fox Pelts on the World Market
About five million fox pelts go onto the world market each year. Finland is the world's biggest producer of farmed fox pelts, about half the world's supply. China and Russia are also leading producers. The number of China's farmed

foxes is growing annually; it was estimated at 3.5 million for 2005 (Dying For Fur), overtaking Finland. See Table 2.

Top Ten Fur-bearers Trapped in N America
People in the United States trap over seven million wild fur-bearing animals a year (Table 3). Far more fur-bearers are trapped in the US than in Canada (compare with Table 4), possibly because the US has a much larger human population and therefore many more trappers. The US International Trade Commission report that the US is the world's largest "volume" producer of pelts trapped in the wild. Racoons and Muskrats are the most commonly trapped fur-bearers (also see Table 4).

Top Ten Fur-bearers Trapped in Canada
Muskrat, beaver and marten are the most commonly trapped fur-bearing animals in Canada and well over a million wild fur-bearers are trapped annually. See Table 4.

Notes for the Tables
Tables 1, 2 and 3 are from *Furskins*. Industry & Trade Summary. US International Trade Commission, publication 3666, 2004. Table 4 is from *Fur Statistics 2004*, vol 2, no 1. Statistics Canada, Agriculture Division.

Table 1. Number of Farmed Mink Worldwide 1998 - 2002. Numbers are in millions.					
	1998	**1999**	**2000**	**2001**	**2002**
Denmark	11.9	10.5	10.9	12.2	12.2
Netherlands	2.7	2.7	2.8	3.0	3.0
United States	2.9	2.8	2.7	2.6	2.6
Russia	3.3	2.7	2.2	2.5	2.7
Finland	2.1	1.9	2.0	2.0	2.0
China	1.2	1.5	1.7	2.0	1.7
Sweden	1.3	1.3	1.2	1.3	1.4
Canada	1.0	0.9	1.0	1.2	1.2
All Others*	3.7	3.5	3.7	3.8	4.1
World Total	30.1	27.8	28.2	30.6	30.9

* Other mink farming countries include Baltic States, Spain, Norway, Italy, Germany, Ireland, France, Iceland, Belgium and Argentina.

Table 2. Number of Farmed Fox Pelts on the World Market 1998 - 2002.
Numbers are in million.

	1998	1999	2000	2001	2002
Finland	2.7	2.1	1.9	2.1	2.1
Other Scandinavian*	0.7	0.5	0.4	0.4	0.4
China	0.4	0.8	0.9	1.0	1.2
Russia	0.7	0.4	0.4	0.4	0.4
All Others	0.3	0.4	0.4	0.4	0.4
World Total	4.8	4.2	4.0	4.3	4.5

* Norway, Sweden and Denmark. Source: see Notes for the Tables.

Table 3. Number of Wild Fur-bearers Trapped in the United States 1997/98 Season.

Racoon	2,896,000
Muskrat	2,183,000
Beaver	429,000
Coypu	398,000
Mink	190,000
Red Fox	164,000
Coyote	159,000
Otter	29,000
Other	613,000
Total	7,062,000

Source: see Notes for the Tables.

Table 4. Number of Top Ten Fur-bearers Trapped in Canada, 1999/00 - 2001/02				
	1999/00	**2000/01**	**2001/02**	**Average***
Muskrat	400,100	207,300	291,300	300,000
Beaver	215,200	221,100	260,400	223,000
Marten	141,100	149,700	119,100	137,000
Squirrel	83,500	63,600	77,100	75,000
Coyote	44,400	54,700	55,400	52,000
Racoon	26,500	30,000	71,800	43,000
Fox	33,700	44,000	48,500	42,000
Mink	40,600	28,800	34,900	34,000
Weasel	38,900	25,800	30,100	32,000
Fisher	16,600	16,100	23,500	19,000
Total*	1,000,000	800,000	1,000,000	1,000,000

* Averages and totals are rounded to avoid spurious accuracy.
Source: see Notes for the Tables.

References & Other Useful Sources
You can find all these on the Web.

- Andrew Linzey. *The Ethical Case Against Fur Farming.* 2002.
- Hsieh-Yi, Yi-Chiao, Yu Fu, B Maas & Mark Rissi: *Dying For Fur: a report on the fur industry in China.* EAST International/Swiss Animal Protection SAP. January 2005 (revised April 2006). (Similar to *Fun Fur? A report on the Chinese fur industry,* by the same authors.)
- *The Socio-Economic Impact Of European Fur Farming.* European Fur Breeders Association / International Fur Trade Federation. (Undated but latest figures are for 2004.)
- International Fur Trade Federation (IFTF) web site.
- *Furskins.* Industry & Trade Summary. US International Trade Commission. Publication 3666. 2004.

Chapter	*Numbers of Animals Raised*
7	*& Killed*
	9. Biomedical Animals

Summary
- Countries often keep poor records of the numbers of animals they use in biomedical research.
- Estimates for the number of animals used worldwide for biomedical research range between 40 million and 100 million animals (Table 1).
- Japan and United States use more experimental animals than all other countries combined (Table 1).
- Six countries using the largest numbers of experimental animals are Japan, United States, Britain, Canada, France and Germany; combined they may use around half the experimental animals worldwide (Table 1).
- Britain keeps good records on the numbers of animals used: nearly four million in 2011, up by over a million animals from 2000 (Table 2).

Reliability of Estimates

Estimates for the numbers of animals used in biomedical research are rough because some countries keep incomplete or no records. The United States for example does not count certain animals, such as the much used rats and mice. Britain may keep more reliable and detailed data than any other country on numbers, species and the purpose experimental animals are put to and some of these details are summarised below. Britain is said to have the most stringent laws concerning laboratory animals. However, this strength is only relative to other countries.

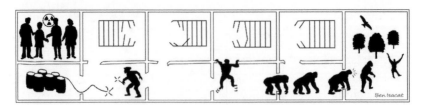

Number of Experimental (Laboratory) Animals (Table 1)
- Various estimates of the total number of animals used for experimental purposes range between 40 million and 100 million animals.

- Japan and United States are by far the biggest users of experimental animals.
- Six countries using the largest numbers of experimental animals are Japan, United States, Britain, Canada, France and Germany.
- These six countries combined use around about half the experimental animals worldwide.

Numbers of Animals Used in Biomedical Research.

True and reliable numbers of animals used for experimental purposes in biomedical research are difficult to find or do not exist. Estimates from various sources range between 40 million and 100 million animals.

Statistics show that the six countries using the largest numbers of experimental animals are Japan, United States, Britain, Canada, France and Germany. Combined they might use around about half the experimental animals worldwide. China would is one of the big players, "...using lab animals...in scientific research - 16 million a year, compared to 12 million in the 25 European Union countries in 2005..." (*Analysis of Current Laboratory Animal Science Policies and Administration in China.* Qi Kong & Chuan Qin. ILAR e-Journal, 51:2010).

Table 1. Numbers of Animals in Biomedical Research Six Highest-using Countries & Worldwide, for 2000. ...don't forget China's position.	
Japan	12,000,000+
United States	12,000,000+
Britain	2 - 3,000,000
Canada	2 - 3,000,000
France	2 - 3,000,000
Germany	2 - 3,000,000
Worldwide	40,000,000 to 100,000,000

Number and Kind of Experimental Animals in Britain

Britain records possibly the most detailed inventory of experimental animals, and thus is a good example of a country's population of biomedical research animals. Table 2 shows that nearly four million animals are used annually as experimental animals, up by well over a million animals from ten years earlier. The vast majority of experimental animals are rodents, then fish and birds.

About three per cent - but nevertheless something like 80,000 - are other mammals.

Table 2. Number & Kind of Experimental Animals in Britain in 2000 & 2011		
Kind of Animal	Number 20000	Number 2011
Mice	1,605,722	2,679,763
Fish	242,757	563,903
Rats & other rodents (eg hamsters & guinea-pigs)	593,967	289,466
Birds	120,505	162,618
Sheep	16,078	37,714
Amphibians	9,661	15,915
Rabbits	27,389	15,461
Horses & donkeys	452	8,380
Cattle	6,801	5,102
Dogs	4,745	4,552
Pigs	8,326	4,340
Primates	2,951	3,020
Other carnivores	663	795
Ferrets	1,358	691
Reptiles	63	383
Other mammals	457	269
Cats	613	235
Goats	325	196
Deer	160	50
Total	2,642,993	3,792,857

Source: for 2000: *Statistics of Scientific Procedures 1987-00*. Home Office. Source for 2011: *Statistics of Scientific Procedures on Living Animals, Great Britain 2011*. Home Office, 2012 (Table 3). www.homeoffice.gov.uk (accessed July 2012).

Number of Procedures on Animals in Britain

This table shows the annual number of procedures by primary purpose, a procedure being a single experiment on one animal (the same animal can be used more than once, of course). Experimenters in Britain annually carry out around four million procedures on animals. Toxicity testing is for protecting humans from potentially harmful chemicals, for instance eye and skin irritants and finding out a substance's concentration that causes death.

Table 3. Number of Procedures in Britain for 2000 & 2011		
Primary Purpose	**2000**	**2011**
Breading	699,600	1,614,000
Research	872,800	1,311,300
Medicine	929,700	658,000
Toxicity testing	161,200	116,200
Education & Other	51,400	1,500
Total	2,600,000 +	3,700,000 +

Numbers are rounded. Source: same as Table 2.

Chapter	Five Extras
8	1. Universal Declaration on Animals

We address questions about human welfare and nature conservation at the highest levels of government, debate them at international meetings, and codify agreements among nations in binding Charters. The *United Nations Convention on the Rights of the Child* and the *Convention on Biodiversity* are examples. Animal rights is more difficult to champion than animal welfare. Yet animals have no worldwide protection, possibly because they are so basic and important a part of human economic exploitation.

The lack of success in shaping internationally binding charters on animal rights has not been for want of trying. People in modern times have attempted to identify and advance the rights of animals at least since the 18th century. Credit usually goes to Henry Salt (1851 - 1939) for writing the first book on animal rights, published in 1892 and subsequently (1). Salt traces animal rights efforts back to John Lawrence (1753 - 1839), one of the earliest modern writers on animal rights and welfare. Lawrence argued that we have to care for animals and common law should support this principle in practice:

> "I therefore propose, that the Rights of Beasts be formally acknowledged by the state, and that a law be framed upon that principle, to guard and protect them from acts of flagrant and wanton cruelty, whether committed by their owners or others." (2)

The 20th century saw a number of international declarations supporting animal rights. Perhaps the most prominent venture was the announcement (*The Times*, 17 October) in 1978 by the United Nation's Educational, Scientific and Cultural Organization (UNESCO) of the *Universal Declaration of Animal Rights*. Among the Declaration's pronouncements were that all animals have the same rights to existence, no animal shall be ill-treated or subject to cruelty, animals shall command the protection of law, and dead animals shall be treated with respect. The Declaration, however, waned and faded away before it could reach significant levels of international agreement.

Declaration on Animal Welfare
More recently some of the leading animal welfare organisations started campaigning for the United Nations to adopt a new declaration. This time the declaration is on the welfare of animals: the *Universal Declaration on Animal*

Welfare. Why welfare and not rights? Probably because welfare is a softer option than rights and therefore easier for people to accept. Thus it has a better chance of endorsement and enduring.

The animal organisations behind this new declaration envisage that signatory countries to the document will recognise animals as sentient beings. They hope their declaration will make animal welfare an important global issue, pioneer the way for legally binding international agreements on animal welfare and hasten a better deal for animals worldwide. Their declaration would also underscore the importance of animal welfare as part of the moral development of humanity. So far a number of United Nations member states are acting as a steering group to advance the initiative at the UN.

The animal organisations behind this new declaration envisage that signatory countries to the document will recognise animals as sentient beings. They hope their Declaration will make animal welfare an important global issue, pioneer the way for legally binding international agreements on animal welfare and hasten a better deal for animals worldwide. The Declaration would also underscore the importance of animal welfare as part of the moral development of humanity. So far a number of United Nations member states are acting as a steering group to advance the initiative at the UN. But achieving this Declaration for animals will be a long and twisting journey. To illustrate, the *Convention on the Rights of the Child* took thirty years of effort before the United Nations adopted it.

References
(1) Salt, Henry. *Animals' Rights: Considered in Relation to Social Progress.* G Bell & Sons: London, 1894. Reprinted 1980 by Macmillan & Co: New York and by Centaur Press: London.
(2) John Lawrence , *A Philosophical and Practical Treatise on Horses and the Moral Duties of Man Towards Brute Creation*, 1796, vol 1, chapter 3, p123. T N Longman: London.

The following is a draft copy of the Universal Declaration on Animal Welfare, composed by a number of animal welfare organisations.

Universal Declaration on Animal Welfare

PREAMBLE

The Manila Conference on Animal Welfare recognizes:

That animal welfare is an issue worth consideration by governments.

That the promotion of animal welfare requires collective action and all stakeholders and affected parties must be involved.

That work on animal welfare is a continuous process

A PROPOSAL FOR A DECLARATION ON ANIMAL WELFARE ARISING FROM THE MANILA CONFERENCE

RECOGNIZING that animals are living, sentient beings and therefore deserve due consideration and respect;

RECOGNIZING that animal welfare includes animal health;

RECOGNIZING that humans share this planet with other species and other forms of life and that all forms of life co-exist within an interdependent ecosystem;

RECOGNIZING that, although there are significant social, economic, religious and cultural differences between human societies, each should care for and treat animals in a humane and sustainable manner;

AGREEING that the term nation includes peoples, civil society and the state;

ACKNOWLEDGING that many nations already have a system of legal protection for animals, both domestic and wild;

SEEKING to ensure the continued effectiveness of these systems and the development of better and more comprehensive animal welfare provisions;

ACKNOWLEDGING that the humane use of animals can have major benefits for humans;

AWARE that the "five freedoms (freedom from hunger, thirst and malnutrition; freedom from fear and distress; freedom from physical and thermal discomfort; freedom from pain, injury and disease; and freedom to express normal patterns of behaviour) " and the "three Rs (reduction in numbers of animals, refinement of experimental methods and replacement of animals with nonanimal techniques)" provide valuable guidance for the use of animals;

RECOGNIZING that the provisions contained in this declaration do not affect the rights of any nation;

PRINCIPLES OF THE DECLARATION:

1. The welfare of animals shall be a common objective for all nations;
2. The standards of animal welfare attained by each nation shall be promoted, recognized and observed by improved measures, nationally and internationally, respecting social and economic considerations and religious and cultural traditions;
3. All appropriate steps shall be taken by nations to prevent cruelty to animals and to reduce their suffering;
4. Appropriate standards on the welfare of animals be further developed and elaborated such as, but not limited to, those governing the use and management of farm animals, companion animals, animals in scientific research, draught animals, wildlife animals and animals in recreation.

Chapter	Five Extras
8	*2. The Five Freedoms*

The Five Freedoms are basic ideals of welfare for farm animals, like livestock and poultry, wherever the animals may be, such as at farms, markets, slaughterhouses, or in transit, and should be applied by anyone in charge of the animals or handling them. The Freedoms make good common sense and are broad enough to apply to all farm animals anywhere in the world (indeed, to all animals, see Animal Friendly Traveller, Chapter 4).

The Five Freedoms were first proposed in Britain in the 1960's. The Farm Animal Welfare Council, established by the British government in the late 1970's to advise it on legislative and other changes for farm animals, subsequently affirmed them. The Council was conservatively made up of individuals with connections to agriculture: farmers, animal farming company directors, veterinary surgeons and academics specialising in agriculture. Other bodies concerned with animal welfare have approved the Freedoms.

The Five Freedoms are:

1. **Freedom from Hunger and Thirst** - by ready access to fresh water and a diet to maintain full health and vigour.
2. **Freedom from Discomfort** - by providing an appropriate environment including shelter and a comfortable resting area.
3. **Freedom from Pain, Injury or Disease** - by prevention or rapid diagnosis and treatment.
4. **Freedom to Express Normal Behaviour** - by providing sufficient space, proper facilities and company of the animal's own kind.
5. **Freedom from Fear and Distress** - by ensuring conditions and treatment which avoid mental suffering.

The Farm Animal Welfare Council say the Five Freedoms are a framework for viewing and improving animal welfare "within the proper constraints of an effective livestock industry." The Council stress that well trained and supervised stockmanship is the key to farm animal welfare: "...without competent, diligent stockmanship the welfare of animals cannot be adequately safeguarded."

However, the Five Freedoms are not inevitably applied, being more honoured in the breach. How much animal farming and stockmanship concede toward applying the Five Freedoms to animals is demonstrated by the brutal realities of factory farming, such as the chicken industry and veal production. Nor are the Five Freedoms widely applied to animals farmed for their fur.

Chapter	Five Extras
8	3. Human Overpopulation

What's the Problem?

Earth's huge human population has a colossal influence on animal rights. Human overpopulation destroys wildlife and imposes suffering on animals. Sources say that as the human population grows, three or more species go extinct every hour.

In 1798 the Englishman Thomas Malthus published *An Essay on the Principle of Population* voicing apprehension about human population growth. He pointed out that the human population grows more quickly than can be matched by food production and was already overtaking its food supply. He predicted environmental degradation leading to massive famine, disease and war. Malthus was writing in response to the optimism of the Enlightenment that humanity can tame the environment and that human potential was limitless.

The disaster Malthus anticipated did not happen, agricultural and industrial revolutions saw to that. But the spectre of Malthus has not gone away. His warning seems even more applicable today and on a worldwide scale. The global human population as it grows is ever increasing its use of resources. Even the most fundamental resources like water, land and air are in short supply and being polluted. Estimates are that humans already use over half the world's accessible fresh surface water and have changed or degraded up to half of Earth's land surface through agriculture and urban building. By 2030 there could be one billion cars - 100 million of them in China alone - choking Earth's atmosphere and considerably contributing to global warming.

The Overflowing Human Population

The human population reached 0.3 billion in year 0 (two thousand years ago). Then it took 1,800 years to reach its first billion. But from there on the pace of human population growth burst its barriers and in the last few decades a billion more people are added to the population every few years, as Table 1 shows.

At the present rate of human increase, three babies are added to Earth every second, making a quarter of a million more people each day or 80 million more people annually. Over half (about 60 per cent) of humanity lives in just ten countries - see Table 2.

Human numbers at the current rate of expansion might reach 300 billion in another 15 decades. However, Earth's resources cannot sustain anything near this number of people and humanity would die off before achieving this mass. Wars for diminishing resources, breakdown of societies followed by disease and starvation would consume humanity first. Fortunately, for some of the world's people, influences like family planning, modern contraception, education and prosperity create a desire to bear fewer children. Consequently, population growth is slowing to some extent.

Table 1. Landmarks in Human Population Growth Worldwide	
Year	Number of People
0 AD	300,000,000
1804	1,000,000,000
1927	2,000,000,000
1960	3,000,000,000
1974	4,000,000,000
1987	5,000,000,000
1998	6,000,000,000
2011	7,000,000,000
2025	8,000,000,000
2043	9,000,000,000
2083	10,000,000,000

Source: The World at Six Billion. United Nations Population Division. Also, World Population Prospects, the 2010 Revision, UN Dept of Economic and Social Affairs (accessed online July 2012).

Overpopulation & Animals

A massive human population goes against animals gaining rights. Billions of more humans mean people kill billions of more animals (livestock and wild). As the human population expands, worldwide meat consumption has increased three and a half times in the last four decades: from about 70 million tonnes to nearly 250 million tonnes a year. Ever more people will deplete resources that wildlife need. Water is becoming increasingly scarce in more parts of the world as people channel it off for agriculture, industry, leisure and

domestic use. Forests are logged to make anything from pencils to buildings and the animals in the forests are turned out and die. Growing cereals denies the use of the land to animals, and the animals themselves may be killed if they eat the crops or trample them. The worldwide consumption of cereals will increase by 66 per cent and consumption of forest products by 120 per cent from 2000 to 2050 (Living Planet Report 2002, WWF).

Table 2. Top Ten Human Populations by Country	
Country	Number of People
China	1,300,000,000
India	1,100,000,000
United States	300,000,000
Indonesia	200,000,000
Brazil	190,000,000
Pakistan	160,000,000
Russian Federation	140,000,000
Bangladesh	140,000,000
Nigeria	130,000,000
Japan	130,000,000
TOTAL	3,790,000,000

Source: World Population 2004. Population Division.
Department of Economic and Social Affairs. United Nations.

Chapter	*Five Extras*
8	*4. Zoos*

When you think of a zoo you might picture one of the few prestigious institutions. But most zoos are small insignificant collections in towns or situated by roadsides or in people's private backyards. A 'zoo' is simply a collection of animals. Most zoos are geared to make money by attracting paying visitors, give trivial or no thought to animal rights or welfare, and the quality of life for their animals varies from lethal to scarcely adequate.

The earliest significant animal collections date back at least 3,500 years to the Middle East. The animals came from faraway places and were objects of curiosity. The animals were given to rulers, the rich and the powerful in return for political favours and the animals' new owners used their collections as displays of status.

Enthusiasts with a passion for collecting animals started the first big zoos as we know them today. They trapped animals from the wild and sometimes killed mother animals to take their young. Young animals are easier to keep and transport because they eat less, take up little room and are more manageable than adults. The animal catchers killed animals who got in their way and many of the animals they trapped died on the long and hard journey to the zoo.

There is a zoo in nearly all large cities today and the bigger the zoo the prouder the citizens. Among the first major city zoos were Vienna, founded in 1752, and Paris, founded about 40 years later. London Zoo, founded in 1828, claims to be the world's first zoo for the study of animals. Later in the nineteenth century Philadelphia and Adelaide zoos were set up in the US and Australia.

Statistics

- Over 10,000 zoos exist worldwide, holding about a million vertebrate animals.
- The number of animals per zoo ranges from a handful to several thousand.
- Over 600 million people a year visit zoos.

These figures (from *Guide to the World Zoo Conservation Strategy*, 1993) no doubt exclude animals from the innumerable small roadside tourist stops and small private collections. Some sources claim there are more like five million vertebrate animals in zoos.

Changing Attitude to Zoos

In living memory the collectors of zoo animals treated their charges as items or specimens, especially treasured if rare or unusual, and prized as public attractions. The animals themselves typically lived in small bare cages with nothing to do and no place to retreat from human gaze or disturbance.

Leading and distinguished zoos set a trend from the 1950's as popular attractions to entertain the mass public. However, in the 1970's people's attitudes really started changing. A few people began expounding the view that animals have mental and physical needs that their inadequate living conditions cannot support. One charity, Zoo Check, was especially prominent. Zoo critics challenged the role of zoos making zoo animal welfare an issue and consequently zoos were forced to justify their existence to the public.

Basic Arguments for Zoos

Zoos justify their existence in four ways:

1. Scientific Research
    Zoos contribute substantially to scientific knowledge by researching animals living at the zoo.
2. Nature Conservation
    Zoos play a key role saving species from extinction by breeding endangered animals and returning them to the wild.
3. Public Education
    Zoo exhibits are a valuable source for the public to learn about animals and their natural habitat.
4. Public Entertainment
    Zoos offer entertainment and recreation for the public. Zoos cannot rely entirely on grants and public donations so must earn their way like any other business.

So what arguments do zoo critics muster against these assertions?

Arguments Against Zoos

1. Scientific Research
Few zoos finance research that may benefit their animal occupants and by far the majority of zoos have neither the means nor the will to carry out research.

Nor is research necessarily always significant and worthwhile in the few zoos that do it and can be misleading. For example, zoo animals make unreliable subjects for behavioural research. Their living conditions are artificial and many zoo animals are mentally deranged (more below). We now know from field studies on wild-living animals, like wolves and chimpanzees, that the social organisation of animals in the wild where humans do not disturb them are completely different from their zoo counterparts.

2. Nature Conservation
The vast majority of zoos have no desire or resources to be effective means for conservation. It is only the few leading zoos or ones with conservation-minded owners that pay tribute to nature conservation.

Zoos have reintroduced successfully only a handful of animals back to the wild. Notable successes are the golden lion tamarin to the rain forest in Brazil, the Arabian oryx to the deserts of Arabia, the tarpan (Przewalski horse) to the Mongolian steppes and the field cricket to Britain. But these exceptions, although important, do not justify the captivity of a million other animals at zoos. In fact, removing rare animals from the wild to stock zoos can influence the survival of the animals' wild population. The major zoos today breed most of their animals from existing zoo-held animals but still occasionally take animals from the wild and there is a highly damaging trade to nature conservation in wild animals for smaller animal collections and for private zoos.

Some zoo animal species, such as the charismatic crowd-pulling ones like pandas, chimpanzees and snow leopards, are in danger of extinction, but most species in most zoos are not pending extinction. The purpose of many of zoo animals, especially the large ones like African lions, elephants and giraffes, is to acquire money at the gate from paying visitors. Zoos breed cute baby animals for the same reason, too pull in crowds, but then have a surplus of animals once they are grown-up and must get rid of them.

Even if a zoo wants to return animals to their wild environment, it is not always possible to do so because people destroy or seriously degrade natural habitats. Few zoos support in situ conservation projects, yet the priority for conservation should be to conserve animals in their natural habitat. There is no space or money in zoos to accommodate and look after even a tiny fraction of the many and growing numbers of endangered species. Nor is there any certainty that animals in zoos will breed successfully, survive debilitation from lack of genetic variety, or resist extinction from infectious diseases.

3. Public Education

Throngs of people visit zoos. So the potential is there to educate people about animals, their rights, welfare and conservation. Some zoos fix up information plaques or recorded talks next to exhibits, and a few of the big zoos supply videos and publications. However, even at the small number of zoos where good educational material is available, the public absorb little of it and most zoo-goers disregard it.

Zoo animals cannot possibly act genuinely in their enclosures and may even be psychotic (more below). Unnaturally housed or insane animals cannot be representative of their species. The zoo-going public learn only what cowed, mad or withdrawn animals are like and that it is normal and acceptable that humans should control animals.

4. Public Entertainment

There were virtually no televisions in the 1950's when people flocked to the big zoos, but good wildlife television programmes today can show normal behaviour of animals in their natural surrounds. And many people today go on safari or working holidays in wild animal habitat to experience nature in the flesh. We do not need to confine animals in zoos to lean about them or be entertained by them. Zoo animals are not necessary as educators or entertainers of the public.

Conclusion

What do zoos really teach people? Zoos teach people at least three things:

1. It is all right to keep animals locked up so long as you can justify it with an excuse ('we need zoo animals for conservation / research / public education / to earn money').
2. Humans are superior to animals because we can capture and control them.
3. Animals exist for human purposes and not as individuals who control their own lives.

Morality of Zoos

Zoo animals live in conditions where outlets for their natural instincts are continually frustrated. Lack of adequate environment is not a mental or emotional problem for invertebrates, like giant stag beetles and tarantula spiders. But it is a serious problem for animals like wolves, bears and eagles. How can animals who normally run or fly great distances express their urges when confined?

Animals in zoo usually have nothing to do. They have no tasks to exercise their intelligence or other skills. Animals can be bored, depressed and listless. In short, zoo animals become institutionalised, helplessly dependent on humans.

In their restricted zoo-world many animals succumb to ailing mental health and go mad. It is easy to see animals with unnatural behaviour in zoos. You can see self-mutilation, such as tail chewing or excessive plucking out of fur or feathers, see listless indifference, and see abnormal repetitive behaviours (stereotypies) like pacing up and down or rocking back and forth for ages. Some animals go crazy in zoos. These behaviours indicate neurosis or insanity brought on by boredom, deprivation, frustration and stress. The animals are telling us they are suffering from inadequate lives - even though they may look physically healthy, well fed, clean and otherwise cared for. Humans in mental homes express the same kind of behaviour, but mental health problems in zoo animals usually go unnoticed by the passing public.

Zoos encourage the (often illegal) trade in animals and endangered species through stocking zoos with wild-caught animals.

Where do old and surplus zoo animals go? For some zoos the temptation is to sell animals they do not want to practices like the exotic meat industry, such as bushmeat or canned hunts.

Animals in zoos in war zones may stave slowly to death in their cages through neglect because no one can care for them. Deliberately condemning animals to death like this is outrageous neglect and an abandonment of moral consideration.

Locking up animals encourages indifference and lack of respect for animal life. Zoos teach people that it is all right to use animals, even for purposes we assume are virtuous (education and conservation). Zoos inspire people with false ideas by inadvertently teaching them that humans are superior to animals, physically dominant over them, and that it is proper to live apart from nature, not as part of it (see Human Superiority and Anthropocentrism).

All in all, humans use zoo animals as a dubious means to further human ends, in particular for the conservation of species for human posterity, research for human knowledge, education for human betterment, and for the pursuit of earning a living. Conservation, research, education and employment are noble ideals, but if you believe that animals should have rights then zoos are a raw deal for them.

For & Against: argue your case

1. Research

- Claim: Zoos contribute valuable knowledge and expertise to our understanding of wildlife and to the needs of wildlife through their research on animals.
- Claim: Research on abnormally disturbed animals kept in barren conditions can only provide reliable information on abnormally disturbed animals kept in barren conditions. The best place to study wildlife is in the wild.

2. Breeding Species

- Claim: Zoos support conservation of endangered populations. They breed these animals so they can return their offspring to the wild.
- Claim: Only a tiny number of zoos breed animals effectively for conservation and release extremely few animals to the wild. This does not justify the captivity of millions of animals.

3. Life Quality vs Sanity

- Claim: Zoo animals live healthy lives in elaborate enclosures and fulfil their natural behaviours. We feed them good diets and dedicated staff look after them.
- Claim: Zoos drive many animals into aberrant behaviour and insanity, even in the better zoos.

4. Longevity

- Claim: Zoos protect animals by keeping them safe, so they live longer than animals in the wild.
- Claim: Zoos may protect animals but they have a poorer quality of life in confinement and longevity is not a guide to good mental health.

5. Stewardship

- Claim: People have severely degraded of destroyed the environment of many species. So the only hope of survival for many wild animals is in zoos and captive breeding centres.

- Claim: All the zoos in the world cannot keep a large enough number of animals with sufficient genetic variation to save endangered species from going extinct. The only way to save species is to preserve them in the wild with their natural habitat.

6. Taking Wild Animals

- Claim: It is wrong for zoos or their agents to capture animals from the wild, kill their parents to get them, and destroy their communities.
- Claim: That is largely in the past, for reputable zoos at least. Animals collected from the wild today are for specific conservation and educational purposes.

7. Education

- Claim: Visitors to zoos are interested in learning about the animals they see and are therefore receptive to education. Zoos offer lots of educational material about their animals and nature.
- Claim: If they bother to provide anything, zoos display the most meagre information about their animals. Most visitors drift from one group of animals to another without leaning anything about them.

8. Creating Awareness

- Claim: Zoos stimulate public interest in animals and their conservation by leading campaigns to save animals and by presenting exhibits to the public to get their conservation message across.
- Claim: Many organisations effectively stimulate public interest in animals and their conservation without imprisoning animals. Local nature trusts and the World Wildlife Fund are examples.

9. Zoos vs TV

- Claim: You can understand animals better from TV films taken in the animals' natural surroundings without having to confine animals.
- Claim: You can see and experience animals at zoos that you would have no other opportunity to meet. Television does not allow you to get close to live animals or smell them.

10. Surplus Animals

- Claim: Zoos destroy surplus animals or send them to disreputable traders for base purposes, like canned hunts.
- Claim: Reputable zoos send surplus animals to other responsible zoos and institutions. They practice birth control or regulate population size in some other suitable manner.

11. Money-pullers

- Claim: Many zoo species are not in danger of extinction so have no conservation value. Zoos use these animals merely to attract the paying public. These animal should not be in zoos.
- Claim: Zoos must attract visitors for revenue so that zoos can carry out their research, conservation and education. These animals can double a zoo's income.

12. Business

- Claim: Zoos exist to make a profit. The money goes to the zoo's owner or investors. There is no justification for zoos.
- Claim: Zoos must make a profit if they are to run successfully and the best zoos invest in the welfare of their animal stock.

Five Extras

5. Climate Change

The Problem

The average temperature of Earth's air and sea is warming. This is called climate change or global warming. We can see climate change happening all around us, including melting Polar ice caps, dissolving permafrost, increasingly serious regional storms and changes in wild animal behaviour. Earth's climate naturally changes slowly over thousands of years in response to changes in solar activity, Earth's orbit around the Sun, volcanic emissions, and other natural phenomena. But climate change is happening very fast, too rapidly for species to adapt to the changing conditions. Consequently, climate change will wipe out millions of species and is the greatest burden on our moral behaviour because we, humanity, are responsible for it.

The Greenhouse Effect

Climate change is powered by the greenhouse effect. The land and sea absorb most of the Sun's heat reaching Earth. The heat then passes to the atmosphere and is lost to outerspace. However, some of the heat gets trapped by certain gases, so called greenhouse gases, in the atmosphere and remains next to Earth's surface.

One of the first people to recognise the greenhouse effect was Frenchman Jean-Baptiste Fourier in the 1820's. He coined the analogy with a greenhouse. The window panes of a greenhouse are like Earth's atmosphere, allowing the Sun's warmth in but prevent some warmth getting out, raising the temperature of the greenhouse.

The greenhouse effect is natural and without it Earth would be too cold for life to evolve the way it has. However, humanity has been releasing huge quantities of greenhouse gases and this has caused an unnatural, accelerating and fast warming of the climate. Currently humans release 22 billion tons of greenhouse gases into the atmosphere annually.

Cataclysms in the Offing

Climate change can trigger major cataclysmic events within the next 200 years.

- Greenland Ice Sheet Meltdown

The ice sheet covering Greenland is Earth's second largest ice cap, containing about 10 per cent of the world's fresh water. It is currently melting and can raise the sea level at least six metres (about 20 feet). The rising sea will engulf lowland coastal areas where countless creatures and billions of people live, including Shanghai, London, New York, Mumbai and Sidney. Millions of people and animals will be forced to move to higher land. Species that cannot migrate will go extinct as they drown.

- Gulf Stream Switch-off

The Gulf Stream (also known as the Atlantic Conveyor) is a major current in the Atlantic between the Caribbean and Europe. It conveys 20 times more water than all the rivers on land. Within its body of water it carries heat and distributes it to the atmosphere across the globe. The Gulf Stream can shut off swiftly and permanently by ice cold water from the melting Arctic and Greenland Ice Sheet colliding with it. If this happens, north-west Europe would suddenly be thrust into an uninhabitable Arctic climate. A mass die off of most fauna and flora in Europe would be inevitable and millions of people would be forced to migrate south that would cause massive civil conflict and ensuing wildlife destruction. The climatic change would not be confined to Europe but impact on other parts of the world because all parts of Earth's climate are connected.

- Permafrost Melt

Permafrost is ground a few inches below the surface that is normally constantly frozen solid, although the top few inches can thaw in summer. Permafrost occupies up to a fifth of Earth's land surface, circling the globe mostly in the far Northern Hemisphere. In some places it is around 1,000 m (3,000 feet) thick. The permafrost contains enormous amounts of carbon dioxide and methane. When the permafrost thaws it will release massive amounts of these gases into the atmosphere precipitously speeding up global warming with no control possible.

- Amazon Conflagration

Climate change could dry up the Amazon rain forest turning it into one huge combustion holocaust. Since trees are made mostly of carbon, a burning Amazon will release vast amounts of carbon into the atmosphere suddenly driving up global warming. The majority of land species on Earth live in rain forests. When the Amazon is destroyed most terrestrial species will die with it.

- Ocean Death

The surface of the sea absorbs carbon dioxide from the air above it. Increasing amounts of carbon dioxide in the air are turning the oceans into a dilute acid (carbon dioxide plus sea water makes carbonic acid, HCO_3) and most marine life will perish - from microscopic plankton to coral reefs and whales. Marine death by acidification is already happening.

- Methane Hydrates Release

Methane hydrates are vast quantities of frozen methane gas under the sea floor. There could be trillions of tonnes of it. Rising temperatures in the sea will trigger its release to surge up as methane gas into the atmosphere. Earth's warming climate will get an abrupt gigantic boost. When this happens, global warming will be out of all control and a mass extinction of life inevitable. Methane is several times more powerful as a global warming gas than carbon dioxide.

Biosphere Wipe-Out

How will global warming leave the Earth? The cumulative effect of all these cataclysmic events when they happen will be a climate change that destroys the biosphere, the realm of all living things between the atmosphere above and the lithosphere of rock below. Without the Arctic ice, creatures dependent on the ice will die off. As the jungles dry up most land species on Earth will vanish. The oceans and almost all life in them will be dead. Virtually all life on Earth will come to an end. Possibly the only life to survive might be micro-organisms already adapted to live in extreme environments.

Can We Stop Climate Change?

Once changes to large bodies, like the oceans and ice caps, are set in motion they take hundreds of years to slow down and stop. Nevertheless, some people hope to avoid the worst scenario: global warming accelerating so fast that it is impossible to slow. But can we slow global warming significantly? Politicians say we can reduce global warming without giving up our standard of living or aspiration for a higher standard. This is false because slowing global warming depends on:

- The amount of global warming fuel (oil, wood, etc) that humanity uses.
- The number of people on Earth and its rate of increase.
- New technology saving us.
- Enormously costly and widespread unpopular economic changes.

But humanity continues to use fossil fuels and shows no sign of seriously limiting its usage. Humanity's population is over seven billion and increasing without significant control. New technology is a reverie; it does not exist and probably could not be delivered in time if it were invented. And no one is going to give up resources unless the other guy/country does so first; people cannot divest themselves of their biological imperative to behave in their own short-term self-interests.

What you can do as an animal rights activist
You can try and help by joining organisations involved with climate change. At a personal level you can do two major things: do not make babies (more people more destruction) - or at the least make fewer babies - and give up your car (10 to 25 per cent of carbon emissions come from motor vehicles). Set a good example to others.

| Epilogue on Doing Animal Rights | *...on feelings of pointless inadequacy and ineptitude* |

Animal suffering caused by humanity is so vast that it is easy to feel dismayed sometimes at its scale and one's seemingly ineffectual struggles to relieve it. How can we tackle feelings of pointless inadequacy and ineptitude we may stumble into? We have to arm ourselves with the right attitude.

Attitude 1: I fight my corner

We must choose a bit of the overall picture and do what we can, no matter how small our effort seems. You are not alone; everyone's input makes for the greater whole.

Attitude 2: I will not be a slave to my emotions

Emotions are not sacrosanct and we can learn to supervise them (if only to put them aside from time to time as best we can). Biologists tell us that our emotions evolved to help our ancestors survive and reproduce (and thus pass on emotion-mediating genes to posterity); and that a key function for having emotions may be that they prioritise our behaviour (for instance, we may be grieving a loss, but when we spot a predator, fear takes first rank, we put grieving aside and flee!). So emotions motivate (not dominate) us and we can strive for a reasonable balance with them.

Attitude 3: Perspective is calming

Cosmologists tell us that we live in an ageless multiverse. What does this mean for animal rights? Animal suffering induced by intelligent creatures exists through eons on endless planets in countless universes. There is nothing we can do about this. Our planet Earth, and our whole universe, is just a fleeting wisp of next to nothingness. We cannot do any more than keep calm and do our best.

Attitude 4: I shall not give up

Often there is no headway changing someone's attitude. Then all we can do is gently try to plant an idea in their mind and hope it matures, perhaps years later, while we set a good example.

Attitude 5: I count my blessings and keep a sense of humour

When all else fails, this always helps!

| *Appendix* | *World Scientists' Warning to Humanity* |

From Chapter 1: Mass Extinction.

Over 1,500 leading scientists from around the world published this World Scientists' Warning to Humanity in 1992 to alert everyone to the coming global catastrophe. Their Warning is reproduced below.

World Scientists' Warning to Humanity

Human beings and the natural world are on a collision course. Human activities inflict harsh and often irreversible damage on the environment and on critical resources. If not checked, many of our current practices put at serious risk the future that we wish for human society and the plant and animal kingdoms, and may so alter the living world that it will be unable to sustain life in the manner that we know. Fundamental changes are urgent if we are to avoid the collision our present course will bring about.

The Environment

The environment is suffering critical stress:

The Atmosphere

Stratospheric ozone depletion threatens us with enhanced ultraviolet radiation at the earth's surface, which can be damaging or lethal to many life forms. Air pollution near ground level, and acid precipitation, are already causing widespread injury to humans, forests and crops.

Water Resources

Heedless exploitation of depletable ground water supplies endangers food production and other essential human systems. Heavy demands on the world's surface waters have resulted in serious shortages in some 80 countries, containing 40% of the world's population. Pollution of rivers, lakes and ground water further limits the supply.

Oceans

Destructive pressure on the oceans is severe, particularly in the coastal regions which produce most of the world's food fish. The total marine catch is now at or above the estimated maximum sustainable yield. Some fisheries have already shown signs of collapse. Rivers carrying heavy burdens of eroded soil into the seas also carry industrial, municipal, agricultural, and livestock waste -- some of it toxic.

Soil

Loss of soil productivity, which is causing extensive Land abandonment, is a widespread by-product of current practices in agriculture and animal husbandry. Since 1945, 11% of the earth's vegetated surface has been degraded -- an area larger than India and China combined -- and per capita food production in many parts of the world is decreasing.

Forests

Tropical rain forests, as well as tropical and temperate dry forests, are being destroyed rapidly. At present rates, some critical forest types will be gone in a few years and most of the tropical rain forest will be gone before the end of the next century. With them will go large numbers of plant and animal species.

Living Species

The irreversible loss of species, which by 2100 may reach one third of all species now living, is especially serious. We are losing the potential they hold for providing medicinal and other benefits, and the contribution that genetic diversity of life forms gives to the robustness of the world's biological systems and to the astonishing beauty of the earth itself.

Much of this damage is irreversible on a scale of centuries or permanent. Other processes appear to pose additional threats. Increasing levels of gases in the atmosphere from human activities, including carbon dioxide released from fossil fuel burning and from deforestation, may alter climate on a global scale. Predictions of global warming are still uncertain -- with projected effects ranging from tolerable to very severe -- but the potential risks are very great. Our massive tampering with the world's interdependent web of life -- coupled with the environmental damage inflicted by deforestation, species loss, and climate change -- could trigger widespread adverse effects, including unpredictable collapses of critical biological systems whose interactions and dynamics we only imperfectly understand.

Uncertainty over the extent of these effects cannot excuse complacency or delay in facing the threat.

Population

The earth is finite. Its ability to absorb wastes and destructive effluent is finite. Its ability to provide food and energy is finite. Its ability to provide for growing numbers of people is finite. And we are fast approaching many of the earth's limits. Current economic practices which damage the environment, in both developed and underdeveloped nations, cannot be continued without the risk that vital global systems will be damaged beyond repair.

Pressures resulting from unrestrained population growth put demands on the natural world that can overwhelm any efforts to achieve a sustainable future. If we are to halt the destruction of our environment, we must accept limits to that growth. A World Bank estimate indicates that world population will not stabilize at less than 12.4 billion, while the United Nations concludes that the eventual total could reach 14 billion, a near tripling of today's 5.4 billion. But, even at this moment, one person in five lives in absolute poverty without enough to eat, and one in ten suffers serious malnutrition.

No more than one or a few decades remain before the chance to avert the threats we now confront will be lost and the prospects for humanity immeasurably diminished.

Warning

We the undersigned, senior members of the world's scientific community, hereby warn all humanity of what lies ahead. A great change in our stewardship of the earth and the life on it, is required, if vast human misery is to be avoided and our global home on this planet is not to be irretrievably mutilated.

What We Must Do

Five inextricably linked areas must be addressed **simultaneously**:

1. We must bring environmentally damaging activities under control to restore and protect the integrity of the earth's systems we depend on. We must, for example, move away from fossil fuels to more benign, inexhaustible energy sources to cut greenhouse gas emissions and the pollution of our air and water. Priority must be given to the development of energy sources matched to third world needs -- small scale and relatively easy to implement. We must halt deforestation, injury to and loss of agricultural land, and the loss of terrestrial and marine plant and animal species.

2. We must manage resources crucial to human welfare more effectively. We must give high priority to efficient use of energy, water, and other materials, including expansion of conservation and recycling.

3. We must stabilize population. This will be possible only if all nations recognize that it requires improved social and economic conditions, and the adoption of effective, voluntary family planning.

4. We must reduce and eventually eliminate poverty.

5. We must ensure sexual equality, and guarantee women control over their own reproductive decisions.
The developed nations are the largest polluters in the world today. They must greatly reduce their over-consumption, if we are to reduce pressures on resources and the global environment. The developed nations have the obligation to provide aid and support to developing nations, because only the developed nations have the financial resources and the technical skills for these tasks.

Acting on this recognition is not altruism, but enlightened self-interest: whether industrialized or not, we all have but one lifeboat. No nation can escape from injury when global biological systems are damaged. No nation can escape from conflicts over increasingly scarce resources. In addition, environmental and economic instabilities will cause mass migrations with incalculable consequences for developed and undeveloped nations alike.

Developing nations must realize that environmental damage is one of the gravest threats they face, and that attempts to blunt it will be overwhelmed if their populations go unchecked. The greatest peril is to become trapped in spirals of environmental decline, poverty, and unrest, leading to social, economic and environmental collapse.

Success in this global endeavour will require a great reduction in violence and war. Resources now devoted to the preparation and conduct of war -- amounting to over $1 trillion annually -- will be badly needed in the new tasks and should be diverted to the new challenges.

A new ethic is required -- a new attitude towards discharging our responsibility for caring for ourselves and for the earth. We must recognize the earth's limited capacity to provide for us. We must recognize its fragility. We must no longer allow it to be ravaged. This ethic must motivate a great movement, convince reluctant leaders and reluctant governments and reluctant peoples themselves to effect the needed changes.

The scientists issuing this warning hope that our message will reach and affect people everywhere. We need the help of many.

- We require the help of the world community of scientists -- natural, social, economic, political;
- We require the help of the world's business and industrial leaders;
- We require the help of the world's religious leaders; and
- We require the help of the world's peoples.
- **We call on all to join us in this task.**

Printed in Great Britain
by Amazon